Pediatric Psychopharmacology

Pediatric Psychopharmacology

Combining Medical and Psychosocial Interventions

LeAdelle Phelps, Ronald T. Brown,
and Thomas J. Power

American Psychological Association
Washington, DC

Published by
American Psychological Association
750 First Street, NE
Washington, DC 20002
www.apa.org

To order   Tel: (800) 374-2721, Direct: (202) 336-5510
APA Order Department   Fax: (202) 336-5502, TDD/TTY: (202) 336-6123
P.O. Box 92984   Online: www.apa.org/books
Washington, DC 20090-2984   Email: order@apa.org

In the U.K., Europe, Africa, and the Middle East, copies may be ordered from
American Psychological Association
3 Henrietta Street
Covent Garden, London
WC2E 8LU England

Typeset in Goudy by EPS Group Inc., Easton, MD

Printer: United Book Press, Inc., Baltimore, MD
Cover Designer: NiDesign, Baltimore, MD
Technical/Production Editor: Jennifer L. Macomber

The opinions and statements published are the responsibility of the authors, and such opinions and statements do not necessarily represent the policies of the American Psychological Association.

Library of Congress Cataloging-in-Publication Data
Phelps, LeAdelle.
    Pediatric psychopharmacology : combining medical and psychosocial interventions /
LeAdelle Phelps, Ronald T. Brown, Thomas J. Power.
        p. ; cm.
    Includes bibliographical references and index.
    ISBN 1-55798-813-7 (alk. paper)
    1. Pediatric psychopharmacology.   I. Brown, Ronald T.   II. Power, Thomas J.
III. Title.
    [DNLM: 1. Mental Disorders—drug therapy—Adolescence.   2. Mental Disorders—
drug therapy—Child.   3. Psychotherapy—methods—Adolescence.
4. Psychotherapy—methods—Child.   5. Psychotropic Drugs—therapeutic use—
Adolescence.   6. Psychotropic Drugs—therapeutic use—Child.
WS 350.2 P539p 2001]
RJ504.7 .P48 2001
618.92'8918—dc21

                                                                        2001022963

British Library Cataloguing-in-Publication Data
A CIP record is available from the British Library.

Printed in the United States of America
First Edition

To Andrei H. and his family, for their courage and strength in fighting the battle of childhood-onset bipolar disorder.—*LeAdelle Phelps*

In memory of Karen H. Tolley,
for her humor and spirit. —*Ronald T. Brown*

To my wife Barbara and our children Joshua, Thomas,
and Leah, for the love that sustains me.—*Thomas J. Power*

CONTENTS

ACKNOWLEDGMENTS

We are deeply indebted to Elizabeth A. Botzer and Karen J. Fitting for their distinguished library research and assistance. Each devoted countless hours when surely more refreshing activities beckoned. We also acknowledge the superb work of the Psychopharmacology Curriculum Committee of the Board of Educational Affairs of the American Psychological Association Education Directorate and the excellent working relationships among the prescribing psychologists in the armed services branches, particularly during the development of the psychopharmacology examination. Last, we acknowledge our families, friends, and colleagues. We extend immeasurable gratitude for their support and encouragement throughout this process.

Pediatric
Psychopharmacology

1

OVERVIEW OF COLLABORATIVE PRACTICES IN MEDICATION MANAGEMENT

Psychologists serve critical roles in the pharmacological management of children and adolescents who require medication. Although prescription privileges for psychologists have yet to be widely accepted, these professionals are often involved in the initial pharmacological treatment of school-age children. Yet few practitioners are experts in psychotropic practice, especially in reference to pharmacological options, standard dosages, and possible adverse effects. This book was written to inform nonphysician practitioners about these factors, as well as about the collaborative options in the provision of pediatric psychopharmacology.

Many disorders are treated with a variety of classes of medications (e.g., stimulants, antidepressants, and anticonvulsants), making professional communication among medical and mental health professionals essential. There is strong movement in the field toward identifying and strongly recommending the use of empirically supported psychosocial and pharmacological interventions. By combining medications that have proven efficacy shown in double-blind clinical trials with psychosocial interventions that have demonstrated empirical support, treatments are likely to be more successful. Of course, such multimodal interventions require close coordination among professionals and should be objectively evaluated for effectiveness on an ongoing basis. Thus, we advocate for an intervention model that is multimodal (i.e., psychosocial and pharmacological), interdisciplinary, and collaborative in nature. This combined model will likely result in better treatment planning and monitoring for children and adolescents requiring such services.

As psychologists have become increasingly involved in research and practice related to the pharmacological management of mental health disorders, the movement within the profession to grant psychologists prescription privileges has strengthened. The American Psychological Association (APA) recently developed guidelines and specific curricula for the preparation of psychologists in medication management (APA, 1996, 1997). Likewise, the presidential miniconvention at the 2000 APA Annual Convention in Washington, DC, was devoted entirely to prescription privileges, with 3 full days of sessions provided by leading experts in the field (Rabasca, 2000). Nevertheless, further research that justifies pediatric pharmacological interventions is sorely needed. For example, recent reports on the use of psychotropic medications with preschool children presenting with behavioral and emotional concerns warrant further examination. Zito et al. (2000) reported a dramatic increase of stimulants, antidepressants, and neuroleptics prescribed for children ages 2 through 4 years between the years of 1991 and 1995. These alarming findings resulted in a White House conference on March 20, 2000, in which APA participated. The following conclusions were reached:

1. Proper diagnosis by qualified professionals is essential,
2. psychosocial interventions generally should be implemented prior to psychotropic treatment,
3. such interventions should continue even if a medication trial is activated, and
4. collaborative practice among medical, mental health, and school professionals is essential (Rabasca, 2000).

INTENDED READERSHIP

This book has been prepared primarily for psychologists addressing the needs of children and adolescents in diverse settings, including community-based private practice and mental health centers, as well as pediatric and psychiatric hospitals in inpatient and outpatient venues. Psychologists with a wide range of specialties, including clinical psychology, pediatric psychology, counseling psychology, community psychology, and school psychology, will find this volume useful. Also, this book will be a helpful resource for other health services providers, including nurse practitioners, nurses, social workers, and school counselors, who are involved in the care of children with mental health problems. In addition, faculty in university training programs for graduate and undergraduate students and postdoctoral fellows will find the text beneficial in preparing students for practice and applied research related to the treatment of psychiatric disorders. Because this book is intended for nonphysicians who may not be highly knowledgeable about psychopharmacology, a glossary of medical terms is provided at the end of the book.

UNIQUE FEATURES OF THIS BOOK

This volume explains the options for the pharmacological treatment of children and adolescents. Although considerably more research on psychopharmacology has been conducted with adults compared with children and adolescents, there has been a wealth of research pertaining to pediatric psychopharmacology since 1980. Understanding the research literature on pediatric psychopharmacology is critical for clinicians providing services to individuals younger than age 21, because response to medication among children and adolescents can differ markedly from that in adults and may vary among children of different ages.

Most books written about psychopharmacology are organized according to classifications of medication (e.g., antidepressants, neuroleptics, and stimulants). There are notable disadvantages to this approach, in particular, that the same class of medications (e.g., antidepressants) is often used to treat children with different disorders (e.g., mood disorders, anxiety disorders, and attention deficit disorders). Also, because a relatively high percentage of children have more than one mental health disorder, decisions about the optimal drug agent are often complex, and occasionally a polypharmacy approach may be indicated. In addition, when clinicians consider pharmacological approaches to care, they typically think about options as a function of the primary problems and disorders presented by these individuals.

One unique feature of this volume is that it is organized according to mental health disorder. Knowing the primary problem or problems presented by a child or adolescent, clinicians can review a variety of medication options and consider advantages and limitations associated with each approach.

For nearly every mental health disorder that arises among children and adolescents, there are viable pharmacological as well as psychosocial methods of intervention. Most volumes consider only pharmacological approaches and do not introduce readers to psychosocial methods. Clinicians are thus not afforded the opportunity to consider the relative merits of a pharmacological-only, a psychosocial-only, and a combined approach to treatment. Another unique feature of this book is that both pharmacological and psychosocial interventions for each disorder are presented, and factors pertaining to the use of a single versus a combined approach to care are outlined.

Providing services for children and adolescents with one or more psychiatric disorders raises numerous professional issues. Given that all medications are associated with beneficial and adverse effects and that it is impossible to predict a priori an individual's response to treatment, the continuous evaluation of a wide range of outcomes in diverse settings, such as home and school, is essential. Also, given that children and adolescents and their caregivers vary greatly in their perceptions of the acceptability of medication and that adherence to drug therapy can vary markedly, it is essential to understand the social validity of medication and to use the interventions when families are ready for them. Furthermore, treating mental health problems often involves the use of multiple intervention approaches provided by clinicians from a variety of disciplines. Effective practice requires the coordination of services across systems, such as the health, educational, and family systems, and the collaboration of providers from a variety of disciplines. This book is unique in its coverage of these professional issues and includes a focus on monitoring intervention effects, understanding and managing barriers to treatment, and promoting interdisciplinary collaboration.

ROLES OF PSYCHOLOGISTS IN MEDICATION MANAGEMENT

Deciding to initiate pharmacotherapy is complex and requires the consideration of many factors. Furthermore, monitoring intervention effectiveness and maintaining treatment adherence can be challenging for professionals and families. The following is a description of the many roles that practicing professionals may serve in making medication decisions, evaluating treatment effectiveness, and maintaining family involvement in the change process.

Assessing Emotional and Behavioral Problems

Assessing emotional and behavioral problems requires a determination of the types of difficulties the child is having, the function of the presenting problems, and the level of functional impairment associated with the problems (American Psychiatric Association, 1994). Numerous methods are available to identify the types of problems experienced by children; these include direct observation procedures, rating scales completed by adult informants, child self-report measures, interview techniques, and psychometric testing (Mash & Terdal, 1997; Shaffer, Lucas, & Richters, 1999). Although it is important to understand the topography of a child's emotional and behavioral problems, this level of analysis is not sufficient. Clinicians also need to understand the function and meaning of a child's behavior, which requires an assessment of contextual variables operating in the family, school, and community that have an influence on the child. Furthermore, for a behavior to become a symptom or problem, it must be associated in some way with a functional impairment. Therefore, assessments need to include an examination of the extent to which emotional and behavioral issues experienced by the child are affecting the family and school as well as peers.

Psychologists are extremely well prepared to assess emotional and behavioral problems. They can take credit for developing many of the tools for assessing these problems, and virtually every aspiring applied psychologist receives extensive training in this area. Psychologists have also been prepared to examine the function and context of behavior by examining contextual factors in the family, school, and community that affect the child.

Identifying Intervention Goals

The types of interventions needed to assist children and their families depend greatly on the goals of treatment and target behaviors exhibited by the child. Families often present with multiple problems and a wide range of needs and goals. Clinicians need to identify the primary goals of treatment and to plan their interventions accordingly. For example, for a child with oppositional defiant disorder and generalized anxiety disorder, the intervention will vary greatly depending on whether the primary goals of treatment pertain to the alleviation of oppositional behavior or to the symptoms of anxiety. Psychologists generally have extensive training in generating problem lists and collaborating with parents and children to identify priority areas most in need of intervention.

Selecting Empirically Supported Interventions

After clinicians assess a child's problems and generate a list of primary intervention goals, the next step is to select the interventions that have been demonstrated through empirical research to be successful in addressing the targets of treatment. Clinicians need to be cognizant of the research literature pertaining to both pharmacological and psychosocial interventions for the problems being treated. The chapters of this book review the literature on the effectiveness of pharmacological and psychosocial agents in the management of a wide range of psychological disorders. With regard to psychosocial treatments, the APA Society of Clinical Psychology has developed specific guidelines for determining whether these interventions are efficacious or probably efficacious (see Chambless & Hollon, 1998;

Chambless et al., 1996). Through the efforts of the APA Division of Child Clinical Psychology, these guidelines have been applied to evaluate research relating to several types of child and adolescent disorders (Kazdin & Weisz, 1998). For example, researchers have identified empirically supported interventions for depressive disorders (Kaslow & Thompson, 1998), phobias and anxiety disorders (Ollendick & King, 1998), autistic disorders (Rogers, 1998), conduct disorder (Brestan & Eyberg, 1998), and attention deficit hyperactivity disorder (ADHD; Pelham, Wheeler, & Chronis, 1998).

Psychologists clearly are committed to the use of clinical strategies that have a strong theoretical and empirical foundation (Beutler, 1998). Working as a team member, the psychologist can serve a vital role in summarizing research findings related to the use of pharmacological and psychosocial interventions. With this information, the treatment team can then determine which approach is most likely to be successful in addressing the problems presented and in achieving the goals of intervention.

Assessing Readiness for Change and Social Validity

For an intervention to be effective, families need to be ready for change, and they should view the goals, treatments, and outcomes of intervention as reasonable and appropriate (Kazdin, 1996; Prochaska, DiClemente, & Norcross, 1992; see also this volume, chapter 3). Families often vary greatly with regard to their views about the acceptability of pharmacological intervention and their willingness to initiate this type of treatment. Failure by clinicians to incorporate the perceptions of each family member in the development of a treatment plan may result in outright treatment refusal, inconsistent adherence, or premature discontinuation of intervention. During the design of the intervention plan, psychologists can serve a critical role in determining a family's readiness for intervention and in assessing their views about the acceptability of various treatment options, which may include medication. In this way, the treatment team is likely to develop a plan of intervention in which family members are willing to become invested. Furthermore, the psychologist can continue to monitor family attitudes during the course of intervention and recommend modifications that will enable the child and caregivers to maintain their commitment to the change process.

Designing Medication-Monitoring Protocols

Because response to psychotropic medication may be idiosyncratic and because of the risk of adverse effects, it is essential that both the efficacy and adverse effects of medication be monitored carefully. As described in chapter 2, methods of behavioral assessment and single-subject research design are extremely useful in assessing whether a medication is effective and in determining the optimal dose. These procedures can also be used to evaluate the relative superiority of a pharmacological, a psychosocial, or a combined approach to intervention (Blum, Mauk, McComas, & Mace, 1996; Hoza, Pelham, Sams, & Carlson, 1992). Psychologists typically are well trained in the use of measures that are effective in monitoring the effects of medication on academic, behavioral, emotional, and social functioning, as well as in the use of single-subject designs for evaluating an intervention approach's efficacy. Psychologists, therefore, can make important contributions by delineating a protocol for conducting a trial of medication and developing a plan to ensure that participants are monitored throughout the treatment (DuPaul & Barkley, 1993).

Interpreting Results of Medication-Monitoring Protocols

Medication-monitoring procedures yield a wealth of data that can be challenging to interpret. The results can differ greatly depending on the domain of functioning that is being assessed (Power, Blum, Jones, & Kaplan, 1996; Rapport, Denney, DuPaul, & Gardner, 1994). It may be difficult for clinicians to determine whether the changes demonstrated are due to chance factors and whether the changes are clinically meaningful. A psychologist with expertise in data analysis can assist the treatment team in evaluating whether treatment effects in a specific domain are statistically significant (DuPaul & Barkley, 1993) and whether intervention has been successful in changing behavior to the point at which the child's functioning is essentially the same as normally functioning peers (Rapport et al., 1994).

Coordinating the Intervention Team

Children coping with psychological disorders often require specialized management from many individuals, including caregivers, multiple school professionals, one or more mental health specialists, and a primary care pediatric provider (Osman, 2000). These individuals can provide useful data in assessing the child's problems, delineating a suitable course of intervention, and monitoring the effects of intervention. Coordinating family members and professionals so that they operate as a well-integrated team, however, can be challenging. In many cases, caregivers must assume the role of coordinating communications among busy professionals. Psychologists can serve a valuable function by establishing collaborative relationships among professionals and caregivers and by coordinating information that is useful in assessing problems and evaluating intervention effectiveness (Drotar, 1995; Power, Atkins, Osborne, & Blum, 1994).

THE DEBATE ABOUT PRESCRIPTION PRIVILEGES

Since the 1980s, psychologists have debated the merits and viability of obtaining prescription privileges for their profession. The APA has taken an active role in soliciting feedback from its members about this issue. Furthermore, the APA has been supportive of its affiliated state organizations in advocating for prescription privileges for psychologists. The debate has addressed both theoretical and pragmatic issues pertaining to the profession. The following is a summary of some of the major positions being advanced to support and to temper the movement of psychologists to obtain prescription privileges.

The Position for Prescription Privileges

Research supporting the biological bases for psychological disturbances, such as psychotic disorders, mood disorders, anxiety disorders, tic disorders, and ADHD, has accumulated over the past 30 years at a rapid rate. Furthermore, research supporting the efficacy of pharmacological interventions for mental health disorders has exploded in recent years. Numerous psychologists have made significant contributions to these developments, conducting outstanding research on the neurobiology of psychiatric disorders and the efficacy of pharmacotherapies for emotional and behavioral disturbances. The profession has also been active in exploring new roles and domains of practice for psychologists in the medication management of psychiatric disorders, such as those described earlier in this chapter.

However, some experts have asserted that the profession of psychology historically has overemphasized the environmental influences on human behavior and has overfocused on training clinicians in psychotherapy and behavior management strategies to alter the environment. The profession has failed to incorporate sufficiently advances made in the neurosciences and to translate these findings into the development of new models of practice (Hayes & Heiby, 1996). Obtaining prescription privileges would affirm the commitment of the profession of psychology to understanding both the psychosocial and biological bases of behavior. In addition, this status would make available to psychologists a powerful set of techniques for improving psychological functioning, and hence improving human welfare.

Granting prescription privileges to psychologists may help to address the concern that medication is being used in cases in which it is not needed. With the dramatic increase in the use of pharmacological interventions for children in the school-age and preschool years during each decade since the 1960s (Safer, Zito, & Fine, 1996; Zito et al., 2000), there has been a growing concern about overdiagnosis and the overuse of medication. At this point, most of the prescriptions to treat psychiatric disorders are written by primary care providers (e.g., pediatricians and family care practitioners) who are not psychiatrists or who do not have extensive training in psychopathology or psychopharmacology (DeLeon & Wiggins, 1996). It is hoped that permitting appropriately trained psychologists the privilege of writing prescriptions will help to ensure that only individuals who need and could benefit from medication get this treatment. Furthermore, given their training in the assessment of contextual factors that influence behavior and given their knowledge of empirically supported psychosocial interventions, psychologists with prescription privileges are in an excellent position to determine whether psychosocial interventions can be effective in addressing a child's problems and whether medication may be indicated. As noted by several advocates, the real power that comes with this privilege is the power *not* to prescribe medication when it may not be indicated (DeLeon & DeNelsky, 1993). Not only can psychologists have an impact on the direction of treatment at the outset of the intervention process, but they can also alter the course of treatment for those who have already been treated for psychopathology (Pachman, 1996).

The rise of the managed care movement since the late 1980s has emphasized the importance of providing treatment in a time-efficient and cost-effective manner (Humphreys, 1996). For many disorders, in particular ADHD, medication can be highly effective and can be provided in a relatively efficient and cost-effective manner (e.g., see Multimodal Treatment Study for Children With Attention-Deficit/Hyperactivity Disorder, 1999). Obtaining prescription privileges would provide psychologists with some powerful intervention tools that are efficient and relatively inexpensive. This privilege would enable psychologists to be positioned well with managed care organizations to provide comprehensive interventions for children with psychiatric disorders (Hayes & Heiby, 1996).

As described earlier in this chapter, services for children with mental health disorders are often fragmented. Professionals providing pharmacological interventions frequently do not provide care in a manner that is coordinated well with those who provide psychosocial interventions. Granting prescription privileges to psychologists would help to provide services to children and families in a more integrated fashion (DeNelsky, 1996). Finally, it is well-known that many children and adolescents do not receive behavioral health services. By allowing psychologists prescription privileges, more children with psychological disorders may have access to needed services.

The Case Against Prescription Privileges

Granting prescription privileges to psychologists, it has been argued, will change the identity of the profession in significant ways. The field will shift from a profession based in the science of psychology to one that is based in the science of both psychology and medicine (Hayes & Heiby, 1996). Increasingly, the profession of psychology will relinquish what is unique to the field and become essentially indistinguishable from psychiatry (DeNelsky, 1996).

For many years, the fields of psychology and psychiatry have engaged in a relationship that at times has been strained and competitive. The granting of prescription privileges to psychologists in all likelihood will exacerbate the tension in this relationship and impede progress in developing a complementary relationship between the professions. This development could serve as an obstacle for psychologists who have invested a considerable amount of energy building strong working alliances with their colleagues in psychiatry.

It has also been argued that prescription privileges would alter the goals and structure of psychology training programs dramatically. Given the enormous knowledge base in psychopharmacology that is needed for effective, responsible, and ethical practice in medication management, training programs will be required to reduce their emphasis on preparing students in the areas of psychosocial intervention, consultation, and prevention. By so doing, training in areas that have been the hallmarks of applied psychology may become diluted (DeNelsky, 1996). Thus, in striving to prepare students to make outstanding contributions in pharmacological management, training programs will reduce their commitment to prepare outstanding psychotherapists, consultants, and preventionists. Some have argued that training in pharmacotherapy should occur at the postdoctoral level to minimize the potential for disrupting the structure of psychology training programs.

For some psychiatric disorders (e.g., anxiety disorders, depression, and autism), psychosocial interventions have been demonstrated to be particularly effective (Kazdin & Weisz, 1998) and, especially for children and adolescents, may be more effective than pharmacological treatments (Barkley et al., 1990; Kubiszyn, 1994). Even in cases in which pharmacological treatments are likely to be more effective than psychosocial interventions, some children and families strongly prefer nonpharmacological interventions (Pelham, 1999). Thus, there is a strong need to continue to develop and refine empirically supported interventions for a wide range of psychiatric disorders. With the granting of prescription privileges to psychologists, concerns have been raised about the shift of emphasis away from research investigating empirically supported methods of psychosocial intervention (Hayes & Heiby, 1996).

A related concern is that psychologists with prescription privileges will become so concerned with issues of medication management that their skills as psychotherapists and consultants will erode. The example of psychiatry is often used to illustrate how clinicians with prescription privileges spend a disproportionate amount of time devoted to pharmacological management of mental health disorders and as a result devote less time providing psychotherapeutic interventions (DeNelsky, 1996).

IMPLICATIONS FOR TRAINING

Regardless of how the movement for prescription privileges unfolds, psychologists can serve important roles in the pharmacological treatment of children with mental health disorders. Training in psychopharmacology is essential to prepare psychologists for effective practice related to medication management. APA (1992) has identified three levels of training in psychopathology: Level I focuses on basic education related to psychopharmacology, Level II provides training in skills needed to engage in collaborative practice with prescribing clinicians, and Level III provides intensive training to psychologists seeking prescription privileges. Curriculum guidelines for training have been developed for both Level I and Level II training (APA, 1995, 1997).

Level I training is designed to provide the minimum basic knowledge base in psychopharmacology needed by all practicing psychologists to function responsibly and effectively in clinical practice. Modules contained within this level of training are presented in Exhibit 1.1. This level of training should be offered in the context of a doctoral training program in psychology or through continuing education at the postdoctoral level for individuals who have already attained licensure for independent practice. The curriculum is designed to be flexible and responsive to the learning needs of the individual. Trainees who have demonstrated mastery in one or more curriculum modules do not need to get additional training in that module (APA, 1995).

EXHIBIT 1.1
Modules of Level I Training in Psychopathology

1. Biological Bases of Psychopharmacological Treatment
2–3. Principles of Psychopharmacological Treatment
4. General Introduction to Clinical Psychopharmacology
5. Introduction to the Psychopharmacological Treatment of Psychoactive Substance Use Disorders
6. Introduction to the Psychopharmacological Treatment of Psychotic Disorders
7. Introduction to the Psychopharmacological Treatment of Mood Disorders
8. Introduction to the Psychopharmacological Treatment of Anxiety Disorders
9. Introduction to the Psychopharmacological Treatment of Developmental Disorders

Note. From *Final Report of the BEA Working Group to Develop a Level I Curriculum for Psychopharmacology Education and Training*, by the American Psychological Association, 1995, p. 1. Copyright 1995 by the American Psychological Association. Reprinted with permission.

Level II training provides the knowledge base needed for the subset of psychologists who intend to collaborate with prescribing providers in the delivery of pharmacotherapy. This level of training provides information that is valuable in (a) developing professional collaborations, (b) conducting clinical practice in an ethical manner, (c) understanding the pharmacokinetics of different classes of medication, (d) determining when to use medication versus psychosocial interventions, (e) understanding the potential effects and adverse effects of various psychotropic medications, (f) monitoring the beneficial effects and adverse effects of medication, (g) improving adherence with treatment, and (h) becoming informed consumers of psychopharmacology research and conducting clinical research (APA, 1997). Training modules have been created for four populations of clients: children and adolescents, older adults, adults with serious mental illness, and individuals with developmental disabilities. A summary of the topics addressed in the module developed for children and adolescents is presented in Exhibit 1.2. The curriculum for each module is self-contained and independent of the curricula in the other modules, so that individuals can pursue training in the modules related to their areas of clinical practice. Level II training can be adapted for application in internship, postdoctoral fellowship, and continuing education programs.

Level III training provides the extensive knowledge base and skill set required by psychologists who seek prescription privileges. In 1996, the APA Task Force on Prescription Privileges issued recommendations for Level III training based on curricula and guidelines developed by the Department of Defense demonstration project curriculum, the report of the Blue Ribbon Panel of the Professional Education Task Force of the California Psychological Association and the California School of Professional Psychology—Los Angeles, and the American College of Neuropsychopharmacology. Level III is intended as a postdoctoral training experience for professionals who currently hold a state license for independent practice and who practice as health service providers. It consists of intensive training in the areas of neuroscience, pharmacology, physiology, physical assessment and laboratory examinations, and legal and ethical issues (APA, 1996). Level III also involves extensive, supervised clinical experiences. Exhibit 1.3 summarizes the didactic and practicum requirements for this level of training. The APA Practice Directorate has designated several sites around the United States as providers of this level of training.

IMPLICATIONS FOR RESEARCH

Although an extensive body of research currently exists to guide psychologists in their roles as consultants in the medication management of children and adolescents, additional research is clearly needed. Research

EXHIBIT 1.2
Summary Outline of Topics in Level II Training in Psychopathology of Children and Adolescents

  I. Professional and Legal Issues
    a. Interdisciplinary collaboration
    b. Ethical and legal issues
 II. Assessment
    a. Physical assessment
    b. Psychological assessment
    c. Ecological assessment of family, school, and community systems
    d. Outcome assessment of effects and side effects
III. Pharmacological Issues and Pediatric Variations
    a. Childhood disorders and medications used to treat them
    b. Distribution and elimination of pharmacological substances
    c. Pharmacokinetics and pharmacodynamics
    d. Onset and duration of effects
    e. Mechanisms of drug action
    f. Issues of tolerance and dependence
IV. Issues of Children With Developmental Disabilities or Chronic Illnesses
    a. Unique physical, cognitive, and behavioral effects
    b. Pharmacological factors
    c. Unique negative side effects
 V. Treatment Issues
    a. Intervention planning
    b. Initiation of pharmacological treatments
    c. Monitoring of effects and side effects
    d. Maintenance of pharmacological interventions
    e. Discontinuation of medication
    f. Follow-up care
    g. Use of medication separately and in combination with psychosocial treatments
    h. Assessing and improving adherence
VI. Research
    a. Strategies for conducting a thorough literature review
    b. Strategies for planning single-subject and group research designs
    c. Models of drug development
    d. Measurement issues
    e. Safety/abuse liability
    f. Assessing consumer satisfaction and cost effectiveness
    g. Conducting multimodal treatment studies
    h. Meta-analytic research strategies

Note. From *Curriculum for Psychopharmacological Training for Particular Populations Using a Collaborative Practice Model,* by the American Psychological Association, 1997, pp. 1–13. Copyright 1997 by the American Psychological Association. Reprinted with permission.

identifying empirically supported psychosocial and pharmacological treatments for children with specific disorders has been extremely useful. However, studies that investigate the differential effects of empirically supported psychosocial versus pharmacological treatments compared with combined interventions for children with specific disorders but varying patterns of comorbidity are very much needed. An excellent example of the kind of research needed is the recently completed Multimodal Treatment Study for

EXHIBIT 1.3
Recommended Didactic and Practicum Requirements for Postdoctoral Training in Psychopharmacology for Prescription Privileges

Didactic Requirements
- Neuroanatomy, neurophysiology, neurochemistry
- Pharmacology, developmental psychopharmacology, chemical dependency, pain management
- Pathophysiology, including effects of alterations in anatomical and physiological processes on bioavailability and biodisposition of drugs
- Introduction to physical assessment and laboratory examinations
- Clinical pharmacotherapeutics, including ethical and legal issues, combined pharmacological and psychosocial interventions, and pharmacoepidemiology

Practicum Requirements
- Diverse patient mix preferably from outpatient and inpatient settings, with emphasis on patient population related to current and anticipated future practice
- Minimum of 100 patients treated with medication
- Minimum of 2 hours of individual supervision per week under the direction of qualified practitioners

Note. From *Recommended Postdoctoral Training in Psychopharmacology for Prescriptive Privileges*, by the American Psychological Association, 1996, pp. 3–5. Copyright 1996 by the American Psychological Association. Reprinted with permission.

Children With Attention-Deficit/Hyperactivity Disorder (1999), the largest clinical trial sponsored by National Institute of Mental Health, which compared the effects of medication versus behavior therapy in comparison with a combined treatment and a control group receiving care in the community. This study examined the effects of varying treatments on children with different subtypes of ADHD and patterns of comorbid disorders, as well as intervention effects using multiple outcome measures assessing many domains of functioning. The results of this study have enabled investigators to address the question of which treatment approach is most effective for which subset of ADHD children with specific types of academic, behavioral, and social problems. Although this study was not designed to investigate the incremental effects of a pharmacological versus behavioral approach to intervention, these types of studies have been conducted by researchers in previous investigations (e.g., see Pelham et al., 1993).

Research studies examining treatments for ADHD have provided guidelines for determining the types of children who are most likely to benefit from a pharmacological, a behavioral, or a combined approach to intervention. Studies of this kind are needed for other disorders to delineate decision-making rules and algorithms for initiating the process of intervention and changing the treatment plan in response to outcome data.

Determining the optimal approach to intervention depends on numerous factors, although major considerations include a child's and caregiver's readiness for change and their perceptions of the intervention plan. As described earlier, psychologists can serve an important role in assessing caregiver and child attitudes about treatment options and planning an approach to intervention that is suitable to the family. To guide psychologists in this role, research investigating family readiness for change, assessing the family's willingness to engage in pharmacological versus psychosocial interventions for various psychiatric disorders, and identifying factors that can facilitate a family's preparation for intervention is needed. Furthermore, research investigating factors that facilitate adherence with pharmacological and psychosocial treatments for a wide range of mental health disorders would help to guide practice.

Although it seems clear that a psychologist with expertise in psychopharmacology and single-subject research design can serve an important role in the delivery of services to children with mental health disorders, it is important that psychologists provide convincing evidence of the value they add to the intervention process. Given the current emphasis on providing services in a highly time-efficient and cost-effective manner in response to reforms in health care, it is imperative that psychologists specify the roles they serve in determining the appropriateness of psychotropic medication, monitoring outcomes, and coordinating services for the child and family. They must also demonstrate that when they serve these functions, children and families achieve better outcomes, are more satisfied with the treatments provided, experience fewer serious adverse effects of intervention, and adhere more consistently with intervention. In addition, practicing psychologists need to demonstrate how their involvement in the medication management process can result in a cost savings to families and managed care companies. With these data, psychologists will be able to demonstrate that primary care physicians, who write most of the prescriptions for behavioral health problems, need the assistance of a mental health professional to determine the appropriateness of medication and to manage the care of children with psychological disorders.

CONCLUSION

Given their training in psychopathology, empirically supported interventions for children with mental health problems, measurement of behavior, research design, and data analyses, psychologists can serve important roles in the pharmacological management of children and adolescents. These roles include (a) determining when pharmacotherapy, psychosocial treatment, or a combined approach to intervention would be best suited for the child; (b) understanding a child's and caregiver's level of readiness for intervention and their perceptions about potentially effective treatments for the problems presented; (c) designing medication-monitoring protocols; (d) analyzing the data generated by these protocols; and (e) facilitating collaboration among professionals and family members so that children receive an integrated approach to care.

In response to the significant advances in the understanding of the biological bases of psychiatric disorders and medical interventions to manage mental disorders, there has been a strong movement to influence state legislators to grant prescription privileges to psychologists. However, opposition to this movement within the field of psychology has also been strong, because of concerns about psychology relinquishing what is unique to the profession and the radical shift in training that would be required. The concern among some academic psychologists is that these new domains of practice could lead to an erosion of skills in psychosocial intervention and prevention. As the profession engages in this debate and decides its future course, many psychologists are rapidly expanding their skill set regarding psychopharmacology and making important contributions to the medication management of children and adolescents in research and in practice.

Given advances in the understanding of the neuropharmacological bases for many psychiatric disorders and the important contribution that medication can make in the treatment of children with mental health problems, the APA Ad Hoc Task Force on Psychopharmacology (APA, 1996) has strongly recommended that the preparation of psychologists at the graduate level include basic training in psychopharmacology. Also, for those individuals who are interested in collaborating with prescribing clinicians, the APA Ad Hoc Task Force has developed specific curriculum guidelines pertaining to children and adolescents and individuals with disabilities, in addition to adults with serious psychiatric problems and older adults. Research is clearly needed to develop decision-making rules for determining when to use pharmacological, psychosocial, and combined approaches to care. It is critical that psychologists demonstrate empirically how their consultation to prescribing clinicians can improve the mental health care of children and do so in a way that results in a more efficient and economical means of providing services to families.

REFERENCES

American Psychiatric Association. (1994). *Diagnostic and statistical manual of mental disorders* (4th ed.). Washington, DC: Author.

American Psychological Association. (1992). *Report of the APA Ad Hoc Task Force on Psychopharmacology*. Washington, DC: Author.

American Psychological Association. (1995). *Final report of the BEA working group* to develop a Level I curriculum for psychopharmacology education and training. Washington, DC: Author.

American Psychological Association. (1996). *Recommended postdoctoral training in psychopharmacology for prescription privileges*. Washington, DC: Author.

American Psychological Association. (1997). *Curriculum for psychopharmacological training for particular populations using a collaborative practice model*. Washington, DC: Author.

Barkley, R. A., Barclay, A., Conners, C. K., Gadow, K., Gittelman, R., Sprague, R., & Swanson, J. (1990). Task Force report: The appropriate role of clinical child psychologists in the prescribing of psychoactive medication for children. *Journal of Clinical Child Psychology, 19*(Suppl.), 1–38.

Beutler, L. E. (1998). Identifying empirically supported treatments: What if we didn't? *Journal of Consulting and Clinical Psychology, 66*, 7–18.

Blum, N. J., Mauk, J. E., McComas, J. J., & Mace, F. C. (1996). Separate and combined effects of methylphenidate and a behavioral intervention on disruptive behavior in children with mental retardation. *Journal of Applied Behavior Analysis, 29*, 305–319.

Brestan, E. V., & Eyberg, S. M. (1998). Effective psychosocial treatments for conduct-disordered children and adolescents: 29 years, 82 studies, and 5,272 kids. *Journal of Clinical Child Psychology, 27*, 146–155.

Chambless, D. L., & Hollon, S. D. (1998). Defining empirically supported therapies. *Journal of Consulting and Clinical Psychology, 66*, 7–18.

Chambless, D. L., Sanderson, W. C., Shoham, V., Bennett Johnson, S., Pope, K. S., Crits-Christoph, P., Baker, M., Johnson, B., Woody, S. R., Sue, S., Beutler, L., Williams, D. A., & McCurry, S. (1996). An update on empirically validated therapies. *Clinical Psychologist, 49*, 5–18.

DeLeon, P., & DeNelsky, G. Y. (1993, January/February). The prescription privilege debate: Will privileges advance psychology? *The National Psychologist, 2*, 12–13.

DeLeon, P. H., & Wiggins, J. G. (1996). Prescription privileges for psychologists. *American Psychologist, 51*, 198–206.

DeNelsky, G. Y. (1996). The case against prescription privileges for psychologists. *American Psychologist, 51*, 198–206.

Drotar, D. (1995). *Consulting with pediatricians: Psychological perspectives*. New York: Plenum Press.

DuPaul, G. J., & Barkley, R. A. (1993). The utility of behavioral methodology in medication treatment of children with attention deficit hyperactivity disorder. *Behavior Therapy, 24*, 47–66.

Hayes, S. C., & Heiby, E. (1996). Psychology's drug problem: Do we need a fix or should we just say no? *American Psychologist, 51*, 198–206.

Hoza, B., Pelham, W. E., Sams, S. E., & Carlson, C. (1992). An examination of "dosage" effects of both behavior therapy and methylphenidate on the classroom performance of two ADHD children. *Behavior Modification, 16*, 164–192.

Humphreys, K. (1996). Clinical psychologists as psychotherapists: History, future, and alternatives. *American Psychologist, 51,* 198–206.

Kaslow, N. J., & Thompson, M. P. (1998). Applying the criteria for empirically supported treatments to studies of psychosocial interventions for child and adolescent depression. *Journal of Clinical Child Psychology, 27,* 146–155.

Kazdin, A. E. (1996). Dropping out of psychotherapy: Issues for research and implications for practice. *Clinical Child Psychology and Psychiatry, 1,* 133–156.

Kazdin, A. E., & Weisz, J. (1998). Identifying and developing empirically supported child and adolescent treatments. *Journal of Consulting and Clinical Psychology, 66,* 7–18.

Kubiszyn, T. (1994). Pediatric psychopharmacology and prescription privileges: Implications and opportunities for school psychology. *School Psychology Quarterly, 9,* 26–40.

Mash, E. J., & Terdal, L. G. (Eds.). (1997). *Assessment of childhood disorders* (3rd ed.). New York: Guilford Press.

Multimodal Treatment Study for Children With Attention-Deficit/Hyperactivity Disorder Cooperative Group. (1999). A 14-month randomized clinical trial of treatment strategies for attention-deficit/hyperactivity disorder. *Archives of General Psychiatry, 56,* 1073–1086.

Ollendick, T. H., & King, N. J. (1998). Empirically supported treatments for children with phobic and anxiety disorders. *Journal of Clinical Child Psychology, 27,* 146–155.

Osman, B. B. (2000). Coordinating care in the prescription and use of Ritalin with attention deficit hyperactivity disorder children/adolescents. In L. L. Greenhill & B. B. Osman (Eds.), *Ritalin: Theory and practice* (2nd ed., pp. 175–190). Larchmont, NY: Mary Ann Liebert.

Pachman, J. S. (1996). The dawn of a revolution in mental health. *American Psychologist, 51,* 213–215.

Pelham, W. E. (1999). The NIMH multimodal treatment study for attention-deficit hyperactivity disorder: Just say yes to drugs alone? *Canadian Journal of Psychiatry, 44,* 981–990.

Pelham, W. E., Carlson, C., Sams, S. E., Vallano, G., Dixon, M. J., & Hoza, B. (1993). Separate and combined effects of methylphenidate and behavior modification on boys with attention deficit-hyperactivity disorder in the classroom. *Journal of Consulting and Clinical Psychology, 61,* 506–515.

Pelham, W. E., Wheeler, T., & Chronis, A. (1998). Empirically supported psychosocial treatments for attention deficit hyperactivity disorder. *Journal of Clinical Child Psychology, 27,* 146–155.

Power, T. J., Atkins, M., Osborne, M., & Blum, N. (1994). The school psychologist as manager of programming for ADHD. *School Psychology Review, 23,* 279–291.

Power, T. J., Blum, N. J., Jones, S. M., & Kaplan, P. E. (1996). Brief report: Response to methylphenidate in two children with Williams syndrome. *Journal of Autism and Developmental Disorders, 27,* 79–87.

Prochaska, J. O., DiClemente, C. C., & Norcross, J. C. (1992). In search of how people change: Applications to addictive behaviors. *American Psychologist, 47*, 1102–1114.

Rabasca, L. (2000, May). APA participates in White House meeting that questions psychotropic drug use among preschoolers. *APA Monitor, 31*, p. 10.

Rapport, M. D., Denney, C., DuPaul, G. J., & Gardner, M. J. (1994). Attention deficit disorder and methylphenidate: Normalization rates, clinical effectiveness, and response prediction in 76 children. *Journal of the American Academy of Child and Adolescent Psychiatry, 33*, 882–893.

Rogers, S. J. (1998). Empirically supported comprehensive treatments for young children with autism. *Journal of Clinical Child Psychology, 27*, 146–155.

Safer, D. J., Zito, J. M., & Fine, E. M. (1996). Increased methylphenidate usage for attention deficit disorder in the 1990s. *Pediatrics, 98*, 1084–1088.

Shaffer, D., Lucas, C. P., & Richters, J. E. (Eds.). (1999). *Diagnostic assessment in child and adolescent psychopathology.* New York: Guilford Press.

Zito, J. M., Safer, D. J., dosReis, S., Gardner, J. F., Boles, M., & Lynch, F. (2000). Trends in the prescribing of psychotropic medications to preschoolers. *Journal of the American Medical Association, 283*, 1025–1030.

2

MONITORING MEDICATION EFFECTIVENESS

Medication can be a highly effective intervention for children with psychological disorders. Unfortunately, pharmacological interventions are sometimes ineffective in addressing target symptoms, and at times these treatments may result in adverse effects that are problematic or even dangerous. Despite numerous efforts, researchers generally have not been successful in identifying factors that are predictive of responsiveness to psychotropic medication. Although research has provided some broad guidelines for predicting those individuals who are likely to experience adverse effects, generally studies have failed to produce a set of indicators that are useful in predicting adverse effects from pharmacological treatments. Furthermore, research regarding the effects of medication has been conducted more extensively among adults than among children and adolescents for most mental health disorders. For these reasons, it is important that clinicians treating children and adolescents carefully monitor the beneficial and adverse effects of medication to determine the outcomes for the individuals being treated.

In this chapter, we describe strategies that are useful for monitoring the beneficial and adverse effects of pharmacological interventions to manage psychological disorders. Procedures are described for assessing outcomes across a broad range of psychological domains of functioning and in a variety of contexts. Methodological issues are delineated that are critical in designing valid medication-monitoring protocols.

IDENTIFYING THE GOALS OF TREATMENT

As with all interventions, the initial step in designing methods to evaluate medication effectiveness is to identify the specific goals of treatment. Medication should be selected to treat a specific set of target symptoms, in specific contexts, to have an impact on certain domains of psychological functioning (Mercugliano, Power, & Blum, 1998).

Clinicians in collaboration with the family need to identify those target symptoms of greatest concern to the child, parents, and educators. They should assess the impact that these problems are having on a child's functioning in the domains of academic, social, emotional, and behavioral functioning. Furthermore, it is useful to know the contexts (e.g., classroom, playground, homework setting, and public settings) within which the child's functioning is being adversely affected. With this information, clinicians can delineate the goals of intervention and provide guidance to the family regarding the potential effectiveness of medication in managing the symptoms targeted for change. Clinicians can also delineate potential adverse effects associated with each of the medication options. Outcome measures should be selected to determine whether progress is being made in attaining the goals of treatment and whether adverse effects are of sufficient severity to preclude the use of a particular medication.

Selecting the optimal medication strategy and designing methods that can be used to monitor treatment effectiveness depend as much on the goals of intervention as they do on the diagnostic profile of the child being treated (Mercugliano et al., 1998). For example, if a child has been diagnosed with attention deficit hyperactivity disorder (ADHD) and Tourette's syndrome, and there is evidence of a depressive disorder, the medication strategy can vary greatly depending on the symptoms targeted for change and the psychological functions that need to be addressed. If the symptoms of greatest concern pertain to ADHD and the domains of psychological impairment most affected are attention and academic functioning, then an initial intervention strategy that includes a trial of stimulant medication, in particular methylphenidate (Ritalin), might be justified (Castellanos et al., 1997; Gadow, Sverd, Sprafkin, Nolan, & Ezor, 1995). In this case, it would be important to monitor carefully effects on ADHD symptoms and academic functioning in both the home and school settings. Given that stimulant medication is sometimes associated with an exacerbation of tics in children with Tourette's syndrome (Castellanos et al., 1997), it would also be important to assess tic behaviors in settings in which the child frequently interacts with peers.

In contrast, if the primary target of intervention is tics and the goal is to reduce tics in social situations, the clinical team may wish to consider an alternative medication, such as a neuroleptic (e.g., haloperidol or pimozide; Castellanos, 1998; Kurlan, 1997). The effects of these medications on tic behaviors manifested in classroom, playground, and other social settings should be assessed. Furthermore, because of the potential for these medications to be associated with sedation (Brown & Sawyer, 1998), the adverse effects of neuroleptic medications need to be carefully monitored. (A *Glossary of Terms* is provided at the end of the book to facilitate an understanding of medical terms.)

SELECTING OUTCOME MEASURES

Clinicians need to select outcome measures that are sensitive to changes in symptoms and domains of psychological functioning targeted for intervention. Because measures of physiological response to medication (e.g., electroencephalogram results, blood levels, and results of brain imaging studies) usually are not predictive of behavioral response to most psychotropic medications, physiological measures are generally not useful in monitoring the behavioral effects of pharmacological intervention. However, physiological measures may be useful with some medications in assessing adverse effects that cannot be reported by the patient (Brown & Sawyer, 1998; DuPaul, Barkley, & Connor, 1998). Also, because each measure is associated with one or more practical and psychometric limitations, multiple measures of treatment outcome should be collected when conducting a medication trial (Brown & Sawyer, 1998; DuPaul & Barkley, 1993). The following is a description of the types of measurement procedures that may be useful in monitoring the effectiveness of medications in the domains of academic functioning, externalizing behavior including ADHD, internalizing symptoms, and social functioning. A summary of these procedures is outlined in Exhibit 2.1. Specific assessment techniques that have been demonstrated to be effective in monitoring medication outcomes are described briefly. Also, procedures for assessing adverse effects and monitoring parent and child views about the acceptability of interventions are discussed.

Academic Functioning

Medication is often used to improve the academic functioning of children. The stimulants, in particular, have been demonstrated to have beneficial effects for on-task behavior, academic productivity and accuracy, working memory, and the ability to engage in strategic, effortful processing (Douglas, Barr, Desilets, & Sherman, 1995; DuPaul & Rapport, 1993;

EXHIBIT 2.1
Measurement Procedures to Assess Treatment Outcomes in Major Domains of Child Functioning

Academic Performance
   Teacher records of academic performance
   Teacher rating scales
   Parent ratings of homework performance
   Measures of cognitive functioning
   Curriculum-based measures of academic functioning
Externalizing Behavior
   Teacher rating scales
   Parent rating scales
   Direct observations in multiple settings
   Clinic-based measures of attention and impulse control
Internalizing Functioning
   Parent rating scales
   Child self-report scales
Social Functioning
   Teacher rating scales
   Parent rating scales
   Child self-report measures
   Direct observations of social behavior

O'Toole, Abramowitz, Morris, & Dulcan, 1997; Rapport, Denney, DuPaul, & Gardner, 1994; Tannock, Ickowicz, & Schachar, 1995). However, research regarding the short- and long-term effects of stimulant medication on academic achievement has not been conclusive (DuPaul, Barkley, & Connor, 1998).

Some medications may be associated with deleterious effects on cognitive and academic functioning. In particular, concerns have been raised about the effects of antipsychotic medications on cognitive and academic functioning (Brown & Sawyer, 1998). For this reason, it is important to assess the effects of medication on cognitive and academic functioning when using medications that have been associated with adverse effects on cognitive performance. Many measures have been developed to assess the effects of medication on cognitive and academic performance. These procedures include teacher records of academic functioning, parent records of homework performance, measures of cognitive functioning, and curriculum-based measures of academic functioning.

Teacher Records of Academic Performance

Teachers are an excellent source of information about the children's academic performance because of numerous opportunities they have to observe the educational functioning of children in relation to their peers. Teachers routinely keep records of academic performance that may be useful in medication monitoring. These records include performance on seat work assignments, performance on tests and quizzes, and completion of homework assignments. In addition, teachers may be asked to complete rating scales pertaining to the academic performance of students. A particularly useful measure is the Academic Performance Rating Scale (DuPaul, Rapport, & Perriello, 1991), which assesses academic productivity, academic success, and level of impulsivity. Because this instrument is brief and can be completed in less than 10 minutes, it is highly suitable for outcome assessment.

Parent Records of Homework Performance

It is important to monitor homework to determine if medication is having beneficial effects on homework performance and to assess whether adverse effects to medication, such as rebound effects when medication is wearing off, may be having a deleterious effect on homework. Parents can provide a wealth of valuable information about homework performance. They record the amount of time the child spent doing homework as well as rates of homework completion and accuracy. Also, parent rating scales, such as the Homework Problems Checklist (Anesko, Schoiock, Ramiriz, & Levine, 1987) and the Homework Problems Questionnaire (Power, Karustis, Mercugliano, & Blum, 1998), can be useful in outcome assessment.

Measures of Cognitive Functioning

Researchers and clinicians often use measures of cognitive functioning to assess the effects of medication. These procedures can be helpful in assessing cognitive processes that are believed to be important in learning. Tasks that involve learning and memory of new information are often used to assess medication effects (Balthazor, Wagner, & Pelham, 1991; O'Toole et al., 1997; Tannock et al., 1995). Examples of these measures include the paired associate learning task (see Douglas, Barr, O'Neill, & Britton, 1986) and the California Verbal Learning Test–Children's Version (Delis, Kramer, Kaplan, & Ober, 1994). Equivalent forms of memory tasks are easy to create, which is helpful when using these procedures repeatedly in a medication-monitoring protocol. However, these procedures have been criticized by some researchers because of the lack of correspondence of these measures to academic tasks presented to children in actual learning situations (Barkley, 1991b).

Curriculum-Based Measures

Research investigating the effects of medication on academic achievement has been characterized by problems with measurement. Many of the early studies (reviewed in Barkley & Cunningham, 1978) have examined medication effects on standardized, norm-referenced tests that do not have sufficient sensitivity to measure academic progress over brief periods of time. Often children's academic performance has been measured using test items that do not correspond closely with curriculum materials, casting doubt about the generalizability of findings to actual learning situations.

Many studies conducted since the mid-1980s have used curriculum-based measures of academic performance, that is, measures that correspond closely with classroom activities and that are brief and easy to administer in a repeated measures protocol. For example, students may be administered a page of math problems or a worksheet of language arts items to complete in a specified period of time. These measures are typically scored for rates of completion and accuracy. Research repeatedly has demonstrated the utility of these procedures in the assessment of medication effects (Rapport et al., 1994; Swanson et al., 1998).

Most of the curriculum-based procedures that have been used in research have assessed changes in work productivity and accuracy in response to medication, but few have examined the effect of medication on rates of learning or skill acquisition. However, curriculum-based measurement (CBM) procedures have been developed to evaluate changes in rates of skill acquisition in response to intervention (see Shinn, 1998). These techniques have been used primarily to assess the effects of academic skills interventions, but researchers have begun to use these procedures in assessing the effectiveness of pharmacological interventions (Roberts & Landau, 1995; Stoner, Carey, Ikeda, & Shinn, 1994). Through the serial assessment of children using brief reading and math probe materials taken directly from the classroom curriculum, CBM procedures have been shown to be highly sensitive in assessing improvements in academic performance over short and long periods of time. The indices used to assess reading progress (i.e., words read correctly per minute) and math progress (i.e., digits calculated correctly per minute), in particular, have been shown to be reliable and valid measures of academic performance and to be highly sensitive to the effects of intervention (Shinn, 1998). When used in medication trials, these indices can be used to calculate a rate of skill acquisition during each phase of treatment to determine whether medication is able to improve rates of learning in relation to baseline performance and to determine the optimal dose of medication. The following is a brief case description derived from Ikeda (1994) that illustrates the potential utility of CBM.

Case Illustration

Ned, an 8-year-old second grader who was diagnosed with ADHD, was administered a trial of methylphenidate to address problems with attention and academic performance. After a 2-week baseline period, he was administered placebo, 5 mg, 10 mg, and 15 mg of medication in double-blind fashion. Each dose of medication/placebo was administered for 1 week. Outcome was assessed using teacher reports of attention and behavior; reports of adverse effects from parent, teacher, and child; and CBM procedures to assess reading and math. Ned was asked to read for 1 minute passages taken from his curriculum. Performance was scored for words read correctly per minute. Math probes were developed to coincide with the curriculum being taught in the classroom. Performance was scored for number of digits calculated correctly in 2 minutes. Ned was administered reading and math probes three times per treatment phase. Performance in each phase was determined to be the median performance on the reading and math probes for that phase.

A review of data obtained from rating scales and CBM procedures revealed that the optimal level of medication for Ned was 10 mg of methylphenidate. Following the medication trial, Ned was placed on 10 mg of medication. CBM techniques were administered on a daily basis over a 2-week period to more carefully assess the effects of medication on academic performance. Figure 2.1 illustrates the changes in performance on curriculum-based measures of reading between the baseline and follow-up phases. During baseline, Ned's performance in reading did not improve; in fact, the slope during this phase was −.69 words correct per day. In contrast, oral reading during follow-up improved at the rate of 2.58 words correct per day, which was dramatically greater than baseline performance and much higher than the rate of performance typically demonstrated by students at his grade level. With regard to math (see Figure 2.2), Ned's performance was essentially unchanged by medication. During baseline,

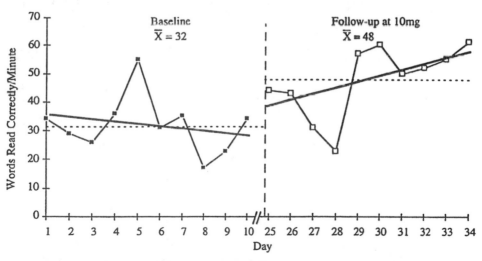

Figure 2.1. Change in rate of oral reading from baseline to follow-up conditions. From *Exploring Dependent Measures for Use in Medication Evaluations for Children Diagnosed as Having ADHD*, by M. J. Ikeda, 1994, p. 101. Copyright 1994 by M. J. Ikeda. Reprinted with permission.

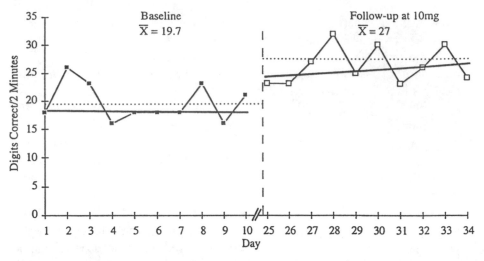

Figure 2.2. Change in rate of math computation from baseline to follow-up conditions. From *Exploring Dependent Measures for Use in Medication Evaluations for Children Diagnosed as Having ADHD*, by M. J. Ikeda, 1994, p. 101. Copyright 1994 by M. J. Ikeda. Reprinted with permission.

performance changed at the rate of $-.02$ digits correct per day, and at follow-up math slope incremented minimally to .20 digits per day.

The results of this case study affirm Stoner et al.'s (1994) findings that CBM can be helpful in determining medication effectiveness and titrating medication dose. The findings also suggest that medication in some cases may have an effect on rate of skill acquisition and that CBM techniques may be highly useful in assessing the effects of medication on learning.

Externalizing Behavior

Several methods have been demonstrated to be effective in evaluating changes in externalizing behavior, including inattention, overactivity, noncompliance with rules, defiance to adults, and conduct problems. The most effective types of procedures are behavior rating scales and direct observations of behavior, although clinic-based measures of attention and impulsivity are also used in clinical practice.

Rating Scales

Both parent and teacher rating scales are highly useful in medication monitoring. Parent-report measures are particularly helpful in assessing behaviors that arise in the home setting, and teacher-report measures are useful in assessing school-based problems. Because concordance rates between parent- and teacher-report measures are relatively low, and because each set of ratings typically makes an independent and important contribution to the assessment of child behavior problems (Power, Andrews, et al., 1998), it is generally recommended that parent- and teacher-report measures be included in a battery to assess externalizing behavioral problems.

Rating scales can be differentiated into those that assess a wide range of behavioral and emotional problems (e.g., inattention, hyperactivity, aggression, conduct problems, anxiety, depression, and social problems) and those that assess specific behaviors associated with a disorder (e.g., symptoms of anxiety only or aggressive behaviors only; Power, Eiraldi, Mercugliano, & Blum, 1998). Wide-range or broad-band scales, many of which have excellent psychometric properties, are particularly useful when clinicians are interested in assessing the effects of medication across a broad range of externalizing and internalizing behaviors. A limitation of broad-band procedures, particularly when used repeatedly in a medication-monitoring protocol, is that they are lengthy and time consuming to complete. Broad-band scales have been developed for use by parents as well as teachers. Examples of broad-band scales include the Child Behavior Checklist (CBCL; Achenbach, 1991a) and CBCL–Teacher Report Form (Achenbach, 1991b), the Behavior Assessment System for Children (BASC; Reynolds & Kamphaus, 1992), and the Devereux Scales of Mental Disorders (DSMD; Naglieri, LeBuffe, & Pfeiffer, 1994).

Narrow-band scales have been developed to assess specific problems in the domain of behavioral functioning. These measures are typically brief, psychometrically sound, and efficient to use when monitoring the effects of medication. Two narrow-band measures that are very useful in assessing improvements in compliance with rules are the 16-item Home Situations Questionnaire, completed by parents, and the 12-item School Situations Questionnaire, completed by teachers (see Barkley, 1991a). For each item, the respondent is asked whether the child has a behavior problem in a particular situation and to rate the severity of the problem. These measures have been demonstrated to be highly effective in detecting changes in externalizing behavior in response to medication (DuPaul, Barkley, & McMurray, 1994). Numerous measures of ADHD symptoms have been developed, and virtually all of these scales have been demonstrated to be sensitive to the effects of stimulant medication. These measures include the ADHD Rating Scale–IV (DuPaul, Power, Anastopoulos, & Reid, 1998), the Conners Rating Scales–Revised (Conners, 1997), and the Attention Deficit Disorder-Hyperactivity: Comprehensive Teacher's Rating Scale (Ullman, Sleator, & Sprague, 1996). Further narrow-band scales have been useful in monitoring the effects of medication on tics. For example, the Tourette Syndrome Severity Scale (Shapiro & Shapiro, 1984) and the Hopkins Motor/Vocal Tic Scale (Walkup, Rosenberg, Brown, & Singer,

1992) have been used to assess the effects of clonidine (Catapres) and desimpramine (Norpramine) on vocal and motor tics (Singer et al., 1995).

Observations of Behavior

Rating scales have the advantage of excellent psychometric properties and efficiency of use, but limitations of these measures include potential problems with rater bias and their relative insensitivity to subtle changes in behavior (Power, Eiraldi, et al., 1998; Rapport et al., 1994). The use of direct observations of behavior provides a more objective source of information about behavior problems and affords an assessment of specific changes in behavioral disturbances. A particularly useful observation procedure that was developed for use in school settings is the ADHD School Observation Code (Gadow, Sprafkin, & Nolan, 1996). This procedure provides an assessment of inattention, overactivity, compliance with rules, aggression, and appropriate social interaction in a variety of school situations, including classroom, playground, and lunchroom. This technique has been demonstrated to have adequate interrater reliability and to be sensitive to the effects of stimulant medication (Nolan & Gadow, 1997). Direct observations and videotaped recordings also have been useful in assessing the effects of medication on tic behaviors (Gadow, Nolan, & Sverd, 1992). Although direct observations of school functioning are a useful source of information about ADHD, tics, and externalizing behaviors, these techniques are time consuming and may be difficult to use on a repeated basis when evaluating the effects of medication.

Another method of conducting direct observations of behavior is to observe the child performing a standardized task in a clinic setting. For example, researchers have conducted systematic observations of behavior during a restricted academic situation in which the child was asked to complete a set of math problems. Behaviors pertaining to inattention, distractibility, and overactivity have been coded with a high level of interrater reliability during these activities. These procedures have been demonstrated to be highly responsive to the effects of stimulants among children with ADHD (DuPaul et al., 1994). Also, procedures have been developed for the observation of young children during standardized play and vigilance activities in clinic settings. These techniques have demonstrated adequate reliability and have been shown to be sensitive to the effects of stimulant medication (Power, Blum, Jones, & Kaplan, 1996).

Clinic-Based Procedures

Many investigators have used tests that are administered in clinic-based settings to evaluate the effects of psychotropic medication. Some of the most commonly used procedures include continuous performance tasks, reaction time tasks, and match-to-sample procedures, which have been developed to assess attention and impulse control. Many of these procedures have been demonstrated to be sensitive to stimulant medication (DuPaul et al., 1994). However, concerns have been raised about (a) the specific functions that these tests actually measure, (b) the relatively low relationship between clinic-based measures and ecological assessments of attention and behavior (Barkley, 1991b), and (c) the relatively high false negative rates on these measures, particularly with older children and adolescents (DuPaul, Anastopoulos, Shelton, Guevremont, & Metevia, 1992).

Internalizing Functioning

Assessing internalizing, emotional functioning (e.g., anxiety or mood) is more challenging than evaluating externalizing behavior because children's emotions cannot be observed directly. The best sources of information about internalizing functioning are informant reports, in particular, parent ratings and child self-reports (Callahan, Panichelli-Mindel, & Kendall, 1996). When assessing internalizing problems, it is generally important to collect information from parents and children, given the lack of concordance between these sources of information (Achenbach, McConaughy, & Howell, 1987) and the independent contribution of each source of data to the prediction of emotional problems (Rubio-Stipec et al., 1994).

Parent Reports

As described earlier, broad-band assessment procedures can be useful in assessing children's emotional problems and changes in internalizing symptoms in response to intervention. The CBCL is the broad-band measure that is most commonly used in clinical practice and research. The BASC and DSMD are also useful in the assessment of internalizing functioning in that they afford an independent assessment of anxiety and depression.

Child Self-Reports

A number of self-report measures are available for the assessment of children's emotional problems. The Youth Self-Report (Achenbach, 1991c) is a broad-band measure that assesses dimensions of functioning that are similar to those assessed by the CBCL and CBCL–Teacher Report Form, which are respectively parent- and teacher-report scales. The BASC also provides a self-report, wide-range measure of emotional functioning. Narrow-band measures of anxiety include the Revised Children's Manifest Anxiety Scale (Reynolds & Richmond, 1985) and the Multidimensional Anxiety Scale for Children (March, Parker, Sullivan, Stallings, & Conners,

1997). Examples of narrow-range measures of depressive symptoms are the Children's Depression Inventory (Kovacs, 1992) and the Reynolds Adolescent Depression Scale (Reynolds, 1987). A useful self-report measure of obsessive–compulsive symptoms is the Leyton Obsessional Inventory–Child Version (Berg, Rapoport, & Flament, 1986).

Social Functioning

Medication often has an effect on the social behavior of children. Medication can alter attempts to engage in social interaction, rates of aggression, and the feedback offered by peers (Granger, Whalen, Henker, & Cantwell, 1996; Hinshaw, Henker, Whalen, Erhardt, & Dunnington, 1989). Measures that are most sensitive to changes in social behavior in response to medication are direct observations, preferably conducted in naturalistic contexts. The ADHD School Observation Code (Gadow et al., 1996) described earlier is a useful measure that assesses positive social interaction as well as various indicators of aggression on the playground and in the lunchroom. Parent, teacher, and child self-report measures, such as the Social Skills Rating System (Gresham & Elliott, 1990), can also be used to assess the effects of medication on social behavior, although rating scales are generally less sensitive in evaluating social outcomes than direct observations of behavior.

Adverse Effects

Every medication may be associated with adverse effects. The adverse effects of medication may vary greatly as a function of the class of medication used, the specific medication selected, and the characteristics of the child treated. Each class of medication (e.g., stimulants, serotonin reuptake inhibitors, tricyclic antidepressants, alpha-2 adrenergic agonists, anxiolytics, and neuroleptics) is associated with a unique side-effect profile. For example, for the management of problems associated with mood, serotonin reuptake inhibitors and tricyclic antidepressants have markedly different adverse effect patterns (Spencer, Biederman, & Wilens, 1998). Furthermore, within each class of medication, medications can vary with regard to their side-effect profile. For example, within the antipsychotic group of medications, haloperidol appears to be associated with a lower level of sedation than other medications in this class (Campbell & Armenteros, 1996), and clonidine (Catapres) and guanfacine (Tenex), which are both alpha-2 adrenergic agonists, may produce a slightly different adverse effect pattern, including differences in levels of sedation and changes in blood pressure (Chappell et al., 1995).

The effects of medication also may vary as a function of characteristics of the child treated. For example, stimulants are frequently used to treat

ADHD symptoms in children with developmental disabilities, and these medications can be effective with this heterogeneous population (Aman, 1996). However, stimulants may be associated with an increased risk of adverse effects and certain unique side effects among children with developmental disabilities (Handen, Feldman, Gosling, Breaux, & McAuliffe, 1991; Power et al., 1996).

Researchers have developed a wide range of measures to assess the adverse effects of various medications. Commonly used measures of the adverse effects of stimulants are the Side Effects Rating Scale (Barkley, 1981) and the Stimulant Side Effects Checklist (see Gadow, 1993). Examples of side-effects measures for medications that are less commonly used are the Subjective Treatment-Emergent Symptoms Scale (National Institute of Mental Health, 1985), which has been used in assessing the adverse effects of antidepressant medications (Biederman, Baldessarini, Wright, Keenan, & Faraone, 1993), and the Naltrexone Side Effects Rating Scale (Barron & Sandman, 1993), which has been used to assess the effects of naltrexone (ReVia) for children with autism (Kolmen, Feldman, Handen, & Janosky, 1997).

An important consideration in the assessment of the adverse effects of medication is a comparison of effects during both active medication and placebo conditions, given the potential placebo effects on ratings of adverse effects (Barkley, McMurray, Edelbrock, & Robbins, 1990). Many children with psychiatric disorders complain of somatic problems when they are not receiving medication (Barkley et al., 1990). In some cases, prescribing clinicians may erroneously conclude that the somatic effects reported by children during medication trials are due to adverse effects of the drug. The use of a placebo can enable a clinician to determine whether the reported symptoms are indeed adverse effects of medication or whether the concerns predate the onset of medication. Also, information about the adverse effects of medication have been shown to vary substantially as a function of informant. For example, parent, teacher, and child self-report data pertaining to the adverse effects of methylphenidate may vary markedly (DuPaul, Anastopoulos, Kwasnik, Barkley, & McMurray, 1996). For this reason, it is generally recommended that clinicians collect data pertaining to adverse effects from multiple informants.

Treatment Acceptability

Assessing a family's perceptions about the acceptability of using a particular medication in the treatment of a set of targeted symptoms can be useful in determining whether the family is ready to implement a trial of medication (for a review, see Brown & Sawyer, 1998, and chapter 3, this volume). Furthermore, information about intervention acceptability can be helpful to clinicians in promoting treatment adherence. Parents and children may differ markedly in their views about the appropriateness and fairness of using medication as a treatment strategy. For this reason, it is good practice to assess both parents' and children's views about intervention acceptability and to take this information into account in planning interventions and monitoring adherence. Because parents' and children's views about treatment acceptability may change markedly during the course of intervention, it is important to assess acceptability on a periodic basis.

DESIGNING MEDICATION-MONITORING PROTOCOLS

Much of the research examining the effectiveness of medication has used group designs that are useful in determining the effects of medication for a group of individuals but may be less helpful in assessing effects for an individual child. Single-subject designs are particularly useful in evaluating the effects of medication for an individual (DuPaul & Barkley, 1993). The following is a discussion of some of the critical components of single-subject designs for evaluating the effects of medication on the functioning of children.

Using Placebo-Controlled, Double-Blind Procedures

Because perceptions of a child's behavior often are affected by the belief that the child is receiving medication, it is important to control for placebo effects in conducting a medication trial. Also, to control for bias effects, one must administer medication in a blinded fashion so that the child, clinician, and all agents involved in data collection are unaware of the intervention being used at a particular point in time. Although placebo-controlled, double-blind medication protocols are considered to be the gold standard in research, practitioners may find it challenging to use these methods in clinical practice. Even when it is not feasible to administer placebo pills or to encapsulate medication to keep the caregivers and child blind to the dose of medication, it may be possible to keep teachers blind to specific intervention procedures and to collect valuable data from them about the behavioral, academic, and social functioning of children (Power, Atkins, Osborne, & Blum, 1994).

Selecting an Appropriate Dosing Range

In conducting a medication trial, clinicians should strive to administer a wide range of doses that are likely to be effective. Although a common clinical practice is to begin with the lowest potentially effective dose and to gradually increase dosage level until clinical effects are evident, this titration approach may fail to detect the incremental benefits of using higher doses of medicine. Also, given that different doses of medication may be associated not only with a differential magnitude of effect within a specific domain of functioning but also with differential effects across domains, it is often useful to explore the magnitude and range of effects at various dosage levels (Rapport et al., 1994).

Timing the Assessment of Outcome

The assessment of medication effects should be conducted during the period of time that the medication is anticipated to have its peak effect on the child. Information regarding the behavioral half-life of medication is important to consider in determining the optimal time to assess the effects of medication (see Bernstein et al., 2000; Pelham, Swanson, Furman, & Schwindt, 1995; Singer et al., 1995).

Selecting Measures That Can Be Administered Repeatedly and Frequently

Single-subject methodologies require multiple data points for each phase of intervention to determine the level of responding within that phase. Typically, data are collected until a stable rate of responding within each phase is achieved. For this reason, clinicians and researchers should strive to use measures that can be repeatedly and frequently administered. Measures that are often useful in single-subject designs are brief ratings of behavior, observations of behavior in naturalistic or analogue situations, and curriculum-based measures of academic performance (Power et al., 1996; Rapport et al., 1994; Stoner et al., 1994).

Controlling for Order Effects

Clinicians typically administer medication in a fixed sequence beginning with the lowest dose and gradually increasing dosage level. The problem with this procedure from a methodological standpoint is that the effects of a particular dose may be affected by the order in which it is administered to a child. For example, 10 mg of Adderall may have a different effect on a child if administered immediately following a trial of 5 mg as opposed to 15 mg of this medication. Ideally, the sequence in which medication is administered to a child should be altered to control for the biasing effects of order (DuPaul & Barkley, 1993). Varying the order of administration is challenging for clinicians in practice, and it may be prohibitive with medications that have relatively long half-lives, such as tricyclic antidepressants and serotonin reuptake inhibitors, for which it may take several hours or days, or even weeks, to achieve a peak level of effectiveness for each dose.

Planning a Replication

In single-subject designs, confidence in the results of a medication trial increases dramatically when the findings are replicated in a second trial (Power et al., 1996). Replicating the effectiveness of short-acting medications, such as the stimulants, by comparing the optimal dose with a placebo generally is advisable to verify that a particular dose indeed is effective. However, conducting a replication of longer acting medications, such as the antipsychotics and antidepressants, may be problematic because of the potentially harmful effects of weaning and reinitiating these medications too quickly. Replication trials, when conducted, need to be supervised closely with careful monitoring of adverse effects.

Determining the Magnitude of the Effect

There are a variety of methods that can be used to evaluate changes in functioning from one phase of intervention to another. A common strategy is to determine the percentage of overlapping data points between phases (Stoner et al., 1994). Ideally, performance during one phase of treatment is clearly and consistently better than performance in the other phases, suggesting the superiority of one level of treatment over the other levels. A more systematic method of evaluating the magnitude of the effect associated with each level of medication is to determine the significance of the difference between performance during each treatment phase and performance during the placebo condition by calculating an effect size, using the Reliable Change Index (RCI; DuPaul & Barkley, 1993). The RCI is the difference between mean level of performance during each treatment phase minus the mean level of performance during placebo divided by the standard error of the difference between the means.

Determining the statistical significance of an intervention effect substantiates that changes in performance are in all likelihood due to the treatment and not to chance factors. However, statistical significance is not always an indicator of clinical significance. For example, it is possible for a medication to significantly reduce aggressive behavior on the playground, but the child may still be more aggressive than the other children in the classroom, resulting in continued rejection by peers. For this reason, it is often useful to evaluate change in relation to a standard reflecting the normal range of behavior for a child (Rapport et al., 1994). Normal functioning often is considered to be performance that is within one standard deviation above the mean for children of similar age and gender. However, for some psychotropic medications, it may not be possible to normalize functioning; in these cases, the goal of treatment is to reduce problematic symptoms and to improve educational, social, or emotional functioning.

Selecting the Optimal Dose of Medication

Determining the optimal dose of medication for a child can be challenging in some cases because the effects may vary greatly as a function of the outcome variables targeted for assessment. For example, it is common for behavioral functioning to be optimized at one level of treatment and for academic functioning to be optimized at a different dosage level. In these cases, clinicians need to clarify the goals of intervention and to select the intervention level associated with the greatest gains in the areas targeted for change.

Collecting Follow-Up Data

The beneficial effects and adverse effects of medication can change markedly over time. For this reason, it is advisable to proactively assess outcomes on an ongoing basis in critical target areas. In this way, clinicians can modify treatments when difficulties begin to arise and avert more serious problems, such as significant adverse effects or failure of the medication to be effective in critical situations for the child and family.

Assessing the Effects of Medication in Relation to Psychosocial Interventions

In clinical practice, it is often important to know whether the optimal management strategy is a pharmacological, psychosocial, or combined approach to treatment. Single-subject methodologies have been useful in determining (a) the benefits of a pharmacological versus a psychosocial approach to treatment, (b) the incremental benefits of a pharmacological treatment when added to a psychosocial intervention, and (c) the incremental benefits of a psychosocial intervention when added to medication (Blum, Mauk, McComas, & Mace, 1996; Hoza, Pelham, Sams, & Carlson, 1992). These procedures have been developed primarily for evaluating stimulant medication in relation to behavioral interventions. Research is needed to develop methodologies for evaluating the separate and combined effects of psychosocial interventions and medications that have relatively long half-lives.

PROMOTING COLLABORATION AMONG PROFESSIONALS

Conducting a systematic evaluation of the effects of medication requires the involvement of family members and many professionals. A clinician is needed to design the medication-monitoring protocol and to determine what types and sources of information are needed. Each parent is typically requested to provide data pertaining to the child's functioning in home and neighborhood settings. In addition, the parents must collaborate with the prescribing clinician in making medication decisions, and parents are needed to monitor the child to maintain ongoing treatment adherence. The child is often asked to provide feedback regarding the emotional effects and potential aversive effects of medication. One or more teachers are needed to provide data pertaining to the child's behavioral, academic, and social functioning. Furthermore, clinicians may attempt to collect direct observation data of a child's functioning in a variety of school settings.

Because several individuals typically are involved in the monitoring of medication effectiveness, it is important that a person be designated to oversee data collection and to organize data as they pertain to outcomes. The prescribing clinician often is the person most suited to this role, but in some cases this professional lacks the time and professional training for this function. It is not uncommon for parents to assume this responsibility, but many parents do not have the resources to be effective in this role. Behavioral health professionals, such as clinical and school psychologists, can make valuable contributions to the design of medication protocols and the collection and analyses of data. Given their training in behavioral assessment and single-subject design, behaviorally oriented psychologists, in particular, can make highly valuable contributions to the monitoring of medication (DuPaul & Barkley, 1993; Power, DuPaul, Shapiro, & Parrish, 1995). For more information about the role of the behavioral health professional in monitoring medication effects, refer to chapter 1.

CONCLUSION

Because children respond to medication in idiosyncratic ways, clinicians should monitor the beneficial and adverse effects of medication carefully. The type of medication used for a child and the methods needed to systematically evaluate treatment effects depend on the goals of intervention, specifically the targets of treatment and the domains of functioning that need to be addressed. Because clinicians and parents typically identify multiple targets and domains for intervention, a multimethod, multi-informant assessment battery is needed to evaluate outcomes. Numerous procedures have been developed to assess outcome. In general, clinicians should attempt to select measures that (a) assess functioning in naturalistic settings, (b) are brief and efficient to use in a repeated measures design, and (c) have been demonstrated to be sensitive to medication effects in the research literature. Single-subject research methods can be extremely useful in evaluating the effects of medication. Although these procedures most commonly have been used in evaluating the effects of stimulants, they can be adapted to the monitoring of medications with a longer time of onset and duration of effect. Monitoring medication effects involves a substantial amount of work on the part of family members and professionals. It is critical that a professional be designated to coordinate data collection and organize the findings of a medication-monitoring protocol. Psychologists with training in behavioral assessment and single-subject design are particularly well suited to designing medication protocols, overseeing data collection, facilitating collaboration among family members and professionals, and managing the data collected in a medication-monitoring protocol.

REFERENCES

Achenbach, T. M. (1991a). *Manual for the Child Behavior Checklist/4–18 and 1991 profile.* Burlington: University of Vermont, Department of Psychiatry.

Achenbach, T. M. (1991b). *Manual for the Teacher's Report Form and 1991 profile.* Burlington: University of Vermont, Department of Psychiatry.

Achenbach, T. M. (1991c). *Manual for the Youth Self-Report and 1991 profile.* Burlington: University of Vermont, Department of Psychiatry.

Achenbach, T. M., McConaughy, S. H., & Howell, C. T. (1987). Child/adolescent behavioral and emotional problems: Implications of cross-informant correlations for situational specificity. *Psychological Bulletin, 101*, 213–232.

Aman, M. G. (1996). Stimulant drugs in developmental disabilities revisited. *Journal of Developmental and Physical Disabilities, 8*, 347–365.

Anesko, K. M., Schoiock, G., Ramiriz, R., & Levine, F. M. (1987). The Homework Problem Checklist: Assessing children's homework difficulties. *Behavioral Assessment, 9*, 179–185.

Balthazor, M. J., Wagner, R. K., & Pelham, W. E. (1991). The specificity of the effects of stimulant medication on classroom learning-related measures of cognitive processing for attention deficit disorder children. *Journal of Abnormal Child Psychology, 19*, 35–52.

Barkley, R. A. (1981). *Hyperactive children: A handbook for diagnosis and treatment.* New York: Guilford Press.

Barkley, R. A. (1991a). *Attention-deficit hyperactivity disorder: A clinical workbook.* New York: Guilford Press.

Barkley, R. A. (1991b). The ecological validity of laboratory and analogue assessment methods of ADHD symptoms. *Journal of Abnormal Child Psychology, 19*, 149–178.

Barkley, R. A., & Cunningham, C. E. (1978). Do stimulant drugs improve the academic performance of hyperkinetic children? A review of outcome research. *Journal of Clinical Pediatrics, 17*, 85–92.

Barkley, R. A., McMurray, M. B., Edelbrock, C. S., & Robbins, K. (1990). The side effects of Ritalin: A systematic placebo controlled evaluation of two doses. *Pediatrics, 86,* 184–192.

Barron, J. L., & Sandman, C. (1993). Pharmacological treatment. In V. B. Van Hasselt & M. Hersen (Eds.), *The handbook of behavior therapy and pharmacotherapy with children: A comparative analysis* (pp. 129–147). Boston: Allyn & Bacon.

Berg, C., Rapoport, J. L., & Flament, M. (1986). The Leyton Obsessional Inventory–Child Version. *Journal of the American Academy of Child and Adolescent Psychiatry, 25,* 84–91.

Bernstein, G. A., Borchardt, M. D., Perwein, A. R., Crosby, R. D., Kushner, M. G., Thuras, P. D., & Last, C. G. (2000). Imipramine plus cognitive–behavioral therapy in the treatment of school refusal. *Journal of the American Academy of Child and Adolescent Psychiatry, 39,* 276–283.

Biederman, J., Baldessarini, R. J., Wright, V., Keenan, K., & Faraone, S. (1993). A double-blind placebo controlled study of desimpramine in the treatment of ADD: Lack of impact on comorbidity and family history factors on clinical response. *Journal of the American Academy of Child and Adolescent Psychiatry, 32,* 199–204.

Blum, N. J., Mauk, J. E., McComas, J. J., & Mace, F. C. (1996). Separate and combined effects of methylphenidate and a behavioral intervention on disruptive behavior in children with mental retardation. *Journal of Applied Behavior Analysis, 29,* 305–319.

Brown, R. T., & Sawyer, M. G. (1998). *Medications for school-age children: Effects on learning and behavior.* New York: Guilford Press.

Callahan, S. A., Panichelli-Mindel, S., & Kendall, P. C. (1996). DSM–IV and internalizing disorders: Modifications, limitations, and utility. *School Psychology Review, 25,* 297–307.

Campbell, M., & Armenteros, J. (1996). Schizophrenia and other psychotic disorders. In J. Weiner (Ed.), *Diagnosis of psychopathology of childhood and adolescent disorders* (2nd ed., pp. 193–227). New York: Wiley.

Castellanos, F. X. (1998). Tic disorders and obsessive–compulsive disorder. In B. T. Walsh (Ed.), *Child psychopharmacology* (pp. 1–28). Washington, DC: American Psychiatric Press.

Castellanos, F. X., Giedd, J. N., Elia, J., Marsh, W. L., Ritchie, G. F., Hamburger, S. D., & Rapoport, J. L. (1997). Controlled stimulant: Treatment of ADHD and comorbid Tourette's syndrome: Effects of stimulant and dose. *Journal of the American Academy of Child and Adolescent Psychiatry, 36,* 589–596.

Chappell, P. B., Riddle, M. A., Scahill, L., Lynch, K. A., Schultz, R., Arnsten, A., Leckman, J. F., & Cohen, D. J. (1995). Guanfacine treatment of comorbid attention-deficit hyperactivity disorder and Tourette's syndrome: Preliminary clinical experience. *Journal of the American Academy of Child and Adolescent Psychiatry, 34,* 1140–1146.

Conners, C. K. (1997). *The Conners Rating Scales–Revised.* North Tonowanda, NY: Multi-Health Systems.

Delis, D. C., Kramer, J. H., Kaplan, E., & Ober, B. A. (1994). *California Verbal Learning Test–Children's version*. San Antonio, TX: Psychological Corporation.

Douglas, V. I., Barr, R., Desilets, J., & Sherman, E. (1995). Do high doses of stimulants impair flexible thinking in attention-deficit hyperactivity disorder? *Journal of the American Academy of Child and Adolescent Psychiatry, 34*, 877–885.

Douglas, V. I., Barr, R. G., O'Neill, M. E., & Britton, B. G. (1986). Short term effects of methylphenidate on the cognitive, learning and academic performance of children with attention deficit disorder in the laboratory and classroom. *Journal of Child Psychology and Psychiatry, 27*, 191–211.

DuPaul, G. J., Anastopoulos, A. D., Kwasnik, D., Barkley, R. A., & McMurray, M. B. (1996). Methylphenidate effects on children with attention deficit hyperactivity disorder: Self-report of symptoms, side effects, and self-esteem. *Journal of Attention Disorders, 1*, 3–15.

DuPaul, G. J., Anastopoulos, A. D., Shelton, T. L., Guevremont, D., & Metevia, L. (1992). Multi-method assessment of attention-deficit hyperactivity disorder: The diagnostic utility of clinic-based tests. *Journal of Clinical Child Psychology, 21*, 394–402.

DuPaul, G. J., & Barkley, R. A. (1993). The utility of behavioral methodology in medication treatment of children with attention deficit hyperactivity disorder. *Behavior Therapy, 24*, 47–66.

DuPaul, G. J., Barkley, R. A., & Connor, D. F. (1998). Stimulants. In R. A. Barkley (Ed.), *Attention-deficit hyperactivity disorder: A handbook for diagnosis and treatment* (2nd ed., pp. 510–551). New York: Guilford Press.

DuPaul, G. J., Barkley, R. A., & McMurray, M. B. (1994). Response of children with ADHD to methylphenidate: Interaction with internalizing symptoms. *Journal of the American Academy of Child and Adolescent Psychiatry, 33*, 894–903.

DuPaul, G. J., Power, T. J., Anastopoulos, A. D., & Reid, R. (1998). *ADHD Rating Scale–IV: Checklists, norms, and clinical interpretation*. New York: Guilford Press.

DuPaul, G. J., & Rapport, M. D. (1993). Does methylphenidate normalize the classroom performance of children with attention deficit disorder? *Journal of the American Academy of Child and Adolescent Psychiatry, 32*, 190–198.

DuPaul, G. J., Rapport, M. D., & Perriello, L. M. (1991). Teacher ratings of academic skills. The development of the Academic Performance Rating Scale. *School Psychology Review, 20*, 284–300.

Gadow, K. D. (1993). A school-based medication evaluation program. In J. L. Matson (Ed.), *Handbook of hyperactivity in children* (pp. 186–219). Boston: Allyn & Bacon.

Gadow, K. D., Nolan, E. E., & Sverd, J. (1992). Methylphenidate in hyperactive boys with comorbid tic disorder: II. Short-term behavioral effects in school settings. *Journal of the American Academy of Child and Adolescent Psychiatry, 31*, 462–471.

Gadow, K. D., Sprafkin, J., & Nolan, E. E. (1996). *Attention deficit hyperactivity disorder school observation code*. Stony Brook, NY: Checkmate Plus.

Gadow, K. G., Sverd, J., Sprafkin, J., Nolan, E. E., & Ezor, S. N. (1995). Efficacy of methylphenidate for attention-deficit hyperactivity disorder in children with tic disorder. *Archives of General Psychiatry, 52,* 444–455.

Granger, D. A., Whalen, C. K., Henker, B., & Cantwell, D. (1996). ADHD boys' behavior during structured classroom social activities: Effects on social demands, teacher proximity, and methylphenidate. *Journal of Attention Disorders, 1,* 16–30.

Gresham, F. M., & Elliott, S. N. (1990). *The Social Skills Rating System*. Circle Pines, MN: American Guidance Service.

Handen, B. L., Feldman, H., Gosling, A., Breaux, A. M., & McAuliffe, S. (1991). Adverse side effects of methylphenidate in children with mental retardation and ADHD. *Journal of the American Academy of Child and Adolescent Psychiatry, 30,* 241–245.

Hinshaw, S. P., Henker, B., Whalen, C. K., Erhardt, D., & Dunnington, R. E. (1989). Aggressive, prosocial, and nonsocial behavior in hyperactive boys: Dose effects of methylphenidate in naturalistic settings. *Journal of Consulting and Clinical Psychology, 57,* 636–643.

Hoza, B., Pelham, W. E., Sams, S. E., & Carlson, C. (1992). An examination of "dosage" effects of both behavior therapy and methylphenidate on the classroom performance of two ADHD children. *Behavior Modification, 16,* 164–192.

Ikeda, M. J. (1994). *Exploring dependent measures for use in medication evaluations for children diagnosed as having ADHD*. Unpublished doctoral dissertation, University of Oregon.

Kovacs, M. (1992). *The Children's Depression Inventory*. North Tonawanda, NY: Multi-Health Systems.

Kolmen, B. K., Feldman, H. M., Handen, B. L., & Janosky, J. E. (1997). Naltrexone in young autistic children: Replication study and learning measures. *Journal of the American Academy of Child and Adolescent Psychiatry, 36,* 1570–1578.

Kurlan, R. (1997). Tourette's syndrome. Treatment of tics. *Neurologic Clinics, 15,* 403–409.

March, J. S., Parker, J., Sullivan, K., Stallings, P., & Conners, C. K. (1997). The Multidimensional Anxiety Scale for Children (MASC): Factor structure, reliability, and validity. *Journal of the American Academy of Child and Adolescent Psychiatry, 36,* 554–565.

Mercugliano, M., Power, T. J., & Blum, N. J. (1998). *The clinician's practical guide to attention-deficit/hyperactivity disorder*. Baltimore: Paul H. Brookes.

Naglieri, J. A., LeBuffe, P. A., & Pfeiffer, S. I. (1994). *Manual for the Devereux Scales of Mental Disorders*. San Antonio, TX: Psychological Corporation.

National Institute of Mental Health. (1985). Subjective treatment emergent symptom scale. *Psychopharmacological Bulletin, 21,* 839–844.

Nolan, E. E., & Gadow, K. D. (1997). Children with ADHD and tic disorder and their classmates: Behavioral normalization with methylphenidate. *Journal of the American Academy of Child and Adolescent Psychiatry, 36,* 597–604.

O'Toole, K., Abramowitz, A., Morris, R., & Dulcan, M. (1997). Effects of methylphenidate on attention and non-verbal learning in children with attention-deficit hyperactivity disorder. *Journal of the American Academy of Child and Adolescent Psychiatry, 36,* 531–538.

Pelham, W. E., Swanson, J. M., Furman, M. B., & Schwindt, H. (1995). Pemoline effects on children with ADHD: A time-response by dose-response analysis on classroom measures. *Journal of the American Academy of Child and Adolescent Psychiatry, 34,* 1504–1513.

Power, T. J., Andrews, T. J., Eiraldi, R. B., Doherty, B. J., Ikeda, M. J., DuPaul, G. J., & Landau, S. (1998). Evaluating attention deficit hyperactivity disorder using multiple informants: The incremental utility of combining teacher with parent reports. *Psychological Assessment, 10,* 250–260.

Power, T. J., Atkins, M. S., Osborne, M. L., & Blum, N. J. (1994). The school psychologist as manager of programming for ADHD. *School Psychology Review, 23,* 279–291.

Power, T. J., Blum, N. J., Jones, S. M., & Kaplan, P. E. (1996). Brief report: Response to methylphenidate in two children with Williams syndrome. *Journal of Autism and Developmental Disorders, 27,* 79–87.

Power, T. J., DuPaul, G. J., Shapiro, E. S., & Parrish, J. M. (1995). Pediatric school psychology: The emergence of a subspecialization. *School Psychology Review, 24,* 244–257.

Power, T. J., Eiraldi, R. B., Mercugliano, M., & Blum, N. J. (1998). Using interviews and rating scales to collect behavioral data. In M. Mercugliano, T. J. Power, & N. J. Blum (Eds.), *The clinician's practical guide to attention-deficit/hyperactivity disorder* (pp. 53–74). Baltimore: Paul H. Brookes.

Power, T. J., Karustis, J. L., Mercugliano, M., & Blum, N. J. (1998). Psychoeducational assessment for children with attention-deficit/hyperactivity disorder. In M. Mercugliano, T. J. Power, & N. J. Blum (Eds.), *The clinician's practical guide to attention-deficit/hyperactivity disorder* (pp. 75–98). Baltimore: Paul H. Brookes.

Rapport, M. D., Denney, C., DuPaul, G. J., & Gardner, M. J. (1994). Attention deficit disorder and methylphenidate: Normalization rates, clinical effectiveness, and response prediction in 76 children. *Journal of the American Academy of Child and Adolescent Psychiatry, 33,* 882–893.

Reynolds, W. M. (1987). *Reynolds Adolescent Depression Scale.* San Antonio, TX: Psychological Corporation.

Reynolds, C. R., & Kamphaus, R. W. (1992). *Manual for the Behavior Assessment System for Children.* Circle Pines, MN: American Guidance Service.

Reynolds, C. R., & Richmond, B. O. (1985). *The Revised Children's Manifest Anxiety Scales: What I think and feel.* Los Angeles: Western Psychological Services.

Roberts, M. L., & Landau, S. (1995). Using curriculum-based data for assessing children with attention deficits [Monograph]. *Journal of Psychoeducational Assessment*, (Special ADHD issue), 74–87.

Rubio-Stipec, M., Canino, G. J., Shrout, P., Dulcan, M., Freeman, D., & Bravo, M. (1994). Psychometric properties of parents and children as informants in child psychiatry epidemiology with the Spanish Diagnostic Interview Schedule for Children (DISC 2). *Journal of Abnormal Child Psychology, 22,* 703–720.

Shapiro, A. K., & Shapiro, E. (1984). Controlled study of pimozide vs. placebo in Tourette's syndrome. *Journal of the American Academy of Child and Adolescent Psychiatry, 23,* 161–173.

Shinn, M. R. (1998). (Ed.). *Advanced applications of curriculum-based measurement.* New York: Guilford Press.

Singer, H. S., Brown, J., Quaskey, S., Rosenberg, L. A., Mellits, E. D., & Denckla, M. B. (1995). The treatment of attention-deficit hyperactivity disorder in Tourette's syndrome: A double-blind placebo-controlled study with clonidine and desipramine. *Pediatrics, 95,* 74–81.

Spencer, T. J., Biederman, J., & Wilens, T. (1998). Pharmacotherapy of ADHD with antidepressants. In R. A. Barkley (Ed.), *Attention-deficit hyperactivity disorder: A handbook for diagnosis and treatment* (2nd ed., pp. 552–563). New York: Guilford Press.

Stoner, G., Carey, S. P., Ikeda, M. J., & Shinn, M. R. (1994). The utility of curriculum-based measurement for evaluating the effects of methylphenidate on academic performance. *Journal of Applied Behavior Analysis, 27,* 101–113.

Swanson, J. M., Wigal, S., Greenhill, L. L., Browne, R., Waslik, B., Lerner, M., Williams, L., Flynn, D., Agler, D., Crowley, K., Fineberg, E., Baren, M., & Cantwell, D. P. (1998). Analog classroom assessment of Adderall in children with ADHD. *Journal of the American Academy of Child and Adolescent Psychiatry, 37,* 519–526.

Tannock, R., Ickowicz, A., & Schachar, R. (1995). Differential effects of methylphenidate on working memory in ADHD children with and without comorbid anxiety. *Journal of the American Academy of Child and Adolescent Psychiatry, 34,* 886–896.

Ullman, R. K., Sleator, E. K., & Sprague, R. K. (1996). *Manual for the Comprehensive Teacher's Rating Scale: Parent form (ACTeRS).* Champaign, IL: MetriTech.

Walkup, J. T., Rosenberg, L. A., Brown, J., & Singer, H. S. (1992). The validity of instruments measuring tic severity in Tourette's syndrome. *Journal of the American Academy of Child and Adolescent Psychiatry, 30,* 472–477.

3

UNDERSTANDING AND OVERCOMING BARRIERS TO TREATMENT UTILIZATION

Researchers have developed many efficacious interventions to treat psychological disorders arising in children and adolescents. For example, stimulant medication and behavior therapy have been demonstrated to be highly effective in the management of attention deficit hyperactivity disorder (ADHD; Klein & Abikoff, 1997; Pelham et al., 1993), and cognitive–behavior therapy is considered to be a "gold standard" in the treatment of anxiety disorders (Beidel & Turner, 1998; Kendall, 1994) Unfortunately, children and families are often unwilling to initiate these interventions or to maintain the use of treatments that have been demonstrated to be efficacious.

Numerous factors have an effect on a family's willingness to seek assistance for psychological problems, including patterns of help-seeking behavior, accessibility of services, affordability of services, and perceptions about the appropriateness of recommended interventions. In this chapter, we explore factors that both facilitate and preclude children and families from initiating or maintaining interventions that have the potential to be helpful. We also describe methods of assessing and overcoming barriers to intervention utilization.

THE PROBLEM OF NONADHERENCE

Children and families frequently fail to adhere to recommendations for health and behavioral health problems (LaGreca & Schuman, 1995). Problems of nonadherence include both a failure to initiate interventions that are potentially helpful and a failure to maintain treatments that have been demonstrated to be effective. In a 4-month follow-up study of 49 families evaluated through a hospital-based ADHD evaluation and treatment center, Bennett, Power, Rostain, and Carr (1996) found that of the 42 families who were provided with a recommendation to pursue some form of counseling or behavior therapy, only 23 families (55%) actually initiated treatment. Similarly, of the 32 families for whom a medication trial was recommended, 23 families (72%) pursued treatment. Joost, Chessare, Schaeufele, Link, and Weaver (1989) found similar rates of adherence to pediatricians' recommendations for counseling to address children's psychological problems.

Research also has shown that families who initiate intervention often terminate prematurely and that rates of adherence decline markedly as the period of follow-up lengthens. For example, studies have shown that about 25% of families do not adhere to medication protocols at 1- to 3-month follow-up and that up to 50% are nonadherent at 9- to 12-month follow-up (Brown & Sawyer, 1998; Johnston & Fine, 1993). With regard to psychotherapy, research has shown that approximately 50% of families terminate treatment prematurely (Kazdin, 1996).

THE MEANING OF NONADHERENCE

Nonadherence has traditionally been viewed by professionals as failure on the part of a family to comply with the expert opinion of the provider. Nonadherence has often been construed in the context of a hierarchical relationship between professional and family (Brown & Sawyer, 1998; LaGreca & Schuman, 1995). This perspective fails to recognize the important role of the child and family in designing intervention plans. More recent perspectives of nonadherence affirm the importance of the child and family in designing treatment plans and emphasize the need for collaboration between provider and family prior to and at various points throughout the intervention process. Within this context, nonadherence is defined as the failure to follow through with an intervention plan that is designed collaboratively with a professional and modified periodically during the course of intervention.

A useful model for conceptualizing nonadherence is the *stages of change* construct (Prochaska, DiClemente, & Norcross, 1992). This model was developed to understand the change process for individuals with addictive behaviors, but it has been demonstrated to be applicable for a wide range of health and behavioral problems (Prochaska et al., 1994). Also, this model has been shown to be applicable in understanding the change process of individuals involved in medication trials for psychological disorders (Wilson, Bell-Dolan, & Beitman, 1997). According to this model, change can occur only when individuals are ready to do so. The effectiveness of intervention is contingent on the match between the readiness of the client to change and the prescribed service being provided.

Prochaska et al. (1992) outlined five stages of change:

1. Precontemplation, which refers to a lack of intention to change behavior, primarily because of the failure to perceive that there is a problem.
2. Contemplation, the stage in which individuals recognize that there is a problem and are attempting to decide whether the effort to overcome barriers to intervention is worthwhile.
3. Preparation, which refers to an intention and commitment to take action in the near future.
4. Action, the stage in which individuals are actively invested in implementing strategies to change behavior.
5. Maintenance, the stage in which individuals consolidate treatment gains and work to prevent relapse.

Individuals advance through the stages in a cyclic as opposed to linear manner. For example, it is common for individuals to advance to the Preparation stage and subsequently, in response to life events, to cycle back to an earlier stage.

Central to the model is the concept that intervention approaches must be appropriate for the stage in which the individual is functioning. A series of studies have affirmed the importance of matching the appropriate intervention to the stage in which an individual is functioning (Beitman et al., 1994; Perz, DiClemente, & Carbonari, 1996; Prochaska et al., 1994). Individuals in the Precontemplation stage generally do not recognize that there is a problem. To assist them in advancing through this stage, therapists often find it helpful to describe the nature and severity of the problem, to provide the individuals with emotional support, and to identify and challenge their beliefs. With individuals in the Contemplation stage, insight-oriented approaches frequently are useful to assist them in understanding themselves and clarifying their values and priorities. It is not until individuals advance to the Preparation stage that they are ready to remove remaining barriers to change and make a commitment to intervention (see Prochaska et al., 1992).

The research of Prochaska and colleagues (Prochaska et al., 1992, 1994) has been conducted primarily with adults in relation to addictive behaviors. Although the findings have been demonstrated to be applicable to other classes of behavioral problems, additional research is needed to confirm the applicability of this model to populations of children and families coping with various forms of psychopathology using pharmacotherapy and psychotherapy. This model holds significant promise in understanding factors that contribute to a family's willingness to initiate and maintain treatments for various childhood disorders (Cunningham, 1997).

FACTORS THAT DETERMINE READINESS FOR CHANGE

Several factors affect a child's or family's readiness to make a commitment to pharmacological or psychosocial intervention. These factors include the social validity of the intervention plan, the feasibility of the plan, and the help-seeking patterns of the family, which are often influenced by cultural determinants.

Social Validity

Social validity refers to perceptions of the participants in intervention about the appropriateness and reasonableness of the goals, techniques, and outcomes of intervention (Wolf, 1978). Participants are more willing to initiate and maintain interventions that they perceive as fair and reasonable than those therapies that are viewed as relatively unfair or inappropriate. Most of the research pertaining to social validity has focused on treatment acceptability, which refers to perceptions held by intervention participants about the appropriateness and fairness of the treatment (Kazdin, 1980).

A considerable body of research relating to treatment acceptability has accumulated since 1980. Research has affirmed repeatedly that behavioral interventions, such as token reinforcement systems, home–school notes, response cost procedures, and time-out, are viewed by parents and teachers as more acceptable and reasonable than pharmacological approaches (Corkum, Rimer, & Schachar, 1999; Liu, Robin, Brenner, & Eastman, 1991; Power, Hess, & Bennett, 1995; Witt & Elliott, 1985). Behavioral techniques involving positive reinforcement have been shown to be more acceptable than reductive, punitive techniques (Power et al., 1995). Interventions that are viewed as time efficient and relatively easy to use are more acceptable than those that are perceived as time consuming and complex (Fantuzzo & Atkins, 1992; Witt, Martens, & Elliott, 1984).

Research has consistently shown that pharmacological approaches to intervention are less acceptable to parents than psychosocial approaches, yet rates of adherence, at least at the outset of treatment, are generally higher with pharmacological interventions than with psychosocial treatments (Bennett et al., 1996; Brown & Sawyer, 1998; Kazdin, 1996). This apparent discrepancy may be related to the higher financial costs and time investment involved in using psychosocial treatments as compared with pharmacological approaches.

Research has shown that intervention approaches that involve a combination of medication and behavioral approaches have consistently been shown to be more acceptable to parents and teachers than approaches using medication only (Liu et al., 1991; Pelham, 1999; Power et al., 1995). In Power et al.'s (1995) study, teachers were asked to indicate the most acceptable and least acceptable intervention approach for ADHD by comparing three treatment plans: behavioral interventions only, stimulant medication only, and a combined treatment approach. Fifty-one percent of teachers rated the combined approach as the most acceptable; 42% rated behavior therapy alone and 7% rated stimulant medication alone as the most reasonable approach. In contrast, only 7% rated the combined approach as the least acceptable intervention plan, whereas 39% rated stimulants alone and 44% rated a behavioral approach alone as the least reasonable method of intervention for the management of ADHD.

Participants' views about the acceptability of intervention techniques vary as a function of several factors. Parents have been shown to view medication as a more acceptable intervention for problems of relatively high severity as compared with problems that are mildly to moderately severe (Pavuluri, Luk, & McGee, 1996; Reimers, Wacker, Cooper, & DeRaad, 1992; Rostain, Power, & Atkins, 1993). Knowledge of a disorder, including its developmental course and effective interventions for treating it, has been demonstrated to be positively associated with perceptions of treatment acceptability (Liu et al., 1991). Parents are more likely to view medication as an acceptable intervention when outcomes are evaluated rigorously and systematically, such as in a controlled clinical trial, as compared with in a less controlled manner (Aman & Wolford, 1995; Johnston & Fine, 1993). The age and developmental level of the child are often important considerations, as adolescents typically differ from younger children in their views about interventions, although the direction of the difference may vary depending on the nature of the problem and the type of intervention used (LaGreca & Schuman, 1995). Gender may also be an important factor, although research in this area is lacking.

Perceptions of intervention acceptability can change during the course of treatment. Views about the acceptability of intervention techniques have been shown to vary in response to outcomes for the child, family, teacher, and peers (Corkum et al., 1999; Liu et al., 1991; Reimers et al., 1992), as well as the adverse effects of treatment (Kazdin, 1981). The use of a collaborative consultation model that involves the parents and child in a partnership with the professional provider and that results in the development and periodic review of intervention plans may also be useful in promoting positive perceptions about the acceptability of pharmacological and psychosocial approaches to treatment (Brown & Sawyer, 1998; Johnston & Fine, 1993).

Attitudes about intervention acceptability may vary as a function of the culture of the family receiving care. Research has shown that there are substantial racial disparities in rates of prescriptions for psychotropic medication (Zito, Safer, dosReis, & Riddle, 1998). Zito and colleagues conducted a study of Medicaid recipients in the state of Maryland and found that African American youths ranging in age from 5 to 14 years were less than 50% as likely to be prescribed psychotropic medication as White youths. This disparity was larger for stimulant medication than it was for other classes of psychotropic medication. The difference in prescription rates for nonpsychotropic medications between these ethnic groups was less striking; African American youths were about 75% as likely to be prescribed nonpsychotropic medications as White youths. The meaning of these findings is unclear and warrants considerable investigation. However, preliminary evidence suggests that African American children do not have lower rates of psychopathology than White children (Zito et al., 1998). In addition, children belonging to these ethnic groups have similar rates of response to psychotropic medication. Variations in prescription practices may be related to ethnic group differences in knowledge about childhood disorders and interventions that may be helpful in treating them (Bussing, Schoenberg, & Perwein, 1998). Furthermore, ethnic group differences may reflect in part variations in how families from these ethnic groups view the mental health system and interventions that are typically recommended by professionals who operate within the system (Zito et al., 1998).

Most of the research on the social validity of intervention strategies has assessed the perceptions of caregivers and teachers. Children's attitudes have often been ignored, although there is evidence to suggest that a sizable fraction of children who are prescribed medication do not view pharmacotherapy as an acceptable way of coping with their problems (Whalen & Henker, 1991). A primary concern of children in taking medication is how it will be viewed by peers. Given that peers often are aware that a child is taking medication and that medication status may affect peer perceptions of a child (Whalen & Henker, 1991), this concern may often be warranted.

Another potentially problematic issue is the message that receiving prescribed, psychotropic medication may have for children. For example, the use of medication may lead a child to attribute success to external causes (e.g., the medication) as opposed to the child's own efforts (Whalen, Henker, Hinshaw, Heller, & Huber-Dressler, 1991). Although these concerns have been raised in the literature, research regarding the attributions of children who take stimulant medication has not supported this hypothesis. Investigators have found that children with ADHD who are prescribed stimulant medication attribute success to their own ability and effort and attribute failure to external causes, an attributional style that is consistent with that of adaptive, healthy functioning (Carlson, Pelham, Milich, & Hoza, 1993; Pelham et al., 1992). In contrast, the attributional style of children with ADHD who do not take medication is often consistent with that of a helplessness orientation (Milich, 1994).

Feasibility

For many families, the primary obstacles to making a commitment to the change process are not their attitudes about intervention but practical issues that restrict their access to care (Bennett et al., 1996). Feasibility issues might include distance from the clinic where services are provided, transportation problems, parking limitations, limited access to child care, inflexible scheduling of clinic hours, and affordability of services (Cunningham, 1998). Managed care may place additional restrictions on access, given the differential insurance benefits available when families are cared for by professionals who operate within as opposed to outside a network of providers. Families may not want services from the providers they can afford to see, and they may not be able to afford services from the providers they want to see.

Families who are economically disadvantaged and socially isolated, and families run by single parents or parents with a history of psychopathology, are the most vulnerable to the limitations imposed by these feasibility factors (Kazdin, Holland, & Crowley, 1997; Kazdin, Mazurick, & Siegel, 1994). Also, families of minority status, including families who are African American and Latino, generally have more problems gaining access to affordable behavioral health services than do White families (Padgett, Patrick, Burns, Schlesinger, & Cohen, 1993). These families often have the most difficulty securing convenient and affordable transportation to clinics, arranging and paying for child care, and scheduling for services at a time that does not interfere with work and family priorities. Furthermore, some of these families may not have health insurance or may have insurance that places severe restrictions on the providers they can afford to see.

Help-Seeking Behavior

When problems arise, families differ in their patterns of seeking help. Family practices in seeking help are influenced strongly by cultural factors. Research has demonstrated that there are ethnic group differences in patterns of help-seeking behavior. In an investigation of the initial help-seeking behaviors of families prior to their presentation at a clinic, McMiller and Weisz (1996) found that African American and Latino families were only 37% as likely to seek help from a professional or agency than were White families. A majority of the preclinic contacts of the minority group families were with family members and community residents, whereas a majority of the preclinic contacts of White families were with professionals and agencies. This research, as well as findings from other studies (Sue, Fujino, & Takeuchi, 1991; Takeuchi, Bui, & Kim, 1993), suggests that families of African and Latino background may be reluctant to present their concerns in clinic settings and may have some level of mistrust toward behavioral health specialists. Even when families of minority background seek help and initiate treatment from professionals in clinic settings, they are more likely to terminate treatment prematurely compared with White families (Sue et al., 1991; Takeuchi et al., 1993).

ASSESSING WILLINGNESS AND ABILITY TO MAKE A COMMITMENT TO INTERVENTION

Several measures have been developed to assess readiness for change and perceptions about the social validity of treatment interventions. A sampling of these measurement methods is described below.

Assessing Readiness for Change

To determine the stage of change in which a family is operating, clinicians often use an interview with a series of questions similar to that outlined in Exhibit 3.1. Prochaska et al. (1994) recommended the following guidelines in determining stage of change. If parents report that their child essentially does not have a problem or that they do not intend to make a commitment to an intervention program for the next 6 months, the family is identified as being in the Precontemplation stage. If the parents acknowledge that there is a problem that needs to be addressed and that they intend to make an investment in treatment within the next 6

EXHIBIT 3.1
Interview Questions for Parents in Determining Readiness for Change

1. Do you think your child is having a problem?
2. If yes, describe your child's problem.
3. How severe do you think the problem is?
4. Do you believe that you and your child need help to overcome this problem?
5. If yes, what kind of help do you think you need?
6. Based on what you know about available interventions, do you think these interventions can help your child and family?
7. If yes, are you ready to make a commitment to intervention at this time (in the next month or so)?
8. If you are not ready now, when do you think you might be ready?
9. What factors will make it difficult for your family to participate in intervention in the near future?

months, they are considered to be in the Contemplation stage. To be in the Preparation stage, families need to indicate that they intend to change within the next month or have already made several attempts at intervention, yet have not achieved an acceptable level of change. Families in the Action stage have already made a commitment to intervention and have achieved a desired level of change within the past 6 months. In the Maintenance stage, families have achieved a desired level of change more than 6 months prior to being interviewed.

A more formal measure of readiness for change is the Stages of Change Scale (McConnaughy, DiClemente, Prochaska, & Velicer, 1989; McConaughy, Prochaska, & Velicer, 1983). This 32-item measure yields scores on four scales: Precontemplation, Contemplation, Action, and Maintenance. Items are rated on a 5-point scale ranging from 1 = *strongly disagree* to 5 = *strongly agree*. Internal consistency for this measure is adequate, and scores on this measure have been shown to be related to level of treatment involvement as well as intervention outcome (Beitman et al., 1994; Wilson et al., 1997).

Assessing Treatment Acceptability

Several measures have been developed to assess the social validity of specific approaches to intervention. The original measure of treatment acceptability, developed by Kazdin (1980), is the Treatment Evaluation Inventory (TEI). This 15-item measure can be administered to a wide range of participants in an intervention program. Sample items are the following: "How consistent is this treatment with common sense or everyday notions about what treatment should be?" and "To what extent do you think there might be risks in undergoing this type of treatment." Each item is rated on a 7-point scale with variable anchor points. Research has demonstrated the factorial integrity and internal consistency of this measure (Kazdin, 1980). The TEI has been modified to make it more appropriate for applications in clinical settings (Reimers et al., 1992) and to create a shorter version of the measure (Kelley, Heffer, Gresham, & Elliott, 1989).

A measure created specifically for the purpose of assessing the acceptability and feasibility of interventions for ADHD is the ADHD Knowledge and Opinion Scale (AKOS; see Power, Karustis, & Habboushe, 2001). This measure consists of 17 true–false items that assess parents' knowledge of ADHD as well as 18 items assessing parents' views about the acceptability of psychotherapy and medication and the feasibility of interventions for ADHD. Items related to intervention acceptability and feasibility are rated on a 6-point scale ranging from 1 = *strongly disagree* to 6 = *strongly agree*. A factor analysis of the AKOS uncovered three factors: Medication Acceptability, Counseling Acceptability, and Counseling Feasibility (Bennett et al., 1996). Sample items for each factor are the following: "I would be reluctant to start our child on a medication for ADHD" (Medication Acceptability), "I could use some professional counseling to help me and my family deal with my child with ADHD in better ways" (Counseling Acceptability), and "Payment problems will make it difficult for our family to follow through with counseling, if recommended, at the present time" (Counseling Feasibility). Internal consistency for each of these factors was well within the acceptable range. Test–retest reliability for the Medication Acceptability and Counseling Feasibility factors was quite high (coefficients above .90), but test–retest reliability for the Counseling Acceptability factor was below an acceptable level (Bennett et al., 1996).

To assess teacher perceptions of treatment acceptability, practitioners may find the Intervention Rating Profile (IRP) useful (see Witt & Elliott, 1985). This 15-item measure requests teachers to rate items on a 6-point scale ranging from 1 = *strongly disagree* to 6= *strongly agree*. Sample items are "I would be willing to use this intervention in the classroom setting" and "This intervention is consistent with those I have used in classroom settings." The IRP has strong factorial integrity and internal consistency (Witt & Elliott, 1985) and has been commonly used in research and practice. Power et al. (1995) created a shorter version of this measure that has a high level of internal consistency (α = .95) and was effective in differentiating teacher perceptions regarding the acceptability of behavioral and pharmacological interventions.

For the assessment of children's views about intervention acceptability, the Children's Intervention Rating Profile (see Witt & Elliott, 1985) is helpful. This seven-item questionnaire requests children to rate the fairness of an intervention strategy on a 6-point scale ranging from 1 = *strongly disagree* to 6 = *strongly agree*. Preliminary research has supported the factorial integrity and internal consistency of this brief measure.

OVERCOMING BARRIERS TO INTERVENTION UTILIZATION

Several strategies may be useful in improving a family's willingness to initiate treatment and to maintain a program of intervention that has been demonstrated to be beneficial. The key ingredients are to design and periodically refine interventions in a collaborative manner with all participants, to improve access to care, and to develop programs of intervention that are responsive to the needs of families in the communities being served.

Matching Interventions to a Family's Stage of Readiness

Research has demonstrated that an individual or a family is more likely to make a commitment to, and derive benefits from, treatment if the intervention is matched to their stage of readiness for change (Prochaska et al., 1992). Interventions that are most useful in the Precontemplation and Contemplation stages are experiential in nature, including approaches that focus on (a) establishing collaborative relationships, (b) providing education about a problem and its treatment, (c) offering support and providing opportunities for emotional catharsis, (d) identifying and challenging deeply held beliefs that serve as obstacles to change, and (e) clarifying individual and family values and priorities. Approaches to treatment that are most useful in the Preparation and Action stages are behavioral in nature and focus on (a) targeting problematic behaviors, (b) identifying the expected outcomes of intervention, (c) identifying methods of assessing outcome, (d) designing an appropriate intervention plan, and (e) evaluating response to treatment and redesigning interventions when needed (Perz et al., 1996). Planning, implementing, and systematically evaluating medication interventions would appear to be most appropriate when families are in the Preparation and Action phases of intervention, although research is needed to confirm this hypothesis. Exhibit 3.2 provides guidelines for selecting approaches to interventions in response to a child's and family's readiness for change.

A critical implication of the research conducted by Prochaska and colleagues is that behavioral approaches to intervention should not be introduced until an individual and family advance to a stage in which they are likely to see the value of this approach and commit to these types of techniques. Another important conclusion derived from this research is

EXHIBIT 3.2
Matching Intervention Approach With Stage of Readiness for Change

Precontemplation Stage
- Educate about problem and effective interventions for problem
- Describe problem severity and expected prognosis
- Provide support and allow opportunities for emotional release
- Identify and challenge deeply held beliefs that are impediments to treatment

Contemplation Stage
- Educate about problem and effective interventions for problem
- Assess parent and child perceptions of the social validity of alternative intervention approaches
- Identify and address potential problems with accessibility to services
- Identify cultural factors that might influence service utilization

Preparation and Action Stage
- Select targets for intervention in collaboration with parents and child
- Identify expected outcomes of treatment with parents and child
- Select intervention strategies with parents and child
- Determine methods of assessing outcome
- Implement intervention and assess outcomes
- Continually reassess social validity of intervention plan and commitment to process of change

that readiness for change can vary greatly during the course of intervention. Children and families who advance to the Preparation and Action phases may regress to earlier phases in response to environmental events. Clinicians need to be responsive to these variations and be prepared to alter approaches to intervention accordingly.

Improving Access to Services

Providing services in clinic settings is convenient and comfortable for providers but at times inconvenient and even anxiety provoking for families. Establishing service delivery systems in school settings is a helpful strategy to improve access to care (Reeder et al., 1997). Schools generally are more accessible and less threatening to families than are clinics. Schools provide innumerable opportunities to build collaborative home–school linkages, which can be important in achieving academic and social success. Furthermore, schools are a rich source of naturalistic data that are useful in diagnostic assessment and outcome assessment (Power, Atkins, Osborne, & Blum, 1994).

Providing interventions in other community settings, such as churches, libraries, and recreational centers, also can improve access to care. An advantage that community centers may have over schools is that they are often open during nonschool hours when caregivers are more available for sessions. Also, some families, particularly those of African American and Latino descent, are more likely to seek help on their own from leaders in community settings (McMiller & Weisz, 1996), so such a strategy builds on their natural patterns of help-seeking behavior. In general, families appear to prefer to receive mental health services in community venues rather than in clinic or school settings (Curran, 1989).

Collaborating With Managed Care Agencies

A major obstacle for many families to receiving the care they need, or in some cases desire, are restrictions imposed by managed health care. Many clinicians adopt a passive posture with managed care agencies, allowing insurance companies to establish the terms of the relationship with providers. A more useful strategy is to establish a partnership with key managed care agencies and to engage in a series of dialogues with them. Clinicians need to learn about the limitations and priorities of managed care agencies. While so doing, they can inform representatives in these agencies about strategies of care that will be more effective or potentially cost-effective (Yates, 1995). For example, it is neither effective nor cost beneficial for a clinician to initiate a trial of medication or a course of behavior therapy when a child and family are in the Contemplation stage of change. A more useful strategy is to assess the stage of change, match the intervention to the stage of change, and frequently monitor progress so that intervention approaches are responsive to the needs of families (Cunningham, 1997).

Improving the Cultural Sensitivity of Professionals

Some families, particularly those of ethnic minority status, do not trust providers because they do not believe that professionals will be able to understand their backgrounds, values, and priorities (McMiller & Weisz, 1996). Establishing programs of service within the community affords clinicians innumerable opportunities to understand the neighborhoods in which they work and the needs of the families they serve. Inviting community leaders to serve on advisory committees that will develop and oversee community-based services is another strategy to improve the community responsiveness of providers. Furthermore, enlisting, training, and empowering community residents to serve as paraprofessionals in community-based centers of care is a valuable resource for improving the cultural sensitivity and effectiveness of clinical providers (Dowrick et al., 2001; Manz, Power, Ginsburg-Block, & Dowrick, 2001).

CONCLUSION

Although many highly efficacious interventions are available for children and families coping with psychological disorders, families often are unwilling to initiate treatment or to consistently adhere with intervention protocols. The stages of change model advanced by Prochaska and colleagues (Prochaska et al., 1992) provides a useful framework for understanding the failure of families to initiate and maintain programs of intervention. This model highlights the importance of matching the intervention approach with a family's readiness for change. Numerous factors contribute to a family's readiness for change, including the parents' and child's perceptions of the social validity of interventions, the accessibility of services, and the family's pattern of help-seeking behavior. Parents and children sometimes differ in their perceptions about interventions and their readiness for change, which can result in problems with treatment adherence and family conflict. For these reasons, it is important for clinicians to understand both parents' and children's attitudes about treatment and to incorporate their perceptions in the development of intervention plans.

Interview procedures and rating scales are helpful to assess parent and child attitudes, as well as teacher perceptions, about the acceptability of intervention approaches. Several strategies are available for overcoming barriers to service utilization. These include matching an intervention strategy to a family's readiness for change, establishing services in school or community settings, collaborating with managed care agencies, improving the cultural sensitivity and community responsiveness of providers, and adjusting treatment approaches in response to feedback from parents and children about the appropriateness of the services being provided. Research regarding family attitudes and readiness for change in using medication to treat psychological problems in children is limited. The research that does exist consists of parent reports related to children and adolescents with ADHD. In the future, research is needed that will focus on understanding readiness for change from the point of view of parents and children as related to both pharmacological and psychosocial methods of care for a wide range of psychological disorders. Furthermore, it is important to understand the influence that age and gender have on children's perceptions of interventions for mental health disorders, particularly pharmacological treatments.

REFERENCES

Aman, M. G., & Wolford, P. L. (1995). Consumer satisfaction with involvement in drug research: A social validity study. *Journal of the American Academy of Child and Adolescent Psychiatry, 34,* 940–945.

Beidel, D. C., & Turner, S. M. (1998). *Shy children, phobic adults: Nature and treatment of social phobia.* Washington, DC: American Psychological Association.

Beitman, B. D., Beck, N. C., Deuser, W. W., Carter, C. S., Davidson, J. R. T., & Maddock, R. J. (1994). Patient stage of change predicts outcome in a panic disorder medication trial. *Anxiety, 1,* 64–69.

Bennett, D. S., Power, T. J., Rostain, A. L., & Carr, D. E. (1996). Parent acceptability and feasibility of ADHD interventions: Assessment, correlates, and predictive validity. *Journal of Pediatric Psychology, 21,* 643–657.

Brown, R. T., & Sawyer, M. G. (1998). Medications for school-age children: Effects on learning and behavior. New York: Guilford Press.

Bussing, R., Schoenberg, N. E., & Perwein, A. R. (1998). Knowledge and information about ADHD: Evidence of cultural differences among African-American and White parents. *Social Science Medicine, 46,* 919–928.

Carlson, C. L., Pelham, W. E., Milich, R., & Hoza, B. (1993). ADHD boys' performance and attributions following success and failure: Drug effects and individual differences. *Cognitive Therapy and Research, 17,* 269–287.

Corkum, P., Rimer, P., & Schachar, R. (1999). Parental knowledge of attention-deficit hyperactivity disorder and opinions of treatment options: Impact on enrollment and adherence to a 12-month treatment trial. *Canadian Journal of Psychiatry, 44,* 1043–1048.

Cunningham, C. E. (1997). Readiness for change: Applications to the management of ADHD. *ADHD Report, 5,* 6–9.

Cunningham, C. E. (1998). A large-group, community-based, family systems approach to parent training. In R. A. Barkley (Ed.), *Attention-deficit hyperactivity disorder: A handbook for diagnosis and treatment* (2nd ed., pp. 394–412). New York: Guilford Press.

Curran, D. (1989). *Working with parents.* Circle Pines, MN: American Guidance Service.

Dowrick, P. W., Power, T. J., Manz, P. H., Ginsburg-Block, M., Leff, S. S., & Kim-Rupnow, S. (2001). Community responsiveness: Examples from under resourced urban schools. *Journal of Prevention and Intervention in the Community, 21,* 71–90.

Fantuzzo, J., & Atkins, M. S. (1992). Applied behavior analysis for education: Teacher-centered and classroom-based. *Journal of Applied Behavior Analysis, 25,* 35–42.

Johnston, C., & Fine, S. (1993). Methods of evaluating methylphenidate in children with attention-deficit hyperactivity disorder: Acceptability, satisfaction, and compliance. *Journal of Pediatric Psychology, 18,* 717–730.

Joost, J. C., Chessare, J. B., Schaeufele, J., Link, D., & Weaver, M. T. (1989). Compliance with a prescription for psychotherapeutic counseling in childhood. *Journal of Developmental and Behavioral Pediatrics, 10,* 98–102.

Kazdin, A. E. (1980). Acceptability of alternative treatments for deviant child behavior. *Journal of Applied Behavior Analysis, 13,* 259–273.

Kazdin, A. E. (1981). Acceptability of child treatment techniques: The influence of treatment efficacy and adverse side effects. *Behavior Therapy, 12,* 493–506.

Kazdin, A. (1996). Dropping out of child psychotherapy: Issues for research and implications for practice. *Clinical Child Psychology and Psychiatry, 1,* 133–156.

Kazdin, A. E., Holland, L., & Crowley, M. (1997). Family experience of barriers to treatment and premature termination from child therapy. *Journal of Consulting and Clinical Psychology, 65,* 453–463.

Kazdin, A. E., Mazurick, J. L., & Siegel, T. C. (1994). Treatment outcome among children with externalizing disorder who terminate prematurely versus those who complete psychotherapy. *Journal of the American Academy of Child and Adolescent Psychiatry, 33,* 549–557.

Kelley, M. L., Heffer, R. W., Gresham, F. M., & Elliott, S. N. (1989). Development of a modified Treatment Evaluation Inventory. *Journal of Psychopathology and Behavioral Assessment, 11,* 235–247.

Kendall, P. C. (1994). Treating anxiety disorders in children: Results of a randomized clinical trial. *Journal of Consulting and Clinical Psychology, 62,* 100–110.

Klein, R. G., & Abikoff, H. (1997). Behavior therapy and methylphenidate in the treatment of children with ADHD. *Journal of Attention Disorders, 2,* 89–114.

LaGreca, A. M., & Schuman, W. B. (1995). Adherence to prescribed medical regimens. In M. C. Roberts (Ed.), *Handbook of pediatric psychology* (2nd ed., pp. 55–83). New York: Guilford Press.

Liu, C., Robin, A. L., Brenner, S., & Eastman, J. (1991). Social acceptability of methylphenidate and behavior modification for the treatment of attention deficit hyperactivity disorder. *Pediatrics, 88*, 560–565.

Manz, P. H., Power, T. J., Ginsburg-Block, M., & Dowrick, P. W. (2001). *Community partners: Improving the effectiveness of urban schools and empowering low-income, ethnically diverse community residents.* Manuscript submitted for publication.

McConnaughy, E. A., Prochaska, J. O., & Velicer, W. F. (1983). Stages of change in psychotherapy: Measurement and sample profiles. *Psychotherapy: Theory, Research, and Practice, 20*, 368–375.

McConnaughy, E. A., DiClemente, C. C., Prochaska, J. O., & Velicer, W. F. (1989). Stages of change in psychotherapy: A follow-up report. *Psychotherapy, 26*, 494–503.

McMiller, W. P., & Weisz, J. R. (1996). Help-seeking preceding mental health clinic intake among African-American, Latino, and Caucasian youths. *Journal of the American Academy of Child and Adolescent Psychiatry, 35*, 1086–1094.

Milich, R. (1994). The response of children with ADHD to failure: If at first you don't succeed, do you try, try again? *School Psychology Review, 23*, 11–28.

Padgett, K., Patrick, C., Burns, B., Schlesinger, H., & Cohen, J. (1993). The effect of insurance benefit changes on use of child and adolescent outpatient mental health services. *Medical Care, 31*, 96–110.

Pavuluri, M. N., Luk, S. L., & McGee, R. (1996). Help-seeking for behavior problems by parents of preschool children: A community study. *Journal of the American Academy of Child and Adolescent Psychiatry, 35*, 215–222.

Pelham, W. E. (1999). The NIMH multimodal treatment study for ADHD: Just say no to drugs? *Clinical Child Psychology Newsletter, 14*, 1–6.

Pelham, W. E., Carlson, C., Sams, S. E., Vallano, G., Dixon, M. J., & Hoza, B. (1993). Separate and combined effects of methylphenidate and behavior modification on boys with attention deficit-hyperactivity disorder in the classroom. *Journal of Consulting and Clinical Psychology, 61*, 506–515.

Pelham, W. E., Murphy, D. A., Vannatta, K., Milich, R., Licht, B. G., Gnagy, E. M., Greenslade, K. E., Greiner, A. R., & Vodde-Hamilton, M. (1992). Methylphenidate and attributions in boys with attention-deficit hyperactivity disorder. *Journal of Consulting and Clinical Psychology, 60*, 282–292.

Perz, C. A., DiClemente, C. C., & Carbonari, J. P. (1996). Doing the right thing at the right time? The interaction of stages and processes of change in successful smoking cessation. *Health Psychology, 15*, 462–468.

Power, T. J., Atkins, M., Osborne, M., & Blum, N. (1994). The school psychologist as manager of programming for ADHD. *School Psychology Review, 23*, 279–291.

Power, T. J., Hess, L., & Bennett, D. (1995). The acceptability of interventions for ADHD among elementary and middle school teachers. *Journal of Developmental and Behavioral Pediatrics, 16*, 238–243.

Power, T. J., Karustis, J. L., & Habboushe, D. F. (2001). *Homework success for children with ADHD: A family–school intervention program*. New York: Guilford Press.

Prochaska, J. O., DiClemente, C. C., & Norcross, J. C. (1992). In search of how people change: Applications to addictive behaviors. *American Psychologist, 47,* 1102–1114.

Prochaska, J. O., Velicer, W. F., Rossi, J. S., Goldstein, M. G., Marcus, B. H., Rakowski, W., Fiore, C., Harlow, L. L., Redding, C. A., Rosenbloom, D., & Rossi, S. R. (1994). Stages of change and decisional balance for 12 problem behaviors. *Health Psychology, 13,* 39–46.

Reeder, G. D., Maccow, G. C., Shaw, S. R., Swerdlik, M. E., Horton, C. B., & Foster, P. (1997). School psychologists and full-service schools: Partnerships with medical, mental health, and social services. *School Psychology Review, 26,* 603–621.

Reimers, T. M., Wacker, D. P., Cooper, L. J., & De Raad, A. O. (1992). Acceptability of behavioral treatments for children: Analog and naturalistic evaluation by parents. *School Psychology Review, 21,* 628–643.

Rostain, A. L., Power, T. J., & Atkins, M. S. (1993). Assessing parents' willingness to pursue treatment for children with attention-deficit hyperactivity disorder. *Journal of the American Academy of Child and Adolescent Psychiatry, 32,* 175–181.

Sue, S., Fujino, H., & Takeuchi, D. (1991). Community mental health services for ethnic minority groups: A test of the community responsiveness hypothesis. *Journal of Community and Clinical Psychology, 59,* 533–538.

Takeuchi, D., Bui, K., & Kim, L. (1993). The referral of minority adolescents to community mental health centers. *Journal of Health and Social Behavior, 34,* 153–164.

Whalen, C. K., & Henker, B. (1991). Social impact of stimulant treatment for hyperactive children. *Journal of Learning Disabilities, 24,* 231–241.

Whalen, C. K., Henker, B., Hinshaw, S. P., Heller, T., & Huber-Dressler, A. (1991). Messages of medication: Effects of actual versus informed medication status on hyperactive boys' expectancies and self-evaluations. *Journal of Consulting and Clinical Psychology, 59,* 602–606.

Wilson, M., Bell-Dolan, D., & Beitman, B. (1997). Application of the stages of change scale in a clinical drug trial. *Journal of Anxiety Disorders, 4,* 395–408.

Witt, J. C., & Elliott, S. N. (1985). Acceptability of classroom intervention strategies. In T. R. Kratochwill (Ed.), *Advances in school psychology* (Vol. 4, pp. 251–288). Hillsdale, NJ: Erlbaum.

Witt, J. C., Martens, B. K., & Elliott, S. N. (1994). Factors affecting teachers' judgments of the acceptability of behavioral interventions: Time involvement, behavior problem severity, and type of intervention. *Behavior Therapy, 15,* 204–209.

Wolf, M. M. (1978). Social validity: The case for subjective measurement of how applied behavior analysis is finding its heart. *Journal of Applied Behavior Analysis, 11,* 203–214.

Yates, B. T. (1995). Cost-effectiveness analysis, cost–benefit analysis, and beyond: Evolving models for the scientist-manager-practitioner. *Clinical Psychology: Science and Practice, 2*, 385–398.

Zito, J. M., Safer, D. J., dosReis, S., & Riddle, M. A. (1998). Racial disparity in psychotropic medications prescribed for youths with Medicaid insurance in Maryland. *Journal of the American Academy of Child and Adolescent Psychiatry, 37*, 179–184.

4

ANXIETY DISORDERS

Professional knowledge about childhood anxiety disorders has improved notably in the past 20 years. For example, the *Diagnostic and Statistical Manual of Mental Disorders* (3rd ed., *DSM–III*; American Psychiatric Association, 1980) listed three categories within the broad spectrum of child and adolescent anxiety disorders: avoidant disorder, overanxious disorder, and separation anxiety. Since that time, researchers have demonstrated the developmental continuity of these maladies (Allen, Leonard, & Swedo, 1995; Bernstein, Borchardt, & Perwein, 1996). The result is a simplification of the diagnostic codes, with childhood onset of anxiety usually subsumed within adult classifications. Thus, a youngster who may have previously been diagnosed with overanxious disorder by *DSM–III* nosology would now be considered as having generalized anxiety with childhood onset by *DSM–IV* criteria (American Psychiatric Association, 1994). Similarly, avoidant disorder was eliminated in the *DSM–IV* and replaced with childhood onset social phobia. Only separation anxiety has remained a separate category, with an age of onset criterion of younger than age 18. Such a unification of childhood and adult disorders has more clearly articulated early identification, prognosis, and treatment issues (Tracey, Chorpita, Douban, & Barlow, 1997).

The *DSM–IV* divides the anxiety disorders into 12 categories: panic disorder with and without agoraphobia, agoraphobia without panic, specific phobia, social phobia, obsessive–compulsive disorder, posttraumatic stress

65

disorder, acute stress disorder, generalized anxiety disorder, anxiety disorder due to a medical condition, substance-induced anxiety disorder, and anxiety disorder not otherwise specified. In addition, as noted above, separation anxiety disorder is listed separately under other disorders of infancy, childhood, or adolescence. Because empirically supported pharmacological and nonpharmacological interventions are not delineated for each specific type of anxiety disorder, this chapter highlights generalized anxiety, separation anxiety, obsessive–compulsive disorder, panic, phobias, and posttraumatic stress disorder. Generalized anxiety and separation anxiety are considered collectively because of their symptom similarities.

GENERALIZED ANXIETY DISORDER AND SEPARATION ANXIETY DISORDER

Anxiety is commonly manifested as a cluster of related symptoms including apprehension, tension, uneasiness, physical complaints, and the need for reassurance (Masi, Mucci, Favilla, Romano, & Poli, 1999). Symptoms of anxiety are generally considered unremarkable in the pediatric population because of the commonly held cultural expectation that children are relatively shy, anxious, and fearful. When these behaviors become abnormally severe, however, and begin to interfere with the quality of life or emotional comfort of the child, they may be considered pathological (Allen et al., 1995). The most common symptoms of anxiety in preschool children include frequent need for reassurance, fear of the dark, fear of harm to an attachment figure, and health-related concerns (Bernstein et al., 1996). Manifestations of anxiety in older children and adolescents may be seen in poor school achievement, school refusal, social isolation and withdrawal, overconcern or worry about competence or quality of performance, and depressive symptoms (American Psychiatric Association, 1994; Sallee et al., 1998). Whereas separation anxiety disorder (SAD) focuses on separation from the primary attachment figure or figures, generalized anxiety disorder (GAD) is more global and encompasses many situations and circumstances.

The prevalence rate of clinically significant anxiety disorders in non-referred children and adolescents ranges from 2% to 5%. This variability may be accounted for by the various categories within the broad spectrum of anxiety as well as the different definitions used over time. For example, numerous epidemiological studies have reported prevalence rates of 2.4% to 4.6% for GAD and 3.5% to 4.1% for SAD (Benjamin, Costello, & Warren, 1990; Bowen, Offord, & Boyle, 1990; Dadds et al., 1999). Because of the frequent comorbidity of anxiety disorders with disruptive behavioral problems as well as with other internalizing disorders such as depression, several researchers have suggested that underidentification is probable (Ollendick, King, & Yule, 1994; Popper & Gherardi, 1996).

There are various etiological hypotheses for anxiety disorders. Current data suggest both environmental and genetic factors (K. S. Kendall, 1996; Martin, Cabrol, Bouvard, Lepine, & Mouren-Simeoni, 1999). For example, an excessively shy temperament and notable behavioral inhibition in preschoolers are highly predictive of later clinical levels of anxiety (Biederman, Rosenbaum, & Bolduc-Murphy, 1993). Likewise, there is a high concordance rate for anxiety disorders among family members (Hewitt et al., 1997; Manassis, Bradley, Goldberg, Hood, & Swinson, 1995).

OBSESSIVE–COMPULSIVE DISORDER

The *DSM–IV* (American Psychiatric Association, 1994) defines obsessive–compulsive disorder (OCD) as characterized by intrusive thoughts, impulses, or images (i.e., obsessions) that often lead to repetitive behaviors or mental acts (i.e., compulsions) intended to reduce stress or prevent dreaded events from occurring. The obsessions appear to be senseless, difficult to dislodge, and typically involve perceived risk or harm (Scahill, 1996). The compulsions are performed in an attempt to suppress, organize, or ignore the obsessive thoughts (March & Mulle, 1996). For children, common obsessive thoughts involve contamination and fear of harm to self or family members. Customary pediatric compulsions include hand washing, repetitive touching or rearranging of objects, and counting.

OCD usually emerges during childhood or adolescence, with a prevalence in the pediatric population of approximately 1%–2% (Leonard, Swedo, Allen, & Rapoport, 1994; Riddle, 1998). As is evident with many childhood disorders, OCD is likely underdiagnosed, with few caregivers seeking treatment for their children until symptoms of the disorder have escalated (March & Leonard, 1996; Rapoport, Swedo, & Leonard, 1992). Cases are further complicated by the presence of comorbid psychiatric disorders (e.g., anxiety, depression, and Tourette's syndrome) that occur in 62%–84% of youths with OCD (Owens & Piacentini, 1998).

Current findings suggest a strong genetic factor in the etiology of OCD. Although no specific genes have yet been isolated, twin and family aggregation studies document probable biological risk factors that are exacerbated by stress and family role modeling (Pauls & Alsobrook, 1999; Pollock & Carter, 1999). Furthermore, functional neuroimaging studies have documented neurobiological aspects of OCD, suggesting an association of OCD with brain morphology (Scahill, 1996).

PANIC DISORDER

This disorder is manifested by recurrent panic attacks that commonly consist of an accelerated heart rate, sweating, shaking, shortness of breath, feelings of choking, and chest discomfort. In addition, there often is a persistent concern that such an attack is imminent. A panic disorder may occur with or without agoraphobia (i.e., anxiety of being in places wherein escape may be difficult or help may be unavailable if a panic attack occurs; American Psychiatric Association, 1994).

Panic disorder is often associated with the onset of sexual maturity (Hayward, Killen, & Hammer, 1992). For example, the National Institute of Mental Health (NIHM) Epidemiologic Catchment Area data indicated that the peak age of onset was between 15 to 19 years (Bernstein et al., 1996). Unfortunately, the mean interval between an adolescent's first panic attack and the initial diagnosis of panic disorder may be up to 3 years (Wiener, 1996). Prevalence data indicate a 6% rate in referred children and adolescents (Biederman et al., 1997).

Ongoing studies support a strong genetic etiological basis for panic disorders (Bernstein et al., 1996). Although family factors and environmental effects clearly compound risk status, twin and multigenerational DNA studies document the likelihood of a multiple allele or recessive gene interactional model (Knowles et al., 1998; Stein, Jang, & Livesley, 1999). (For technical medical terminology, refer to the *Glossary of Terms* provided at the end of the book.)

PHOBIAS

A diagnosis of specific phobia or social phobia is warranted when exposure or fear of exposure to a circumscribed stimulus (e.g., darkness, spiders, or blood) or social situation (e.g., being called on by a teacher, playing sports, or performing in a play) results in marked and persistent fear. In children, phobias may be expressed by excessive crying, refusal, freezing, and clinging behaviors. Unlike adults, children and young adolescents may not realize that their fears are unreasonable or extreme (American Psychiatric Association, 1994). Regardless, the feared situation or stimulus is avoided whenever possible.

It is important to differentiate between normal apprehensions and excessive fears that seriously affect a youngster's functioning. For instance, young children may often fear strangers, unfamiliar surroundings, animals, or "magical entities" such as ghosts or monsters. Unlike such common concerns, a phobia cannot be logically explained away, is beyond voluntary control, leads to avoidance of the feared stimulus or situation, persists over time, and is age inappropriate (Silverman & Rabian, 1994). In a large epidemiological study, Simonoff et al. (1997) reported that 8% of the child and adolescent catchment area sample had phobias to the extent that functional impairment was evident.

Etiological research suggests a strong familial pattern in the development of phobias (e.g., Smoller & Tsuang, 1998). Environmental factors are apparent in conditioning through direct exposure to a traumatic event as well as vicarious learning (e.g., observing parental or sibling reactions, viewing media coverage). Reinforcement occurs regularly when family members comfort the child or assist in the avoidance behaviors. In addition to the frequent occurrence within family constellations, phobias are often comorbid with panic disorder, depression, and OCD (Simonoff et al., 1997; Stein, Chartier, Kozak, King, & Kennedy, 1998).

POSTTRAUMATIC STRESS DISORDER

Postraumatic stress disorder (PTSD) is the development of characteristic symptoms following exposure to a traumatic event (or events) that involves the threat of death, serious injury, or physical safety of self or others (American Psychiatric Association, 1994). The responses to such exposure may include intense fear, agitated or disorganized behavior, a sense of helplessness, and intense psychological distress to cues that resemble the trauma (American Psychiatric Association, 1994). In young children, PTSD may be displayed in separation difficulties, irritability, anger, repetitive trauma-specific reenactment (e.g., acting out a shooting), generalized nightmares, and psychosomatic symptoms (Pfefferbaum, 1997; Yule & Canterbury, 1994). PTSD symptomatology may occur immediately following the trauma, be delayed for a period of time, or even increase with time (American Psychiatric Association, 1994).

The prevalence rate of PTSD in children and adolescents who have documented cases of physical or sexual abuse is approximately 33% (Ackerman, Newton, McPherson, Jones, & Dykman, 1998). Given the necessary precondition of exposure to serious injury or a life-threatening event, etiological studies are limited. To date, genetic analyses suggest a possible heritable intrapsychic risk factor (Gelernter et al., 1999; True et al., 1993). PTSD is highly comorbid with other affective disorders (Ackerman et al., 1998; Cohen, 1998).

MEDICAL INTERVENTIONS

Although there is substantial information regarding behavioral, cognitive–behavioral, and psychosocial interventions for the treatment of childhood anxiety disorders (e.g., Morris & Kratochwill, 1998; Ollendick

& King, 1998), much less is known about the efficacy of medical management. Few double-blind studies have been completed with the pediatric population, and extrapolating pharmacological treatment strategies from adult efficacy data is precarious at best (Allen et al., 1995). Furthermore, many psychotropic agents prescribed for children are not specifically approved for pediatric use by the U.S. Food and Drug Administration (FDA). Yet the current health care movement toward short-term cost containment has resulted frequently in the sole usage of medication rather than psychological or multimodal treatments for symptom regulation (Kearney & Silverman, 1998).

Although medication may be deemed necessary in cases that have proved refractory to psychological interventions, the indiscriminate use of psychotropic agents as a first line of treatment and without validated efficacy in the pediatric population is difficult to justify (Gadow, 1997). It is advised, therefore, that treatment of pediatric anxiety disorders always incorporate psychological (e.g., behavioral or cognitive–behavioral) intervention components and that medication be considered as a possible augmentation. Below, we provide a summary of the most frequently used medications in the management of childhood anxiety, with the listing in alphabetical order to facilitate reader ease. Tables 4.1 and 4.2 provide a summary of medications clinically validated in double-blind and open studies for use with children and adolescents. The tables list recommended dosage, expected positive outcomes, and possible adverse effects. In Table 4.3, we list the medications that are not clinically validated for children and adolescents.

Clomipramine

Released for use in the United States in 1990, clomipramine (Anafranil) is a tricyclic antidepressant used in the treatment of OCD. Double-blind studies with pediatric participants have documented significant decreases in OCD symptomatology when comparing clomipramine with placebos (DeVeaugh-Geiss et al., 1992; Flament et al., 1985) or desipramine (Leonard et al., 1989, 1991).

The typical starting dosage for children and adolescents is 25 mg per day, with increases of 25 mg per day to a maximum daily dose of 3 mg per kg of body weight (Scahill, 1996). As with all tricyclics, clomipramine requires the evaluation of vital signs, blood levels, liver functioning, and cardiac status (Riddle, Geller, & Ryan, 1993). Adverse effects include risk of seizure onset with prolonged use of more than 1 year at a high dosage (300 mg per day), drowsiness, dizziness, tremors, headaches, dry mouth, and fatigue.

TABLE 4.1
Medications Clinically Validated in Double-Blind Studies for Use With Children and Adolescents With Anxiety Disorders

Generic Name (Trade Name)	Children mg/kg/day or Daily Dose	Adolescents mg/kg/day or Daily Dose	Treatment Outcome	Adverse Effect
Clomipramine (Anafranil)	1–3 mg/kg	1–3 mg/kg	Highly effective in symptom reduction of OCD when compared with placebo and desipramine in double-blind crossover comparisons.	Risk of seizure onset with prolonged use (>1 year) and high dosage (300 mg/day), drowsiness, dizziness, tremors, headaches, dry mouth, and fatigue.
Clonazepam (Klonopin)	.01–.02 mg/kg	.01–.03 mg/kg	Effective in symptom reduction in separation anxiety, GAD, and panic attacks.	Drowsiness, ataxia, and dizziness.
Fluoxetine (Prozac)	10–50 mg	10–50 mg	Effective in symptom reduction of OCD.	Restlessness, insomnia, fatigue, nausea, disinhibition, decreased appetite, and tremors.
Sertraline (Zoloft)	Up to 200 mg	Up to 200 mg	Effective in symptom reduction of OCD.	Nausea, diarrhea, insomnia, reduced appetite, and drowsiness.

Note. Sources include DeVeaugh-Geiss et al. (1992); Flament et al. (1985); Graae, Milner, Rizzotto, and Klein (1994); Kutcher, Reiter, Gardner, and Klein (1992); Leonard et al. (1989, 1991); March, Biederman, et al. (1998); *Physicians' Desk Reference* (1999); and Riddle et al. (1992). OCD = Obsessive–compulsive disorder; GAD = generalized anxiety disorder.

TABLE 4.2
Medications Clinically Validated in Open Studies for Use With Children and Adolescents With Anxiety Disorders

Generic Name (Trade Name)	Children mg/kg/day or Daily Dose	Adolescents mg/kg/day or Daily Dose	Treatment Outcome	Adverse Effect
Buspirone (BuSpar)	Not yet established	Not yet established	Effective in treating GAD and social phobia.	Dizziness and drowsiness. Safety with children under 18 years of age not established.
Clonidine (Catapres)	Not yet established	Not yet established	Effective in treating PTSD.	Dry mouth, drowsiness, approximately 10% decrease in blood pressure. Safety with children under 12 years of age not established.
Fluvoxamine (Luvox)	50–200 mg	50–200 mg	Decline in symptom severity of OCD.	Nausea, drowsiness, insomnia, and headaches.
Paroxetine (Paxil)	Not yet established	Not yet established	Decline in symptom severity in OCD.	Drowsiness. Safety with pediatric population has not been established.
Propranolol (Inderal)	2.0–4.0 mg/kg	2.0–4.0 mg/kg	Effective in treating PTSD.	Reduction in blood pressure, drowsiness, and insomnia.

Note. Sources include Alderman, Wolkow, Chung, and Johnston (1998); Apter et al. (1994); Famularo, Kinscherff, and Fenton (1988); Harmon and Riggs (1996); Kutcher, Reiter, Gardner, and Klein (1992); Moore, MacMaster, Stewart, and Rosenberg (1998); *Physicians' Desk Reference* (1999); and Zwier and Rao (1994). GAD = generalized anxiety disorder; PTSD = posttraumatic stress disorder; OCD = obsessive–compulsive disorder.

TABLE 4.3
Medications Not Clinically Validated for Children and Adolescents With Anxiety Disorders

Generic Name (Trade Name)	Adverse Effects and Cautionary Statement
Desipramine (Norpramin)	Cardiac complications leading to death. Clinicians are encouraged to use safer alternatives.
Imipramine (Tofranil)	Cardiac complications leading to death. More supportive documentation is needed. Clinicians are encouraged to use it only when other more appropriate medications (e.g., clonazepam and fluoxetine) have not achieved treatment efficacy.

Note. Sources include Bernstein et al. (2000); Klein, Koplewicz, and Kanner (1992); Leonard et al. (1989, 1991); Riddle, Geller, and Ryan (1993); Varley and McClellan (1997); Werry (1994, 1995); and Wilens et al. (1996).

Clonazepam

Clonazepam (Klonopin), a benzodiazepine, has received limited attention from the pediatric research community. In one of two double-blind crossover studies, Graae, Milner, Rizzotto, and Klein (1994) compared clonazepam with a placebo in the treatment of SAD and GAD in 12 children. Moderate to marked improvement was noted for 66% of the sample when clonazepam was administered. Likewise, Kutcher, Reiter, Gardner, and Klein (1992) reported successful clonazepam treatment in a double-blind study of adolescents diagnosed with panic disorder. Findings revealed that the frequency of panic attacks and the severity of the anxiety symptoms decreased notably with clonazepam compared with the placebo.

Although considerably more research is necessary, it appears that clonazepam may be helpful in refractory cases of anxiety and panic disorders. Adverse effects are few and include drowsiness, ataxia, and dizziness.

Desipramine

A tricyclic antidepressant that has been used in the treatment of adult anxiety disorders, desipramine (Norpramin) has limited documented efficacy with children and adolescents. For example, double-blind studies with pediatric participants have documented significantly better treatment outcomes with clomipramine than with desipramine when the two medications were compared (Leonard et al., 1989, 1991). In addition, its notable toxicity has resulted in the sudden deaths of six children due to cardiac complications (Riddle et al., 1993; Varley & McClellan, 1997; Werry, 1995). As a result, clinicians are encouraged to use safer alternatives (Werry, 1994).

Fluoxetine

A selective serotonin reuptake inhibitor (SSRI), fluoxetine (Prozac) has been tested in one double-blind (Riddle et al., 1992) and three open studies (Birmaher et al., 1994; Fairbanks et al., 1997; Geller, Biederman, Reed, Spencer, & Wilens, 1995) in the treatment of OCD, GAD, SAD, and social phobia. Outcomes are positive, with notable symptom reduction after at least 4 weeks of treatment. For example, Riddle et al. (1992) used a randomized, double-blind, placebo-controlled fixed-dose (20 mg) trial of fluoxetine in the treatment of OCD in 14 children ages 8–15 years. The medication resulted in significant reduction in compulsive behaviors over the placebo condition. In the open studies, Birmaher et al. (1994) reported an 81% reduction in anxiety symptoms, and Geller et al. (1995) reported a 74% reduction in OCD behaviors with the use of fluoxetine. Mild, transient side effects evidenced in the four trials included insomnia, fatigue, nausea, and motor restlessness.

In conclusion, these few preliminary studies suggest that fluoxetine may be a generally safe and effective short-term treatment for children with anxiety disorders. Data suggest that the typical starting dosage is 5 mg or less in young children and 10 mg for older children and adolescents, with an optimal final dose range of 10–50 mg per day (Biederman et al., 1997; Scahill, 1996).

Imipramine

Imipramine (Tofranil) is a tricyclic antidepressant commonly prescribed for the treatment of anxiety and depression in adults. Yet its efficacy with children has yet to be consistently demonstrated by double-blind studies. For example, Klein, Koplewicz, and Kanner (1992) treated 20 children diagnosed with separation anxiety who had not responded to a 1-month trial of behavioral therapy. The 20 children were evaluated using a double-blind, randomized, 6-week trial of imipramine or placebo. About half of the children improved with either treatment, and no superiority of imipramine was obtained. By comparison, Bernstein et al. (2000) reported imipramine coupled with cognitive–behavioral therapy (CBT) was notably better than the placebo plus CBT condition in the treatment of 47 children manifesting school refusal. Nonetheless, sudden deaths involving cardiac complications in children being treated with imipramine have been reported (e.g., Varley & McClellan, 1997; Wilens et al., 1996). Given these mixed results, far more supportive documentation is necessary before imipramine could be viewed as an appropriate pharmacological alternative with children and adolescents. It is recommended, therefore, that it be considered for use only when other more appropriate medications (e.g., clona-zepam and fluoxetine) have not achieved treatment efficacy.

Sertraline

A SSRI, sertraline (Zoloft) is commonly used in the treatment of anxiety and depression in adults. Efficacy and safety data for the juvenile population are still forthcoming. March, Biederman, et al. (1998) evaluated its effectiveness for treating 187 children and youths ages 6–17 years diagnosed with OCD. Using a multicenter randomized control trial, the researchers reported significantly greater reduction in OCD symptomatology, as measured by the Children's Yale–Brown Obsessive Compulsive Scale and the NIMH Global Obsessive Compulsive Rating Scale, in the children treated with sertraline over those in the placebo condition. Likewise, the medication was well tolerated with only mild adverse effects (insomnia, drowsiness, reduction in appetite). An open study using sertraline in the treatment of OCD indicated similar findings (Alderman, Wolkow, Chung, & Johnston, 1998). These data indicate that further double-blind studies using sertraline are warranted.

Medications Requiring Double-Blind Studies

The effectiveness and safety of other benzodiazepines, SSRIs, and tricyclics in the management of pediatric anxiety disorders have yet to be established by double-blind trials (see Table 4.2). To date, open studies with children and adolescents have documented the effectiveness of other serotonin reuptake inhibitors, including fluvoxamine (Luvox; Apter et al., 1994) and paroxetine (Paxil; Moore, MacMaster, Stewart, & Rosenberg, 1998) in the treatment of OCD without significant adverse effects. Open trials with buspirone (BuSpar) were reported to be effective in the treatment of GAD (Kranzler, 1988; Kutcher et al., 1992) and social phobia (Zwier & Rao, 1994). Finally, few studies have evaluated pharmacological interventions for PTSD. One open trial found clonidine (Catapres) to be efficacious in the treatment of PTSD in preschool children (Harmon & Riggs, 1996), and another open study indicated success with propranolol (Inderal) for children exhibiting PTSD secondary to sexual or physical abuse (Famularo, Kinscherff, & Fenton, 1988). Randomized placebo-controlled trials, however, are necessary to establish the efficacy of these and other medications in relation to empirically supported treatments such as psychological interventions (i.e., behavioral and cognitive–behavioral) and medications such as clomipramine and clonazepam.

PSYCHOSOCIAL INTERVENTIONS

Psychological interventions for the management of childhood anxiety disorders include a plethora of well-developed and empirically supported procedures such as exposure, response prevention, systematic desensitization, anxiety-management/relaxation training, modeling, and contingency reinforcement (Ammerman, Hersen, & Last, 1999; Morris & Kratochwill, 1998; Ollendick & King, 1998). In addition to these mainstays of behavioral therapy, cognitive procedures include the use of coping self-statements, role playing, the identification of positive coping strategies (e.g., exercise, singing a favorite song), social skills training, and homework assignments (Farrell, Hains, & Davies, 1998; March, Amaya-Jackson, Murray, & Schulte, 1998; March & Mulle, 1996). In general, treatment focuses on increasing the child's ability to confront and cope with a feared stimulus or situation. This can be accomplished by either reducing the child's specific fears (e.g., riding the bus, teasing by peers, and leaving home) or by increasing approach strategies. Either approach results in the ultimate goal of reduced anxiety.

Systematic Desensitization, Contingency Management, and Modeling Interventions

Exposure-based treatments rely on the assumption that anxiety usually dissipates after a duration of exposure to the feared stimulus (March, 1995). These procedures have proved most efficacious in the management of anxiety disorders and panic attacks (Bernstein et al., 1996; P. C. Kendall, 1994). Systematic desensitization, the most commonly used technique to treat children's panic and phobia disorders (Ollendick & King, 1998), is designed to decrease progressively the child's fear of the phobic object or situation. After relaxation skills are taught, the child is presented with fear-producing situations in a progressive manner in order from least to most fear provoking (i.e., a fear hierarchy). Each time the child experiences fear in response to a stimulus, he or she is directed to engage in the relaxation skills. Because relaxation is incompatible with fear, there is a concomitant reduction in anxiety.

Systematic desensitization can occur through imagery or in vivo. The child's age, level of visual imagery, and ability to follow directions and perform relaxation exercises are important considerations in therapy selection (Ollendick et al., 1994). Although these procedures work reasonably well with older children and adolescents, younger children may have difficulty with muscle relaxation and following mental imagery sequences. With younger clients, numerous in vivo sessions, beginning with innocuous settings and working progressively up the fear hierarchy will be necessary (Silverman & Rabian, 1994).

Contingency management, particularly shaping and positive reinforcement, may be used to increase approach responses to anxiety-provoking situations by reinforcing successive approximations made by the child. To be most effective, the professional should thoroughly assess the contingencies that are currently maintaining the phobic or panic response. Although the use of contingency management procedures are commonly used, outcome data for this approach are less convincing than data regarding systematic desensitization (Bernstein et al., 1996; P. C. Kendall, 1994, Ollendick & King, 1998).

Modeling techniques are designed to demonstrate to the child methods of approaching the feared stimulus or situation and the positive consequences (or at least the lack of negative consequences) that result from that approach (Morris & Kratochwill, 1998; Silverman & Rabian, 1994). Variables influencing successful outcomes with modeling include the level of initial anxiety, the selection of models who are similar in age and gender, and the use of multiple models (Ammerman et al., 1999). As with systematic desensitization, modeling procedures have been used frequently with strong empirical support (Franklin et al., 1998; Ollendick & King, 1998).

Cognitive–Behavioral Approaches

CBT is based on the assumption that psychological problems result largely from maladaptive cognitive and behavioral antecedents (Southam-Gerow, Henin, Chu, Marrs, & Kendall, 1997). Given this theoretical orientation, the intent of CBT is to remedy the identified problem by altering beliefs and perceptions and focusing on the learning and practicing of new, more effective coping skills (Farrell et al., 1998). The technique of replacing "faulty" cognitive processes with more adaptive thinking is referred to as *cognitive restructuring* (P. C. Kendall, Panichelli-Mindel, & Gerow, 1995). By training the child or adolescent to replace maladaptive thoughts ("If I make a mistake, the whole class will laugh at me") with adaptive thoughts (i.e., cognitive restructuring) and to engage in positive verbalizations (self-instructional training), the treatment enhances constructive behavior change (Treadwell & Kendall, 1996).

Cognitive–behavioral intervention programs typically last 16–20 weeks, with children attending weekly sessions (P. C. Kendall, Krain, & Treadwell, 1999). The first half of the protocol is designed to teach the child or adolescent new skills that will alter the maladaptive reactions to anxiety-provoking situations. This is followed with the identification and modification of anxious "self-talk" with positive statements (e.g., "When the teacher calls on me, I will answer the question with a strong voice"). In addition, alternative behaviors for use in a variety of situations are identified and practiced. The second half of the treatment is dedicated to having the client practice her or his new coping strategies in increasingly anxiety-provoking situations (Southam-Gerow et al., 1997).

Efficacy data support the use of CBT in the treatment of GAD, OCD, and PTSD (Farrell et al., 1998; Franklin et al., 1998; P. C. Kendall, 1994; P. C. Kendall et al., 1997; March, Amaya-Jackson, et al., 1998). For example, in P. C. Kendall's (1994) trial, which treated 47 children who were diagnosed with anxiety disorders, 66% of the children no longer met diagnostic criteria at the termination of the intervention. These gains were maintained at 1-year follow-up assessments. Likewise in Kendall's second randomized clinical trial (P. C. Kendall et al., 1997), 53% of the children no longer had a diagnosed anxiety disorder following treatment, and self-report measures yielded concomitant decreases in negative self-statements and significant increases in coping skills that were still evident at 1-year follow-up.

Exposure and Response Prevention

Response prevention requires the blocking of compulsive ritual or avoidance behaviors upon exposure to feared objects or situations (Dar & Greist, 1992). Thus, a child who is afraid of contamination must not only practice touching "contaminated" objects (exposure) but must not be allowed to engage in compulsive hand washing following such exposure (response prevention). For this strategy to work, the therapist must train caregivers and teachers to interrupt or prevent the ritual behaviors from occurring (March, 1995). The procedure works best if the child is not only aware of, but also gives permission for, exposure and response prevention to occur (Geffken, Pincus, & Zelikovsky, 1999). Because most anxiety-provoking situations typical of childhood OCD occur in the natural environment, it is not problematic to find opportunities for exposure (American Academy of Child and Adolescent Psychiatry, 1998). What is more difficult is the training of primary adults in the child's environment to *consistently* interrupt or prevent compulsive behaviors (March, 1995). (For an excellent OCD treatment manual designed for children and adolescents, refer to March & Mulle, 1998.)

Response prevention has proved most efficacious in the treatment of childhood OCD (American Academy of Child and Adolescent Psychiatry, 1998; King, Leonard, & March, 1998; Piacentini, 1999). For example, in a study which randomly assigned 22 children diagnosed with OCD to either an exposure/response prevention behavioral intervention or a clomipramine trial, the behavioral intervention produced stronger therapeutic changes as measured by the Children's Yale–Brown Obsessive Compulsive

Scale (de Hann, Hoogduin, Buitclaar, & Keijsers, 1998). Likewise, a meta-analysis comparing five SSRIs (clomipramine, fluoxetine, sertraline, paroxetine, and fluvoxamine) to exposure/response prevention found the behavioral intervention superior to the medications in initial efficacy ratings (Kobak, Greist, Jefferson, Katzelnick, & Henk, 1998).

CONCLUSION

Childhood anxiety disorders are more prevalent than once thought, are often comorbid with other childhood disorders, and usually persist over time (Ollendick & King, 1998). Although anxiety disorders are one of the most prevalent categories of psychopathology in children and adolescents, there are scant research studies evaluating pharmacological treatments with this population. Given the considerable empirical support for behavioral and cognitive–behavioral interventions in the amelioration of pediatric anxiety disorders, it is generally recommended that pharmacological treatments be used only after cases prove refractory to such psychological approaches. When psychotropic medication augmentation is necessary, it is advisable to limit its use to a short interval, with desired outcomes (e.g., symptom reduction) clearly specified and frequently measured on an ongoing basis.

One of the most pressing issues in drug therapy is inadequate clinical management (Gadow, 1997). All too frequently, psychopharmacological treatments are prescribed without an explicitly developed and defined treatment protocol, which includes a rigorous monitoring system and delineated measures to evaluate symptom reduction. Nowhere may this be more evident than in the treatment of childhood anxiety disorders wherein the symptoms are vague and often include behaviors that may not be evidenced in adult anxiety (e.g., school refusal, irritability, poor scholastic performance, psychosomatic symptoms such as headaches and stomachaches, clinginess, and agitation). Psychologists may facilitate appropriate treatment with pediatric clients evidencing an anxiety disorder by ensuring that the intervention model follows empirically supported practices and that, owing to the demonstrated efficacy of behavioral therapy and CBT, pharmacological interventions be only initiated after behavioral or cognitive–behavioral interventions have not resulted in satisfactory symptom reduction. When a medication trial is selected, we recommend that it be in conjunction with continued psychological interventions, that the medical and psychological treatments be coordinated and collaborative in nature, and that the treatment protocol include objective measures to assess treatment efficacy. Although follow-up studies have indicated that complete remission of symptoms seldom occurs in childhood onset anxiety disorders (Bernstein et al., 1996; Leonard et al., 1993), an empirically driven treatment protocol that is multimodal, coordinated, and objectively evaluated may well result in significant symptom reduction.

REFERENCES

Ackerman, P. T., Newton, J. E., McPherson, W. B., Jones, J. G., & Dykman, R. A. (1998). Prevalence of PTSD and other psychiatric diagnoses in three groups of abused children. *Child Abuse and Neglect, 22,* 759–774.

Alderman, J., Wolkow, R., Chung, M., & Johnston, H. (1998). Setraline treatment of children and adolescents with obsessive–compulsive disorder or depression: Pharmacokinetics, tolerability, and efficacy. *Journal of the American Academy of Child and Adolescent Psychiatry, 37,* 386–395.

Allen, A., Leonard, H., & Swedo, S. (1995). Current knowledge of medications for the treatment of childhood anxiety disorders. *Journal of the American Academy of Child and Adolescent Psychiatry, 34,* 976–989.

American Academy of Child and Adolescent Psychiatry. (1998). Practice parameters for the assessment and treatment of children and adolescents with obsessive–compulsive disorder. *Journal of the American Academy of Child and Adolescent Psychiatry, 37S,* 27–44.

American Psychiatric Association. (1980). *Diagnostic and statistical manual of mental disorders* (3rd ed.). Washington, DC: Author.

American Psychiatric Association. (1994). *Diagnostic and statistical manual of mental disorders* (4th ed.). Washington, DC: Author.

Ammerman, R. T., Hersen, M., & Last, C. G. (Eds.). (1999). *Handbook of prescriptive treatments for children and adolescents.* Boston: Allyn & Bacon.

Apter, A., Ratzoni, G., King, R., Weizman, A., Iancu, I., Binder, M., & Riddle, M. (1994). Fluvoxamine open-label treatment of adolescent inpatients with obsessive–compulsive disorder or depression. *Journal of American Academy of Child and Adolescent Psychiatry, 33,* 342–349.

Benjamin, R. S., Costello, E. J., & Warren, M. (1990). Anxiety disorders in a pediatric sample. *Journal of Anxiety Disorders, 4,* 293–316.

Bernstein, G. A., Borchardt, C. M., & Perwein, A. (1996). Anxiety disorders in children and adolescents: A review of the last 10 years. *Journal of the American Academy of Child and Adolescent Psychiatry, 35,* 1110–1120.

Bernstein, G. A., Borchardt, C. M., Perwien, A. R., Crosby, R. D., Kushner, M. G., Thurbas, P. D., & Last, C. G. (2000). Imipramine plus cognitive–behavioral therapy in the treatment of school refusal. *Journal of the American Academy of Child and Adolescent Psychiatry, 19,* 276–283.

Biederman, J., Farmone, S. V., Marrs, A., Moore, P., Garcia, J., & Ablon, S. (1997). Panic disorder and agoraphobia in consecutively referred children and adolescents. *Journal of the American Academy of Child and Adolescent Psychiatry, 36,* 214–223.

Biederman, J., Rosenbaum, J. F., & Bolduc-Murphy, E. A. (1993). A 3-year follow-up of children with and without behavioral inhibition. *Journal of the American Academy of Child and Adolescent Psychiatry, 32*, 814–821.

Birmaher, B., Waterman, G., Ryan, N., Cully, M., Balach, L., Ingram, J., & Brodsky, M. (1994). Fluoxetine for childhood anxiety disorders. *Journal of American Academy of Child and Adolescent Psychiatry, 33*, 993–999.

Bowen, R. C., Offord D. R., & Boyle, M. H. (1990). The prevalence of overanxious disorder and separation anxiety: Results from the Ontario Child Health Study. *Journal of the American Academy of Child and Adolescent Psychiatry, 29*, 753–758.

Cohen, J. (1998). Summary of the practice parameters for the assessment and treatment of children and adolescents with posttraumatic stress disorder. *Journal of the American Academy of Child and Adolescent Psychiatry, 37*, 997–1002.

Dadds, M. R., Holland, D. E., Laurens, K. R., Mullins, M., Barrett, P. M., & Spence, S. H. (1999). Early intervention and prevention of anxiety disorders in children: Results at 2-year follow-up. *Journal of Consulting and Clinical Psychology, 67*, 145–150.

Dar, R., & Greist, J. (1992). Behavior therapy for obsessive–compulsive disorder. *Child and Adolescent Psychiatric Clinics of North America, 15*, 885–894.

de Hann, E., Hoogduin, K. A., Buitclaar, J. K., & Keijsers, G. P. J. (1998). Behavior therapy versus clomipramine for the treatment of obsessive–compulsive disorder. *Journal of the American Academy of Child and Adolescent Psychiatry, 37*, 1022–1029.

DeVeaugh-Geiss, J., Moroz, G., Biederman, J., Cantwell, D., Fontaine, R., Griest, J., Reichler, R., Katz, R., & Landau, P. (1992). Clomipramine hydrochloride in childhood and adolescent obsessive–compulsive disorder: A multicenter trial. *Journal of the American Academy of Child and Adolescent Psychiatry, 31*, 45–49.

Fairbanks, J. M., Pine, D. S., Tancer, N. K., Dummit, E. S., Kentgen, L. M., Asche, B. K., & Klein, R. G. (1997). Open fluoxetine treatment of mixed anxiety disorders in children and adolescents. *Journal of Child and Adolescent Psychopharmacology, 7*, 17–29.

Famularo, R., Kinscherff, R., & Fenton, T. (1988). Propanolol treatment for childhood posttraumatic stress disorder, acute type: A pilot study. *American Journal of Diseases of Children, 142*, 1244–1247.

Farrell, S., Hains, A., & Davies, W. (1998). Cognitive behavioral interventions for sexually abused children exhibiting PTSD symptomatology. *Behavior Therapy, 29*, 241–255.

Flament, M., Rapoport, J., Berg, C., Sceery, W., Kilts, C., Mellstrom, B., & Linnoila, M. (1985). Clomipramine treatment of childhood obsessive–compulsive disorder. *Archives of General Psychiatry, 42*, 977–983.

Franklin, M., Kozak, M., Cashman, L., Coles, M., Rheingold, A., & Foa, E. (1998). Cognitive–behavioral treatment of obsessive–compulsive disorder: An open clinical trial. *Journal of American Academy of Child and Adolescent Psychiatry, 37*, 412–419.

Gadow, K. D. (1997). An overview of three decades of research in pediatric psychopharmacology. *Journal of Child and Adolescent Psychopharmacology, 7,* 219–236.

Geffken, G. R., Pincus, D. B., & Zelikovsky, N. (1999). Obsessive compulsive disorder in children and adolescents: Review of background, assessment, and treatment. *Journal of Psychological Practice, 5,* 15–31.

Gelernter, J., Southwick, S., Goodson, S., Morgan, A., Nagy, L., & Charney, D. S. (1999). No association between D2 dopamine receptor alleles, or DRD2 haplotype, and PTSD. *Biological Psychiatry, 45,* 620–625.

Geller, D., Biederman, J., Reed, E., Spencer, T., & Wilens, T. (1995). Similarities in response to fluoxetine in the treatment of children and adolescents with obsessive–compulsive disorder. *Journal of the American Academy of Child and Adolescent Psychiatry, 34,* 36–44.

Graae, F., Milner, J., Rizzotto, L., & Klein, R. (1994). Clonazepam in childhood anxiety disorders. *Journal of American Academy of Child and Adolescent Psychiatry, 35,* 372–377.

Harmon, R., & Riggs, P. (1996). Clonidine for posttraumatic stress disorder in preschool children. *Journal of the American Academy of Child and Adolescent Psychiatry, 35,* 1247–1230.

Hayward, C., Killen, J., & Hammer, L. (1992). Pubertal stage and panic attack history in sixth- and seventh-grade girls. *American Journal of Psychiatry, 149,* 1239–1243.

Hewitt, J. K., Silberg, J. L., Rutter, M., Simonoff, E., Meyer, J. M., & Pickles, A. (1997). Genetics and developmental psychopathology: I. Phenotypic assessment in the Virginia Twin Study of Adolescent Behavioral Development. *Journal of Child Psychology, Psychiatry, and Allied Disciplines, 38,* 943–963.

Kearney, C., & Silverman, W. (1998). Critical review of pharmacotherapy for youth with anxiety disorders: Things are not as they seem. *Journal of Anxiety Disorders, 12,* 83–102.

Kendall, K. S. (1996). Major depression and generalized anxiety disorder: Same genes, partly different environments-revisited. *British Journal of Psychiatry, 30,* 68–75.

Kendall, P. C. (1994). Treating anxiety disorders in children: Results of a randomized clinical trial. *Journal of Consulting Clinical Psychology, 62,* 100–110.

Kendall, P. C., Flannery-Schroeder, E., Panchelli-Mindel, S. M., Southam-Gerow, M., Henin, A., & Warman, M. (1997). Therapy for youths with anxiety disorders: A second randomized clinical trial. *Journal of Consulting and Clinical Psychology, 65,* 366–380.

Kendall, P. C., Krain, M., & Treadwell, K. R. H. (1999). Generalized anxiety disorders. In R. H. Ammerman, M. Hersen, & C. G. Last (Eds.), *Handbook of prescriptive treatments for children and adolescents* (pp. 155–171). Boston: Allyn & Bacon.

Kendall, P. C., Panichelli-Mindel, S. M., & Gerow, M. A. (1995). Cognitive–behavioral therapies with children and adolescents: An integrative overview.

In H. P. van Bilsen, P. C. Kendall, & J. H. Slavenburg (Eds.), *Behavioral approaches for children and adolescents: Challenges for the next century* (pp. 1–18). New York: Plenum Press.

King, R. A., Leonard, H., & March, J. (1998). Practice parameters for the assessment and treatment of children and adolescents with obsessive–compulsive disorder. *Journal of the American Academy of Child and Adolescent Psychiatry, 37S*, 27–45.

Klein, R. G., Koplewicz, H. S., & Kanner, A. (1992). Imipramine treatment of children with separation anxiety disorder. *Journal of the American Academy of Child and Adolescent Psychiatry, 31*, 21–28.

Knowles, J. A., Fyer, A. J., Vieland, V. J., Weissman, M. M., Hodge, S. E., & Heiman, G. A. (1998). Results of a genome-wide genetic screen for panic disorder. *American Journal of Medical Genetics, 81*, 139–147.

Kobak, K. A., Greist, J. H., Jefferson, J. W., Katzelnick, D. J., & Henk, H. J. (1998). Behavioral versus pharmacological treatments of obsessive–compulsive disorder: A meta-analysis. *Psychopharmacology, 136*, 205–216.

Kranzler, H. (1988). Use of buspirone in an adolescent with overanxious disorder. *Journal of the American Academy of Child and Adolescent Psychiatry, 27*, 789–790.

Kutcher, S., Reiter, S., Gardner, D., & Klein, R. (1992) The pharmacotherapy of anxiety disorders in children and adolescents. *Psychiatric Clinics North America, 15*, 41–67.

Leonard, H., Swedo, S., Allen, A., & Rapoport, J (1994) Obsessive–compulsive disorder. In T. Ollendick, N. King, & W. Yule (Eds.), *International handbook of phobic and anxiety disorders in children and adolescents* (pp. 207–222). New York: Plenum Press.

Leonard, H., Swedo, S., Lenane, M., Rettew, D., Cheslow, D., Hamburger, S., & Rapoport, J. (1991). A double-blind desipramine substitution during long-term clomipramine treatment in children and adolescents with obsessive–compulsive disorder. *Archives of General Psychiatry, 48*, 922–927.

Leonard, H., Swedo, S., Lenane, M., Rettew, D., Cheslow, D., Hamburger, S., & Rapoport, J. (1993). A 2- to 7-year follow-up study of 54 obsessive–compulsive children and adolescents. *Archives of General Psychiatry, 50*, 429–439.

Leonard, H., Swedo, S., Rapoport, J., Koby, E., Lenane, M., Cheslow, D., & Hamburger, S. (1989). Treatment of obsessive–compulsive disorder with clomipramine and desipramine in children and adolescents: A double-blind crossover comparison. *Archives of General Psychiatry, 46*, 1088–1092.

Manassis, K., Bradley, S., Goldberg, S., Hood, J., & Swinson, R. P. (1995). Behavioral inhibition, attachment, and anxiety in children of mothers with anxiety disorders. *Canadian Journal of Psychiatry, 40*, 87–92.

March, J. S. (1995). Cognitive–behavioral psychotherapy for children and adolescents with OCD: A review and recommendations for treatment. *Journal of the American Academy of Child and Adolescent Psychiatry, 34*, 7–19.

March, J. S., Amaya-Jackson, L., Murray, M. C., & Schulte, A. (1998). Cognitive–behavioral psychotherapy for children and adolescents with posttraumatic stress disorder after a single-incident stressor. *Journal of the American Academy of Child and Adolescent Psychiatry, 37,* 585–589.

March, J. S., Biederman, J., Wolkow, R., Safferman, A., Mandekian, J., Cook, E. H., Cutler, N. R., & Dominguez, R. (1998). Sertraline in children and adolescents with obsessive–compulsive disorder: A multicenter randomized controlled trial. *Journal of the American Medical Association, 280,* 1752–1756.

March, J. S., & Leonard, H. L. (1996). Obsessive–compulsive disorder in children and adolescents: A review of the past 10 years. *Journal of the American Academy of Child and Adolescent Psychiatry, 35,* 1265–1273.

March, J. S., & Mulle, K. (1996). Banishing OCD: Cognitive behavioral psychotherapy for obsessive–compulsive disorders. In E. G. Hibbs & P. S. Jensen (Eds.), *Psychosocial treatment for child and adolescent disorders: Empirically based strategies for clinical practice* (pp. 83–102). Washington, DC: American Psychological Association.

March, J. S., & Mulle, K. (1998). *OCD in children and adolescents: A cognitive–behavioral treatment manual.* New York: Guilford Press.

Martin, C., Cabrol, S., Bouvard, M. P., Lepine, J. P., & Mouren-Simeoni, M. C. (1999). Anxiety and depressive disorders in fathers and mothers of anxious school-refusing children. *Journal of the American Academy of Child and Adolescent Psychiatry, 38,* 16–22.

Masi, G., Mucci, M., Favilla, L., Romano, R., & Poli, P. (1999). Symptomatology and comorbidity of generalized anxiety disorders. *Comprehensive Psychiatry, 40,* 210–215.

Moore, G., MacMaster, F., Stewart, C., & Rosenberg, D. (1998). Case study: Caudate glutamatergic changes with paroxetine therapy for pediatric obsessive–compulsive disorder. *Journal of the American Academy of Child and Adolescent Psychiatry, 37,* 663–668.

Morris, R. J., & Kratochwill, T. R. (1998). *The practice of child therapy* (3rd ed.). Boston: Allyn & Bacon.

Ollendick, T., & King, N. (1998). Empirically supported treatments for children with phobic and anxiety disorders: Current status. *Journal of Clinical Child Psychology, 27,* 156–157.

Ollendick, T., King, N., & Yule, W. (Eds.). (1994). *International handbook of phobic and anxiety disorders in children and adolescents.* New York: Plenum Press.

Owens, E., & Piacentini, J. (1998). Case study: Behavioral treatment of obsessive–compulsive disorder in a boy with comorbid disruptive behavior problems. *Journal of the American Academy of Child and Adolescent Psychiatry, 37,* 443–446.

Pauls, D. L., & Alsobrook, J. P. (1999). The inheritance of obsessive–compulsive disorder. *Child and Adolescent Psychiatric Clinics of North America, 8,* 481–499.

Pfefferbaum, B. (1997). Posttraumatic stress disorder in children: A review of the past 10 years. *Journal of the American Academy of Child and Adolescent Psychiatry, 36*, 1503–1511.

Physicians' Desk Reference. (53rd ed.). (1999). Montvale, NJ: Medical Economics.

Piacentini, J. (1999). Cognitive behavioral therapy of childhood OCD. *Child and Adolescent Psychiatric Clinics of North America, 8*, 599–616.

Pollock, R. A., & Carter, A. S. (1999). The familial and developmental contexts of obsessive–compulsive disorder. *Child and Adolescent Psychiatric Clinics of North America, 8*, 461–479.

Popper, C., & Gherardi, P. (1996). Childhood anxiety disorders. In J. Weiner (Ed.), *Diagnosis and psychopharmacology of childhood and adolescent disorders* (pp. 293–347). New York: Wiley.

Rapoport, J. L., Swedo, S. E., & Leonard, H. L. (1992). Childhood obsessive–compulsive disorder. *Journal of Clinical Psychiatry, 53*, 11–16.

Riddle, M. (1998). Obsessive–compulsive disorder in children and adolescents. *British Journal of Psychiatry, 173*, 91–96.

Riddle, M., Geller, B., & Ryan, N. (1993). Another sudden death in a child treated with desipramine. *Journal of the American Academy of Child and Adolescent Psychiatry, 32*, 792–797.

Riddle, M., Scahill, L., King, R., Hardin, M., Anderson, G., Ort, S., Smith, J., Leckman, J., & Cohen, D. (1992). Double-blind, crossover trial of fluoxetine and placebo in children and adolescents with obsessive–compulsive disorder. *Journal of the American Academy of Child and Adolescent Psychiatry, 31*, 1062–1069.

Sallee, F., Richman, H., Sethuraman, G., Dougherty, D., Sine, L., & Altman-Hamamdzic, S. (1998). Clonidine challenge in childhood anxiety disorder. *Journal of the American Academy of Child and Adolescent Psychiatry, 37*, 655–663.

Scahill, L. (1996). Contemporary approaches to pharmacotherapy in Tourette's syndrome and obsessive–compulsive disorder. *Journal of Child and Adolescent Psychiatric Nursing, 9*, 27–44.

Silverman, W., & Rabian, B. (1994). Specific phobia. In T. Ollendick, N. King, & W. Yule (Eds.), *International handbook of phobic and anxiety disorders in children and adolescents* (pp. 87–110). New York: Plenum Press.

Simonoff, E., Pickles, A., Meyer, J. M., Silberg, J. L., Macs, H. H., & Loeber, R. (1997). The Virginia twin study of adolescent behavioral development. *Archives of General Psychiatry, 54*, 801–808.

Smoller, J. W., & Tsuang, M. T. (1998). Panic and phobic anxiety: Defining phenotypes for genetic studies. *American Journal of Psychiatry, 155*, 1152–1162.

Southam-Gerow, M. A., Henin, A., Chu, B., Marrs, A, & Kendall, P. C. (1997). Cognitive–behavioral therapy with children and adolescents. *Child and Adolescent Psychiatric Clinics of North America, 6*, 111–135.

Stein, M. B., Chartier, M. J., Kozak, M. V., King, N., & Kennedy, J. L. (1998). Genetic linkage to the serotonin transporter protein and 5HT2A receptor genes excluded in generalized social phobia. *Psychiatry Research, 81*, 283–291.

Stein, M. B., Jang, K. L., & Livesley, W. J. (1999). Heritability of anxiety sensitivity: A twin study. *American Journal of Psychiatry, 156,* 246–251.

Tracey, S. A., Chorpita, B. F., Douban, J., & Barlow, D. H. (1997). Empirical evaluation of DSM–IV generalized anxiety disorders criteria in children and adolescents. *Journal of Clinical Child Psychology, 26,* 404–414.

Treadwell, K. R. H., & Kendall, P. C. (1996). Self-talk in youth with anxiety disorders: States of mind, content specificity, and treatment outcome. *Journal of Consulting and Clinical Psychology, 64,* 941–950.

True, W. R., Rice, J., Eisen, S. A., Heath, A. C., Goldberg, J., Lyons, M. J., & Nowak. J. (1993). A twin study of genetic and environmental contributions to liability for PTSD. *Archives of General Psychiatry, 50,* 257–264.

Varley, C., & McClellan, J. (1997). Two additional sudden deaths with tricyclic antidepressants. *Journal of the American Academy of Child and Adolescent Psychiatry, 34,* 390–395.

Werry, J. S. (1994). The safety of desipramine. *Journal of the American Academy of Child and Adolescent Psychiatry, 33,* 588–589.

Werry J. S. (1995). Resolved: Cardiac arrhythmias make desipramine an unacceptable choice in children. *Journal of the American Academy of Child and Adolescent Psychiatry, 34,* 1239–1231.

Wiener, J. (1996). *Diagnosis and psychopharmacology of childhood and adolescent disorders* (2nd ed.). New York: Wiley.

Wilens, T. E., Biederman, J., Baldessarini, R. J., Geller, B., Scheifer, D., Spencer, T. J., Birmaher, B., & Goldblatt, A. (1996). Cardiovascular effects of therapeutic doses of tricyclic depressants in children and adolescents. *Journal of the American Academy of Child and Adolescent Psychiatry, 35,* 1491–1501.

Yule, W., & Canterbury, R. (1994). The treatment of post traumatic stress disorder in children and adolescents. *International Review of Psychiatry, 6,* 141–151.

Zwier, K., & Rao, U. (1994). Buspirone use in an adolescent with social phobia and mixed personality disorder. *Journal of the American Academy of Child and Adolescent Psychiatry, 33,* 1007–1012.

5

ELIMINATION DISORDERS

In this chapter we present a description of the assessment and management of childhood elimination disorders, specifically, enuresis and encopresis. Mellon and Houts (1995) observed that the treatment of elimination disorders is one of the most promising areas in pediatric psychology, with considerable potential for collaborative efforts between mental health and medical personnel. In addition, recent advances in the understanding of the physiological mechanisms of these disorders within the context of social learning and child development have enhanced treatment outcomes (Mellon & Houts, 1995).

FUNCTIONAL ENURESIS

Functional enuresis refers to accidental or uncontrolled wetting in one's clothes or bed by children who are at least age 5 years. The soiling must not be related to a medical condition or a consequence of a specific medication, hence the term *functional* (American Psychiatric Association, 1994). Diurnal enuresis refers to daytime wetting, whereas nocturnal enuresis refers to nighttime bed-wetting. Regardless of whether youngsters wet at night, those children who wet during the daytime typically have more medical problems and generally are more in need of extensive medical assistance than peers who have nocturnal enuresis without daytime wetting

(Loening-Baucke, 1997). Very often, children with diurnal enuresis benefit from antibiotic therapies for urinary tract infections or from antispasmodic medications to reduce bladder contractions. Because behavioral therapies and psychopharmacology are more frequently used for nocturnal enuresis, this chapter focuses primarily on nocturnal enuresis or bedtime wetting.

It has been estimated that approximately 10% of school-age children between ages 5 and 16 wet their beds (Mellon & McGrath, 2000). Yet few of these children have organic conditions that result in incontinence (American Academy of Pediatrics Committee on Radiology, 1980). Because the disorder declines with age, it has been suggested that children with enuresis frequently demonstrate delayed maturation of the nervous system (Jarvelin et al., 1991). Likewise, there is compelling evidence of a genetic component to nocturnal enuresis. Several etiological hypotheses have been posited, including a deficiency in the nocturnal secretion of an antidiuretic hormone, inadequacy of muscular responses necessary for urinary inhibition during sleep, neurological delays, difficulty in sleep arousal, and emotional problems (Mellon & Houts, 1998; Mellon & McGrath, 2000). It has been recommended that future research efforts focus on the various etiological influences of enuresis as this predicts treatment response. In this way, specific treatment programs may be designed for children having different etiologies (Devitt et al., 1999; Jarvelin, 2000). As Mellon and Houts (1995) argued, however, although enuresis is a physical problem, effective management incorporates the application of learning and conditioning principles that alter physiological mechanisms maintaining the actual problem.

Current psychiatric criteria require that children have wetting episodes at least twice per week for a period of at least 3 consecutive months or that the wetting episodes result in distress or impairments in social or academic areas. When children have never attained at least 6 months of continuous nighttime continence, it is referred to as primary enuresis, whereas secondary enuresis refers to the delayed acquisition of nighttime continence (American Psychiatric Association, 1994). Typically, many more boys manifest enuresis than do girls, and epidemiological data suggest that prevalence decreases with age, primarily due to the fact that many children simply outgrow the disorder. Nonetheless, because there are a number of other difficulties associated with bed-wetting, including disruption to family life and problems of emotional and social adjustment, appropriate management clearly is warranted.

Assessment

All children referred for enuresis need careful medical screening and a physical examination to rule out other diseases and problems that may result in poor bladder control (e.g., urinary tract infection, Type I insulin-dependent diabetes mellitus, and structural abnormalities; Jarvelin, 2000). Children with diurnal enuresis have a higher incidence of urinary tract abnormalities or structural impairments (Jarvelin, Huttunen, Seppanen, Seppanen, & Moilanen, 1990; Jarvelin et al., 1991). A urinalysis and renal and urine cultures are considered to be standards of care and should precede any treatment program. In addition to an extensive medical evaluation, a careful clinical interview is imperative (Mellon & Houts, 1995). Data gathered during the interview should include a history of enuresis and current wetting pattern, previous management and treatment, caregivers' attitudes and beliefs regarding the wetting, physical home environment, familial stressors, and behavioral problems. A careful and detailed history can provide important information as to whether the wetting is a function of stressful events or psychosocial pressures. Finally, because the treatment regimen for enuresis frequently may be quite complex, a careful interview provides the psychologist with the opportunity to assess whether the family will likely adhere to the intervention protocol or whether additional assistance will be needed to implement the treatment program. For example, family discord and distress have been found to be important predictors of treatment failure (Dische, Yule, Corbett, & Hand, 1983). Thus, for children presenting with enuresis when there is a complex treatment regimen prescribed, it may be necessary to provide a great deal of therapeutic and social support so that appropriate management may take place. Similarly, for children with high levels of anxiety or oppositional behavior, treatment may need to be postponed until caregivers are able to learn how to better manage their children's behavior. Such behaviors on the part of the child may result in treatment failure that can be devastating for caregivers who have made a significant emotional investment in carrying out the treatment program. For the purposes of assessing children's behavior, the Child Behavior Checklist (Achenbach, 1991a) and Teacher Report Form (Achenbach, 1991b) may prove helpful.

Treatment

Both behavioral and pharmacological therapies have been the gold standard in the management of enuresis when there are no medical complications associated with the disorder. In this chapter, we first review medical approaches followed by behavioral therapies.

Medical Interventions

Table 5.1 provides a summary of medications clinically validated in double-blind studies for use with children and adolescents with enuresis, including recommended dose, expected positive outcomes, and possible adverse effects. The only pharmacological approach for routine use with en-

TABLE 5.1

Medications Clinically Validated in Double-Blind Studies for Use With Children and Adolescents Ranging in Age From 7 to 21 Years for the Treatment of Functional Enuresis

Generic Name (Trade Name)	Children mg/kg/day or Daily Dose	Adolescents mg/kg/day or Daily Dose	Treatment Outcome	Adverse Effect
Desmopressin (DDAVP)	10–40 mg	10–40 mg	Significant reduction in urine output.	Transient headaches and nausea.
Imipramine (Tofranil)	0.9 mg/kg	0.9 mg/kg	Reduction in nocturnal enuresis.	Notable risk for cardiac complications.

Note. Sources include Neveus, Lackgren, Tuvemo, and Stenberg (1999); *Physicians' Desk Reference* (1999); Smellie, McGrigor, Meadow, Rose, and Douglas (1996); and Vertucci et al. (1997).

uresis is desmopressin (DDAVP), which has been demonstrated to be superior to a placebo in the management of enuresis (Jarvelin, 2000). DDAVP is a synthetic version of the naturally occurring hormone vasopressin, a hormone affecting renal functioning (i.e., water retention). DDAVP is also used in the treatment of diabetes and head trauma wherein frequent urination is problematic. Prior to FDA approval of DDAVP, imipramine (a tricyclic antidepressant; Tofranil) was the most frequently used medication for bed-wetting. Because of the low side-effect profile of DDAVP and because of sudden deaths involving cardiac complications in children being treated with imipramine (Varley & McClellan, 1997), DDAVP has been received enthusiastically by many pediatricians and family practice providers. As a result, imipramine is now used far less frequently than DDAVP. Initially, DDAVP was available only as a nasal spray, although more recently it has been available in tablet form (Houts, 2000). Jarvelin (2000) recommended that DDAVP be administered in a dosage range of 10–40 mg for a period of 3 months. Despite the enthusiasm and widespread use of DDAVP in the pediatric community, this pharmacotherapy is not without limitations, the most notable being relapse. That is, the medication does not *stop* bed-wetting and, on cessation of the medication, the child frequently reverts back to bed-wetting (Moffatt, Harlos, Kirshen, & Burd, 1993).

Children who are delayed responders or refractory to traditional behavioral approaches are likely to be good candidates for a combination of behavior therapy and DDAVP. In fact, Bradbury and Meadow (1995) argued that psychopharmacological approaches combined with behavioral therapies to the treatment of enuresis result in fewer relapse rates than do pure operant techniques. Few studies are available to evaluate the efficacy of the combination of behavioral and pharmacological therapies, although the studies that are available have provided encouraging data. For example, Sukhai, Mol, and Harris (1989) compared the combination of a urine alarm and DDAVP with the alarm condition alone and with a placebo pill condition alone. Findings revealed that the combined treatment condition was more efficacious than the alarm condition alone when the number of dry nights was used as a dependent variable. Likewise, Bradbury and Meadow (1995) corroborated this finding and found the combined treatment approach to be particularly successful for children with more severe wetting. It should be noted, however, that none of the aforementioned studies provided longitudinal follow-up data, and dependent measures in both of the studies included only number of wet nights rather than the percentage of children who ceased bed-wetting (Mellon & Houts, 1995). Nonetheless, these studies provide encouraging empirical support for the combination of behavioral and pharmacological therapies. Future clinical trials examining behavioral and pharmacological approaches alone and in combination would be fruitful research endeavors.

Behavioral Interventions

The primary behavioral approaches in the treatment of functional enuresis include (a) a basic urine alarm, (b) urine alarm combined with other behavioral procedures, and (c) behavioral procedures without the urine alarm (Houts, Berman, & Abramson, 1994). There are more than 70 well-controlled trials that examined the efficacy of various behavioral treatment protocols (for reviews, see Mellon & McGrath, 2000). These approaches are based on the principles of classical and operant conditioning.

The urine alarm is the treatment of choice for bed-wetting. It is straightforward, easy to implement, and has a success cure rate of more than 75% (Mellon & Houts, 1995, 1998; Mellon & McGrath, 2000). One alarm method includes the use of a moisture-sensitive pad that is placed under the child at bedtime. The pad registers when urination starts to occur, and a loud alarm is triggered. Because the alarm activates as soon as any moisture is present, the alarm awakens the child early in the voiding process. Likewise, the sound is quite loud and results in muscle contraction (as in a fright response). The child is instructed to immediately get out of bed and visit the bathroom when the alarm is activated. The urine alarm works by a means of active avoidance conditioning (Houts, 1991, 1995). Only after the child has been accident free for 30 days is the urine alarm removed.

Another approach is the more involved Full Spectrum Treatment (FST; Mellon & Houts, 1995). This protocol includes (a) the urine alarm, (b) cleanliness training, (c) retention control training, and (d) overlearning. For the basic urine alarm treatment, children are instructed to get out of bed and stand prior to turning off the alarm. A critical aspect in this step is to assure that the child is actually awake. In some cases, where arousal is difficult, it may be necessary to implement a waking schedule (Azrin, Sneed, & Fox, 1974). After appropriate urination, the child is then instructed to change her or his underwear and to remake the bed even if the sheets are not wet (i.e., cleanliness training). In addition, the child records each night of the training as either wet or dry and receives positive reinforcement for dry nights. Retention control training teaches the child to postpone urination (on a graduated schedule starting at 1 minute and ending at 45 minutes) by means of restriction of the urinary muscles, as well as to practice "stream interruption" wherein the child attempts to start and stop urination several times while voiding. Retention training is believed to enhance the speed of acquisition being conditioned by the urine alarm (Houts, Peterson, & Whelan, 1986). After 14 consecutive dry nights, an overlearning procedure is activated. Intended to prevent relapses, overlearning consists of instructing the child to drink 16 ounces of water during the hour prior to bedtime and to void as necessary in the bathroom but to not wet the bed. This procedure continues until 14 additional consecutive dry nights are attained. More recent approaches have gradually titrated the amount of water consumed prior to bedtime until a maximum amount of water is consumed for a child's given age (i.e., approximately 2 ounces per year in chronological age plus two). Data have demonstrated that relapse rates may be reduced up to approximately 50% with the use of overlearning (Mellon & Houts, 1995). Despite the efficacy of the FST approach, Mellon and McGrath (2000) cautioned that this approach is quite demanding and that a comprehensive evaluation of family and child functioning be assessed prior to implementing this treatment approach.

Other nonpharmacological approaches to the management of enuresis include the use of hypnosis, cognitive–behavioral approaches targeting the child's irrational beliefs that are posited to be etiologic and maintain the wetting, and contingency management (Edwards & Van Der Spuy, 1985; Mellon & McGrath, 2000; Ronen, Wozner, & Rahav, 1992). None of these alternative approaches has proved effective in the treatment of functional enuresis, although research suggests that they may be promising in the treatment of this disorder (Houts, 2000; Mellon & McGrath, 2000).

FUNCTIONAL ENCOPRESIS

Functional encopresis refers to the repeated involuntary passage of feces into places not appropriate for that purpose. It must occur at least once a month for a duration of at least 3 months, the child must be at least age 4 years, and the disorder must not be due to a physical ailment or adverse effects associated with medication (American Psychiatric Association, 1994). As with enuresis, primary and secondary encopresis distinguish children who have been previously trained in comparison with their counterparts who have not been previously toilet trained. The diagnosis of encopresis now requires the determination of whether the soiling is due to constipation (i.e., with constipation or overflow incontinence vs. without constipation and overflow incontinence; American Psychiatric Association, 1994). Soiling with constipation is frequently chronic, with fecal impaction of the colon, reports of abdominal pain, the painful passage of large-diameter stool, and frequent daily accidents (Mellon & Houts, 1995). These subtypes for encopresis are particularly important as they have significant implication for treatment programs (McGrath, Mellon, & Murphy, 2000).

Estimates of the incidence of functional (i.e., nonorganic) encopresis range between 1.5% and 7.5% of school children ranging in age from 6 to 12 years, with the incidence higher in boys than in girls (McGrath et al., 2000; Mellon & Houts, 1995). The incidence generally decreases with chronological age, although the problem may persist into adolescence and adulthood. The disorder can have significant effects on children, particularly in the area of self-esteem and emotional and behavioral development. Mellon and Houts (1995) suggested that the etiology of encopresis be viewed from a biobehavioral perspective in which both physiology and behavioral theories are used to understand the etiology of encopresis. A complete explanation of the physiological mechanisms associated with normal bowel function is not within the scope of this chapter, although the interested reader is encouraged to examine McGrath et al. (2000) and Whitehead and Schuster (1985).

Mellon and Houts (1995) advocated that bowel control is a muscular-coordination skill that is predicated on principles of learning specific skills, including (a) using bodily cues to discriminate when there is a need for defecation and responding appropriately to these bodily cues, (b) finding and discriminating the appropriate and inappropriate place to defecate, (c) undressing and sitting on the toilet, and finally, (e) initiating the valsalva maneuver (tightening the stomach and pushing out as though attempting to defecate). Learning these complex behaviors is contingent on a complex interaction of biopsychosocial processes and learning principles. Encopresis is due to either faulty learning of the aforementioned behaviors or to pain or fear-arousing events whereby the child wishes to escape aversive consequences. As McGrath et al. (2000) pointed out, more than 65% of children with constipation experience pain on defecation. Thus, prior to initiating any treatment program, it is necessary to remove any fecal impaction or to implement dietary changes that may contribute to the painful event of defecation.

Assessment

Godfried and Sprafkin (1974) recommended that assessment of encopresis include a careful analysis of where the soiling occurs, the emotional and social functioning of the child with encopresis, the description of the soiling response, and the consequences of the soiling that may affect its frequency and strength. Thus, both medical and psychological components of assessment are necessary. Because organic syndromes as well as the adverse effects of certain medications may be associated with encopresis (e.g., Hirschprung's disease and anticholinergic medications), a complete physical examination by a physician is absolutely imperative. Such an examination could reveal structural abnormalities that may be causing pain during defecation, which could result in a child withholding stools because of pain associated with defecation.

The assessment for encopresis should also include a clinical interview of the primary caregivers and the child. In addition to the assessment of developmental milestones and evaluation of failed attempts at previous toilet training, Mellon and Houts (1995) recommended that the interviewer determine if appropriate toileting behaviors have been learned and what caregiver and child behaviors may be maintaining soiling. Consistent with the enuresis literature, parental motivation for adherence also should be carefully evaluated. Unreasonable expectations on the part of caregivers as well as familial discord need to be carefully examined as this could affect adherence to the treatment program. Finally, because behavioral interventions for encopresis involve ongoing use of positive reinforcement, a careful assessment of what activities or tangible items constitute rewards for the child is imperative (Mellon & Houts, 1995).

Behavioral observations are also helpful. These observations should include, but not be limited to, specific toileting behavior, including how the child approaches the toilet and how the child undresses. Daily records of bowel movements, accidents, the number of self-initiated bathroom visits, as well as time of day that these activities take place are important. Because caregivers must maintain accurate records, the clinician is wise to develop simple records for caregivers and to carefully train them in the recording of data. Finally, careful monitoring of dietary intake also may be critical, particularly if it is determined that the soiling is related to the child's diet (Mellon & Houts, 1995).

Treatment

Unfortunately, there is a dearth of literature related to controlled trials for the management of encopresis. This is surprising given the incidence of the disorder and the high frequency of referrals to clinicians. The majority of studies include the evaluation of complex behavioral interventions, laxatives, and biofeedback. Medical interventions include dietary manipulation, laxatives, and agents posited to affect musculature involved in defecation. Because the majority of children who experience encopresis have had a history of early painful defecation (thereby leading to a pain-avoidance response), treatment necessarily involves medical aspects of constipation (e.g., dietary change, laxatives, enemas, stool softener, and bowel cleanout).

Because medical management alone is usually not sufficient, behavioral therapies have frequently been used. Behavioral therapies have focused on the teaching of the necessary skills for toileting and altering contingencies for the purpose of increasing toileting and eliminating soiling behaviors. Behavioral treatments that have been used successfully include toileting skills training, discrimination training, overcorrection and punishment for soiling, positive reinforcement for sitting on the toilet, positive reinforcement for defecation in the toilet, and positive reinforcement for clean underwear (Mellon & Houts, 1995). The aforementioned procedures are used in combination, and a blend of procedures has been found to be more efficacious than any treatment used alone (Houts & Abramson, 1990). In fact, Nolan, Debelle, Oberklaid, and Coffey (1991) found a bowel cleanout, followed by maintenance with laxatives, dietary changes, and a sitting schedule to be superior to any medical intervention used alone. Medical therapies used alone (Cox, Sutphen, Borowitz, Dickens, & Singles, 1994; Loening-Baucke, 1997; van der Plas et al., 1996) have not been demonstrated to be particularly effective. Behavioral therapies alone have been demonstrated to be more effective than medical therapies used alone (McGrath et al., 2000). In short, multimodal interventions (i.e., a combination of behavioral and medical procedures) are quite effective, with approximately 60% of treated patients reaching full resolvement of symptoms (Mellon & Houts, 1995).

One particularly promising treatment for encopresis is the use of biofeedback training (Loening-Baucke, 1990; Wald, Chandra, Gabel, & Chiponis, 1987). Specifically, biofeedback has been found to assist in specific anorectal responses involved in defecation and also has been lauded because it reduces the time it takes to resolve problems with soiling in comparison with more traditional medical and behavioral therapies. Specifically, feedback is provided when the child is relaxed (e.g., galvanic skin response), and similar feedback responses are provided for anxiety. Mellon and associates (McGrath et al., 2000; Mellon & Houts, 1995) have argued for the combination of biofeedback training in combination with diet manipulation and laxatives for the purpose of reducing constipation. Finally, biofeedback in combination with behavioral treatment programs has demonstrated efficacy for the purpose of establishing ongoing toileting habits (McGrath et al., 2000).

Mellon and Houts (1995) argued that management will often vary according to the setting where the child is treated as well as the orientation of the clinician. For example, children treated for encopresis in a mental health center will likely be treated with behavior management techniques, and those seen in pediatric practices will frequently be given laxatives and recommendations for sitting on the toilet on a daily basis. In addition, cost is apt to dictate what treatment is provided. As a means of providing the standard of care for all children with encopresis, Houts and colleagues (Houts & Abramson, 1990; Mellon & Houts, 1995) have called for greater collaboration among providers, particularly physicians and psychologists, where standard empirically supported treatments might be provided in specialty clinics. Finally, there have been no studies that have used psychotropic medications for the management of encopresis. At this point, none of the available psychotropics on the market appear to be appropriate for some of the complex physiological and behavioral processes associated with encopresis.

CONCLUSION

Elimination disorders are biobehavioral conditions for which the active efforts of mental health and medical personnel are essential for diagnosis and treatment. The most effective treatments for the management of both enuresis and encopresis are the combinations of medical interventions and behavioral approaches. Although there are no prescription medications recommended for the treatment of encopresis, DDAVP and imipramine have resulted in notable reductions in functional enuresis. Behavioral interventions (e.g., alarm pad) are successful in treating nocturnal enuresis. The use of biofeedback in combination with medical approaches (e.g., laxatives, diet manipulation) seems to be equally promising in the management of encopresis, although more clinical trials are needed.

The elimination disorders must always be managed jointly by the practicing psychologist and pediatrician. Given the opportunity to collaborate with our pediatric colleagues and the availability of empirically supported behavioral and medical treatments for these problems, it is hoped that greater attention will be focused on these disorders and on the quality of life for children who suffer both socially and emotionally from these conditions.

REFERENCES

Achenbach, T. M. (1991a). *Manual for the Child Behavior Checklist and Revised Child Behavior Profile*. Burlington: University of Vermont, Department of Psychology.

Achenbach, T. M. (1991b). *Teacher's Report Form*. Burlington: University of Vermont, Department of Psychology.

American Academy of Pediatrics Committee on Radiology. (1980). Excretory urography for evaluation of enuresis. *Pediatrics, 65,* 644–655.

American Psychiatric Association. (1994) *Diagnostic and statistical manual of mental disorders* (4th ed.). Washington, DC: Author.

Azrin, N. H., Sneed, T. J., & Fox, R. M. (1974). Dry-bed training: Rapid elimination of childhood enuresis. *Behavior Research and Therapy, 12,* 147–156.

Bradbury, M., & Meadow, S. (1995). Combined treatment with enuresis alarm and desmopressin for nocturnal enuresis. *Acta Pediatricia Scandinavica, 84,* 1014–1018.

Cox, D. J., Sutphen, J., Borowitz, S., Dickens, M. N., & Singles, J. (1994). Simple electromyographic biofeedback treatment for chronic pediatric constipation/encopresis: Preliminary report. *Biofeedback & Self Regulation, 19,* 41–50.

Devitt, H., Holland, P., Butler, R., Redfern, E., Hiley, E., & Roberts, G. (1999). Plasma vasopressin and response to treatment in primary nocturnal enuresis. *Archives of Disease in Childhood, 80,* 448–451.

Dische, S., Yule, W., Corbett, J., & Hand, D. (1983). Childhood nocturnal enuresis: Factors associated with outcome of treatment with an enuresis alarm. *Developmental Medicine and Child Neurology, 25,* 67–80.

Edwards, S., & Van Der Spuy, H. (1985). Hypnotherapy as a treatment for enuresis. *Journal of Child Psychology and Psychiatry, 26,* 161–170.

Godfried, M. R., & Sprafkin, J. N. (1974). *Behavioral personality assessment.* Morristown, NJ: General Learning Press.

Houts, A. C. (1991). Nocturnal enuresis as a biobehavioral problem. *Behavior Therapy, 22,* 133–151.

Houts, A. C. (1995). Behavioural treatment for enuresis. *Scandinavian Journal of Urology and Nephrology* (Suppl.), *173,* 83–87.

Houts, A. C. (2000). Commentary: Treatments for enuresis: Criteria, mechanisms, and health care policy. *Journal of Pediatric Psychology, 25,* 219–224.

Houts, A. C., & Abramson, H. (1990). Assessment and treatment for functional childhood enuresis and encopresis: Toward a partnership between health psychologists and physicians. In S. B. Morgan & T. M. Okwumabua (Eds.), *Child and adolescent disorders: Developmental and health psychology perspectives* (pp. 47–103). Hillsdale, NJ: Erlbaum.

Houts, A. C., Berman, J. S., & Abramson, H. A. (1994). The effectiveness of psychological and pharmacological treatments for nocturnal enuresis. *Journal of Consulting and Clinical Psychology, 11,* 513–519.

Houts, A. C., Peterson, J. K., & Whelan, J. P. (1986). Prevention of relapse in Full-Spectrum home training for primary enuresis: A components analysis. *Behavior Therapy, 17,* 462–469.

Jarvelin, M. R. (2000). Commentary: Empirically supported treatments in pediatric psychology: Nocturnal enuresis. *Journal of Pediatric Psychology, 25,* 215–218.

Jarvelin, M. R., Huttunen, N., Seppanen, J., Seppanen, U., & Moilanen, I. (1990). Screening of urinary tract abnormalities among day and nightwetting children. *Scandinavian Journal of Urology and Nephrology, 24,* 181–189.

Jarvelin, M. R., Moilanen, I., Kangas, P., Moring, K., Vikevainen-Tervonen, L., Huttunen, N. P., & Seppanen, J. (1991). Aetiological and precipitating factors for childhood enuresis. *Acta Pediatrica Scandinavica, 80,* 361–369.

Loening-Baucke, V. A. (1990). Modulation of abnormal defecation in chronically constipated children with encopresis. *Journal of Pediatrics, 116,* 214–222.

Loening-Baucke, V. (1997). Urinary incontinence and urinary tract infection and their resolution with treatment of chronic constipation of childhood. *Pediatrics, 100,* 228–232.

McGrath, M. L., Mellon, M. W., & Murphy, L. (2000). Empirically supported treatments in pediatric psychology: Constipation and encopresis. *Journal of Pediatric Psychology,* 225–254.

Mellon, M. W., & Houts, A. C. (1995). Elimination disorders. In R. T. Ammerman & M. Hersen (Eds.), *Handbook of child behavior therapy in the psychiatric setting* (pp. 341–366). New York: Wiley.

Mellon, M. W., & Houts, A. C. (1998). Home-based treatment for primary enuresis. In J. Briesmeister & C. E. Schaefere (Eds.), *Handbook of parent training; Parents as co-therapists for children's behavior problems* (2nd ed., pp. 341–366). New York: Wiley.

Mellon, M. W., & McGrath, M. L. (2000). Empirically supported treatments in pediatric psychology: Nocturnal enuresis. *Journal of Pediatric Psychology, 25,* 193–214.

Moffatt, M. E. K., Harlos, S., Kirshen, A. J., & Burd, L. (1993). Desmopressin acetate and nocturnal enuresis: How much do we know? *Pediatrics, 92,* 420–425.

Neveus, T., Lackgren, G., Tuvemo, T., & Stenberg, A. (1999). Desmopressin resistant enuresis: Pathogenetic and therapeutic considerations. *Journal of Urology, 162,* 136–140.

Nolan, T., Debelle, G., Oberklaid, F., & Coffey, C. (1991). Randomized trial of laxatives in treatment of childhood encopresis with anismus. *Archives of Diseases in Childhood, 79,* 131–135.

Physicians' Desk Reference. (53rd ed.). (1999). Montvale, NJ: Medical Economics.

Ronen, T., Wozner, Y., & Rahav, G. (1992). Cognitive intervention in enuresis. *Child and Family Behavior Therapy, 14,* 1–14.

Smellie, J. M., McGrigor, V. S., Meadow, S. R., Rose, S. J., & Douglas, M. F. (1996). Nocturnal enuresis: A placebo controlled trial of two antidepressant drugs. *Archives of Disease in Childhood, 75,* 62–66.

Sukhai, R. N., Mol, J., & Harris, A. S. (1989). Combined therapy of enuresis alarm and desmopressin in the treatment of nocturnal enuresis. *European Journal of Pediatrics, 148,* 465–467.

van der Plas, R. N., Benninga, M. A., Buller, H. A., Bossuyt, P. M., Akkermans, L. M. A., Redekop, W. K., & Taminiau, J. A. (1996). Biofeedback training in treatment of childhood constipation: A randomized controlled study. *Lancet, 348,* 776–780.

Varley, C., & McClellan, J. (1997). Two additional sudden deaths with tricyclic antidepressants. *Journal of the American Academy of Child and Adolescent Psychiatry, 34,* 390–395.

Vertucci, P., Lanzi, D., Cappese, G., Fano, G. V., Margari, L., Mazzotta, G., & Menegati, E. (1997). Desmopressin and imipramine in the management of nocturnal enuresis: A multicenter study. *British Journal of Clinical Practice, 51,* 27–31.

Wald, A., Chandra, R., Gabel, S., & Chiponis, D. (1987). Evaluation of biofeedback in childhood encopresis. *Journal of Pediatric Gastroenterology and Nutrition, 6,* 554–558.

Whitehead, W. E., & Schuster, M. M. (1985). *Gastrointestinal disorders: Behavioral and physiological basis for treatment.* New York: Academic Press.

6

EXTERNALIZING DISORDERS

The externalizing disorders refer to those behavioral problems of childhood and adolescence that place some children in conflict with their environment (Quay & Hogan, 1999). Dimensional and categorical approaches frequently have identified these children as having antisocial behavior, delinquency, noncompliance, aggression, and hyperactivity (Quay & Hogan, 1999). Those psychiatric disorders that fall under the domain of the externalizing disorders include attention deficit hyperactivity disorder (ADHD), oppositional defiant disorder (ODD), and conduct disorder (CD; American Psychiatric Association, 1994). These specific disorders are the focus of this chapter. Because ADHD has been so extensively and meticulously investigated, particularly with regard to pharmacological treatments, it received the majority of attention in this chapter. (Refer to the *Glossary of Terms* for definitions of medical terms.)

ATTENTION DEFICIT HYPERACTIVITY DISORDER

Current psychiatric nosology clusters the symptoms of ADHD into inattention (e.g., fails to give close attention to assignments, difficulty sustaining attention and effort, and frequent shifts from one activity to another) and hyperactive–impulsive (e.g., fidgets, blurts out answers, and difficulty remaining seated during meals). Six symptoms from either of these clusters or their combination must be present for the purpose of making a diagnosis, and the severity of the symptoms must render a child as functionally impaired (American Psychiatric Association, 1994). In addition, symptoms must be present for a minimum of 6 months, and the age of onset of the disorder must be prior to age 7 years. Finally, there must be evidence that the impairments are present in more than one setting (e.g., home and school).

On the basis of the aforementioned criteria, there are three subtypes of ADHD: primarily inattentive type, primarily hyperactive–impulsive type, and combined type. The ratio of male to female is estimated to range from four to nine boys for every girl, although more girls have been identified in community samples than in clinical samples.

Etiological Influences

Several environmental toxins have been posited to be etiologic or at least contributory to ADHD. These include elevated blood lead levels, food additives including salicylates, food dyes and preservatives, sugar, cigarette smoking, alcohol use during pregnancy, and exposure to fluorescent lighting, to name just a few. It should be noted that a careful review of the literature has cast doubt on the role of any of these agents in the diagnosis of ADHD (American Academy of Pediatrics, 2000).

Although neurological examinations of children with ADHD during routine physical examinations have been found to be generally unremarkable, there has been an accumulating body of research suggesting that children and adolescents with ADHD may differ from their normally developing peers in brain morphology. A particularly seminal study conducted by Zametkin and associates (Zametkin et al., 1990) has provided evidence of reduced glucose metabolism in various areas of the brain of adults with ADHD, including the premotor and superior frontal regions, that have been associated with the regulation of attention, information processing, and motor activity. These data have been interpreted to suggest a connection between the prefrontal areas and the limbic system of the brain. These structures of the brain are implicated in the processing of attention, executive functioning (e.g., behavioral inhibition), emotion, and learning. Other theories have suggested deficiencies in the neurotransmitters, including dopamine and norepinephrine. Because the prefrontal limbic system has been demonstrated to contain high amounts of these neurotransmitters, this neurotransmitter hypothesis is consistent with the findings of Zametkin et al. (1990), lending compelling evidence to a neurophysiological etiology of ADHD.

More recently, investigators have begun to focus on the role of hereditary transmission of ADHD. This research is still in an infancy stage, although an investigation by Biederman and associates (Biederman, Faraone, Keenan, Knee, & Tsuang, 1990) has provided compelling data to indicate that approximately 65% of children with ADHD had at least one relative with ADHD compared with 24% and 15% of a psychiatric and normally developing comparison group, respectively. Of further interest is the finding that other psychiatric disorders were more prevalent in the families of children with ADHD, including antisocial disorders and mood disorders, when compared with control groups. Although additional research studies in this area clearly are needed, ADHD is a familial disorder that may place children and adolescents at later risk for adult psychopathology.

Developmental Issues

The first symptoms of ADHD that include overactive and impulsive behaviors typically emerge during preschool, when there are increased demands for following directions and modulating social behaviors in accordance with same-age peers. The diagnosis of ADHD is likely to persist to the elementary school years, when the symptoms are pervasive and severe and occur in the context of negative parent–child interactions (Johnston & Ohan, 1999). Symptoms during elementary school include distractibility, inability to sustain attention and effort to the tasks at hand, low frustration tolerance, and fidgeting. These symptoms are typically mediated by environmental demands, including the presence of reinforcing contingencies. Frequently, children with ADHD demonstrate impairments in parent–child and peer relationships and poor academic performance.

There is compelling evidence that the core symptoms of ADHD persist into adolescence (Barkley, Fischer, Edelbrock, & Smallish, 1990; Fischer, Barkley, Fletcher, & Smallish, 1993; Weiss & Hechtman, 1993), although hyperactivity and inattention have been found to decrease from childhood to adolescence. Moreover, over the past decade there has been increasing recognition that the disorder continues well into adulthood, with up to 50% of children with ADHD reporting problems as adults.

OPPOSITIONAL DEFIANT DISORDER

ODD has been defined as a pattern of negativistic, hostile, and defiant behavior (e.g., loses temper, argues with adults) that exceeds age norms and results in functional impairments (American Psychiatric Association, 1994). According to current psychiatric nomenclature, at least four symptoms of the following must be present for a minimum of at least 6 months: often loses temper, often argues with adults, often actively defies or refuses to comply with adults' rules, often deliberately does things that annoy other people, often blames others for his or her mistakes, is often touchy or easily annoyed, is often angry and resentful, and is often vindictive (American Psychiatric Association, 1994). Prevalence is estimated to range from 2% to 16%, and the disorder is more frequently diagnosed in boys than in girls, although this is believed to change somewhat at puberty (Johnston & Ohan, 1999).

In terms of etiology and developmental course, there has been little study of ODD except within the context of CD. For this reason, little is know about the etiology. Although the average age of onset for ODD is 6 years, there is an emerging literature to suggest that oppositional and rule-violating behaviors are first present in the preschool years (S. B. Campbell, 1990). In support of this notion, Lahey and associates (Lahey, Loeber, Quay, Frick, & Grimm, 1992) have provided compelling evidence to suggest the onset of behavior problems during the preschool years; the children were described as stubborn as early as age 3 and as being defiant and having tantrums as early as age 5. In addition, although the majority of children with ODD do not necessarily develop symptoms of CD, 90% of children and adolescents with CD have had a history of symptoms associated with ODD (Lahey & Loeber, 1994).

CONDUCT DISORDER

CD refers to a set of behaviors that violate basic rules of the rights of others (e.g., aggression, destruction of property, and authority violations such as lying and cheating during the school years), and three of these behaviors (often bullies, threatens, or intimidates others; often initiates physical fights; has used a weapon that can cause serious physical harm; has stolen with confrontation with a victim; has been physically cruel to people; has been physically cruel to animals; has forced someone into sexual activity; often lies or breaks promises; often stays out at night despite parental prohibitions beginning before age 13; has stolen items of non-trivial value; has deliberately engaged in fire setting; has deliberately destroyed another's property; has run away from home overnight at least twice while living in parental home; often truant from school beginning before age 13; and has broken into someone else's house, building, or car) are required within the past year, whereas one of these behaviors is required within the past 6 months (American Psychiatric Association, 1994). Consistent with the other disruptive behavior disorders, some type of functional impairment must be established. Thus, there must be a significant degree of destruction or disturbance, and the behaviors must occur in more than one setting (e.g., home and school). Psychiatric nomenclature specifies two specific subtypes of CD: childhood onset and adolescent onset. Prevalence rates have been found to vary, although estimates range from approximately 2% to 9% for girls and 6% to 16% for boys.

Etiological Influences

Numerous factors have been posited to be etiologic in CD, including biological factors (i.e., temperament, cognition, genetics, and neurological abnormalities), school-related factors, family adversity (e.g., divorce, marital distress, and violence), family insularity, and parent–child interactions. Although much research has focused on the neuropsychological functioning of children with CD, these data have been primarily inconclusive, and such deficits are probably more likely associated with functional impairments than with the CD per se (Kazdin, 1987). Other physiological factors have been found to distinguish children with CD from their normally developing peers, including resting heart rate, vagal tone, and skin conductance. Finally, the association of genetic contributions to child and adolescent CD has not received a great deal of support, although having a biological parent with antisocial behaviors has been found to increase the risk of conduct disturbances.

Temperament also has been proposed as being etiologic in CD, although findings have generally indicated that temperament alone does not necessarily result in psychopathology, nor does it make the child immune to any specific type of psychopathology (Thomas & Chess, 1977). Other evidence has suggested that conduct problems may be associated with poor academic performance, neuropsychological or cognitive impairments, and low mental abilities (Johnston & Ohan, 1999). The literature generally suggests a bidirectional relationship in which conduct disturbances produce problems at school and resultant academic difficulties and academic problems at school are clearly linked with conduct disturbances. It is more likely that there are significant mediating and moderating variables where familial influences serve as protective factors.

Familial contributions continually have been implicated in the literature as playing a role in the etiology of CD. For example, parental psychopathology, including maternal depression, paternal antisocial behaviors, and a history of paternal substance abuse, has been demonstrated continually to be associated with CD in childhood and adolescence (Williams, Anderson, McGee, & Silva, 1990). Familial discord, including marital distress, has been posited in the etiology of conduct disturbances, although path-analytic techniques have clearly implicated caregivers' psychological adjustment as the major determinant influencing parent–child interactions and the subsequent development of conduct disturbances. Finally, studies that have examined familial adversity, including life stressors associated with low social class, have revealed little association between social class and conduct disturbances. However, families characterized by insularity whereby there is a high frequency of negative and adverse relationships and few social supports have been found to be at marked risk for CD (Webster-Stratton, 1990).

There has been a corpus of research to indicate that parental interactions are the most proximal cause of CD (Webster-Stratton & Dahl, 1995). The data generally indicate that parents of children with CD are more violent and critical in their use of discipline, are more erratic and inconsistent, frequently fail to monitor their children's behavior, and often ignore or punish prosocial behaviors (Webster-Stratton & Spitzer, 1991). Thus, as Patterson (1982) suggested, children learn to escape or avoid parental criticism by escalating their negative behaviors, thereby resulting in an increase in parental interactions.

Although there is clear support for an environmental effect for CD, more recently there has been a burgeoning of literature to suggest a genetic basis for mood disorders as well as externalizing disorders (Biederman, Faraone, Mick, & Moore, 1996). In fact, there also has been support for cormorbidity between mood disorders and externalizing behavioral problems (Biederman et al., 1996), suggesting that both classifications of disorders may be an expression for the same genotype. This remains an exciting area for future research.

Developmental Issues

The average age for onset of CD is 6 years. Symptoms during the elementary school year may include conflicts with authority, overt problems of aggression with peers, parent–child conflict, and covert problems including lying and stealing (Johnston & Ohan, 1999). During the adolescent years, there is a marked increase in the presence of CD symptoms from the elementary school years. Frequently, these adolescents evidence school truancy, delinquency, physical violence, and substance abuse. There also is a second group of adolescents who have demonstrated no history of ODD or CD during childhood; rather the conduct disturbances evidenced in this group are associated with modeling of peer behaviors and a search for autonomy and independence. Although only 25% to 40% of adolescents with CD develop adult antisocial behaviors (Johnston & Ohan, 1999), the histories of adults with antisocial or aggressive behaviors almost always include CD.

Specific risk factors contributing to the continuation of the ODD and CD spectrum include (a) early onset (preschool years), (b) breadth of deviance (across multiple settings including home and school), (c) frequency and intensity of antisocial behavior, (d) diversity of antisocial behavior (several vs. few), and (e) family and parent characteristics (Kazdin, 1987).

Issues Pertaining to Comorbidity

Although the diagnoses of ADHD, ODD, and CD have been reviewed separately for the present chapter, it should be noted that many children and adolescents frequently meet criteria for both ADHD and ODD or ADHD and CD (Barkley, Fischer, Edelbrock, & Smallish, 1991). The issue of comorbidity is important both in predicting prognosis and in developing treatment programs. For example, there is compelling evidence to suggest that when ADHD and ODD or CD co-occur, there is a more guarded prognosis than when either of the disorders occurs alone (Faraone, Biederman, Keenan, & Tsuang, 1991). The hypothesized pathway is that ADHD first occurs, and many of the core symptoms of the disorder including inattention and impulsivity interact with a number of familial risk factors (e.g., marital discord and poor parenting) and increase the probability of ODD and CD. Thus, impulsivity and inattention, the cardinal symptoms of ADHD, are believed to drive the early onset of behaviors associated with ODD and also accelerate some of the more severe symptoms associated with CD.

TREATMENT

In this section, we first discuss the most frequently used medical interventions in the management of externalizing disorders in children and adolescents. These include stimulants, antidepressant and antimanic drugs, neuroleptics, and other medications. Next, the benefits of psychosocial interventions, including behavioral therapies and child-based, family, school, and community interventions, are examined. Finally, we discuss the collaborative approach of combining pharmacotherapy and psychotherapy interventions for children with ADHD, ODD, and CD.

Medical Interventions

Stimulants

Stimulants in children and adolescents have been the most widely researched and used medications in child psychiatry, primarily for the management of ADHD (for a review, see Bennett, Brown, Craver, & Anderson, 1999). In fact, the use of stimulants has increased dramatically over the past two decades (Safer & Krager, 1988), and there is evidence to indicate that there is a significant increase in the use of stimulants for preschoolers (Rappley et al., 1999; Zito et al., 2000). Although stimulant drug therapy is not a panacea and should probably not constitute the only treatment modality provided to children with ADHD, research on its safety and efficacy has been meticulous. In fact, some have concluded (Jensen et al., 1999) that stimulant medication treatments are underutilized in the management of children with ADHD and that physicians and other mental health providers be provided with more education regarding the potential benefits of these pharmacotherapies.

Research consistently has demonstrated the beneficial effects of the stimulants on symptoms associated with ADHD, including inattention, impulsivity, and overactivity (for a review, see Bennett et al., 1999). These findings have been corroborated on laboratory tests, direct observations of behavior with a structured classroom setting, and behavioral rating scales completed by caregivers and teachers. DuPaul and Rapport (1993) provided important data to indicate that methylphenidate (Ritalin), a commonly used stimulant medication, exerts a significant effect on classroom measures of attention and academic efficiency for children with ADHD. Finally, there is a corpus of research to indicate that stimulant medication improves mother–child relationships (Barkley & Cunningham, 1979; Barkley, Karlsson, Strzelecki, & Murphy, 1984).

Anecdotal evidence suggests that when children evidence positive response to stimulants, there is a corollary improvement in their schoolwork; however, the available literature to date is not consistent with these findings. In part, the failure to demonstrate these effects has been attributed to inadequate duration of pharmacotherapy and the use of assessment instruments in clinical trials that are not sufficiently sensitive to stimulant drug effects. The general consensus of researchers in the field is that the stimulants exert their effects on academic efficiency rather than academic achievement, although clearly more investigation is needed because many children with ADHD who are treated with stimulants also have delays in academic achievement.

Studies examining the effects of stimulant medication on children's social behaviors have been somewhat positive (for a review, see Hinshaw, 1991). One controlled trial of the effects of stimulant medication on children's social behaviors has demonstrated that, when compared with their peers who were receiving active medication, children who were receiving placebo doses were more negatively engaged, used more aversive leadership techniques, and were rated as less likable by their peers (Buhrmester, Whalen, Henker, MacDonald, & Hinshaw, 1992).

Because the stimulants are frequently used to manage children with comorbid CD, of particular interest is the effect of the stimulants on aggression. In general, laboratory-based studies of children designated with aggression have suggested that children are little affected by the stimulants (Hinshaw, 1991). However, when the effects of the stimulants have been examined in ecological settings similar to classroom and play settings, there has been substantial support for the efficacy of the stimulants.

Regarding the long-term clinical effects of the stimulants, there have been few studies that have examined the long-term effects of these medications, including their safety and efficacy. Although the recent clinical trial conducted by the National Institute of Mental Health provided evidence to suggest efficacy and safety for a controlled trial over the course of 14 months, more research will be needed, particularly studies that examine the combined effects of stimulant medication and behavioral approaches (Hinshaw, 2000).

Adverse effects of stimulant medication are typically classified according to short- and long-term effects. Because stimulant medication has been prescribed for nearly 50 years, there is an extensive literature addressing the adverse effects of these medications at least in the short term. Barkley, McMurray, Edelbrock, and Robbins (1990) examined parent- and teacher-reported adverse effects in 82 children diagnosed with ADHD for both high (0.5 mg/kg) and low doses (0.3 mg/kg) of stimulant medication. Findings revealed that both doses of stimulant medication resulted in mild levels of decreased appetite, insomnia, anxiety, and irritability in over half of the sample. One third of the sample reported abdominal pains and headaches. Of interest was the finding that some of the adverse symptoms also were present in the placebo group, suggesting that these symptoms may also be characteristic of children with ADHD rather than representing adverse effects of stimulant medication. Other adverse effects, albeit less frequently reported, include mood disturbances, tics, anxiety, nightmares, and social withdrawal (DuPaul, Barkley, & Connor, 1998). These adverse effects generally dissipate following discontinuation of stimulant medication, although the beneficial effects of these medications also dissipate.

The magnitude of adverse effects of the stimulants has been generally associated with dose of medication, with adverse effects increasing linearly with dose. Adverse effects also may differ as a function of informant, with children rating their symptoms as more severe than either caregivers or teachers (DuPaul, Anastopoulos, Kwasnik, Barkley, & McMurray, 1996). These findings underscore the importance of systematically obtaining information from all sources when evaluating adverse effects of the stimulants.

Another adverse effect of stimulant medication is the development of abnormal motor movements or tics, with estimates indicating that fewer than 1% of children receiving stimulant medication also develop tics. Certainly, stimulant medication must be administered judiciously for children with a family history of Tourette's syndrome, although there has been compelling evidence presented by Gadow (1997) to suggest that the stimulants may be used safely for children with comorbid tic disorders. Much more research is needed in this area, and the prudent pediatrician is most wise to judiciously use this class of medication for children with a history of tic or Tourette's syndrome. Another frequent adverse effect of stimulant medication is behavioral rebound, or the deterioration of behavior to a level worse than baseline as the medication wears off. Behavioral rebound is best managed by adjusting the dose of medication and imposing structure during this part of the day by increasing the use of behavior management techniques as the effects of active medication begin to dissipate.

Finally, although the stimulants reduce negative social behaviors in children diagnosed with ADHD, there also has been concern that the stimulants may reduce prosocial behaviors (Whalen, Henker, Hinshaw, & Granger, 1989). Jacobvitz, Sroufe, Stewart, and Leffert (1990) suggested that reduced levels of prosocial behaviors may be associated with relatively high doses of stimulants, although additional research is clearly needed. Until further data are forthcoming, careful monitoring by objective reports should always be the standard of care.

Regarding long-term effects, the majority of studies have focused on height and weight suppression, cardiovascular effects, and drug dependence and abuse. More recent studies have suggested that height and weight suppression, as a function of stimulant therapies, is dose related and transient. In a long-term follow-up study, Klein and Mannuzza (1988) compared the growth in young adults previously treated with methylphenidate (Ritalin) for ADHD with control adults who had a history of behavioral problems but who were not managed with pharmacological intervention. No differences were found between the two groups, leading the investigators to conclude that growth rebound occurs after stimulant medication is discontinued. However, because of the growing trend for the stimulants to be used well into adolescence and even in adulthood, ongoing monitoring of height and weight is imperative (Bennett et al., 1999). Also of concern have been the effects of stimulant medication on cardiovascular functioning, due to the fact that stimulant medication increases heart rate, blood pressure, and respiration in the short term. However, these effects have been found to be clinically insignificant and transient (Zeiner, 1995). Finally, there has been much concern about patients potentially abusing stimulant medication, particularly during adolescence when many youths are at marked risk for drug abuse. This concern is particularly relevant when there is comorbidity of CD. Fortunately, the few available studies suggest that when children and adolescents are managed on appropriate doses of medication, they are at no higher risk for substance abuse than are their peers who are not treated with stimulants (American Academy of Pediatrics, 2000).

Table 6.1 presents the commonly used stimulant medications, doses, treatment outcomes, and adverse effects. These include methylphenidate (Ritalin), dextroamphetamine (Dexadrine), pemoline (Cylert), and amphetamine/dextroamphetamine (Adderall). Because of 10 reports in the United States of acute liver failure, based on discussions with the Food and Drug Administration (FDA), it is recommended that pemoline should not be ordinarily considered a first-line drug therapy for children diagnosed with ADHD (Abbott Pharmaceuticals, 1996). In Table 6.2, we list the medications that may be dangerous or are not effective for children and adolescents with externalizing disorders.

Despite the widespread clinical use of Adderall in the management of children with ADHD, only three investigations have compared it with

TABLE 6.1
Medications Clinically Validated in Double-Blind Studies for the Treatment of Attention Deficit/Hyperactivity Disorder (ADHD)

Generic Name (Trade Name)	Children mg/kg/day or Daily Dose	Adolescents mg/kg/day or Daily Dose	Treatment Outcome	Adverse Effect
Amphetamine and d-amphetamine compound (Adderall)	5–20 mg	5–20 mg	A single dose of Adderall appears to be as effective as two daily doses of methylphenidate (Ritalin) for the reduction of ADHD symptomatology. Improvement in academic productivity and behavior.	Insomnia, dizziness, and headaches.
Bupropion (Wellbutrin)	Not yet established	Not yet established	Reduction in inattentiveness, distractibility, impulsivity, and motor hyperactivity.	Insomnia, dizziness, and constipation.
D-amphetamine (Dexadrine)	5–15 mg	5–15 mg	Reduction in inattentiveness, motor hyperactivity, and impulsivity.	Insomnia, dizziness, appetite suppressant, and headaches.
Fluoxetine (Prozac)	10–80 mg	10–80 mg	Reduction in ADHD, aggression, and mood disturbances.	Restlessness, insomnia, fatigue, nausea, decreased appetite, and tremors.
Methylphenidate (Ritalin)	5–20 mg	5–20 mg	Significant reduction in inattentiveness, distractibility, impulsivity, and motor hyperactivity. Improvement in academic productivity.	Appetite suppressant, insomnia, and irritability.
Nortriptyline (Aventyl, Pamelor)	10–25 mg	10–25 mg	Reduction in inattentiveness, impulsivity, and motor hyperactivity.	Insomnia, dry mouth, headaches, constipation, nausea, and blurred vision.

Note. Sources include Barrickman, Peery, Allen, and Kuperman (1995); Biederman, Baldessarini, Wright, and Knee (1989); Connors (1996); Manos, Short, and Findling (1999); Pelham, Greenblade, and Vodde-Hamilton (1990); Pelham, Swanson, Furman, and Schmidt (1995); *Physicians' Desk Reference* (1999); Swanson et al. (1998); and Wigal et al. (1998).

TABLE 6.2
Medications That Are Dangerous or Not Effective for
Children and Adolescents

Generic Name (Trade Name)	Adverse Effect and Cautionary Statement
Desipramine (Norpramin)	There have been reports of cardiac complications leading to death. Clinicians are encouraged to use safer alternatives.
Pemoline (Cylert)	In addition to appetite reduction, insomnia, tics, and headaches, there have been reports of acute liver failure. Clinicians are advised not to consider this as a first line of drug therapy and to use safer alternatives.

Note. Werry, J. S., and Aman, M. G. (1999). *Practitioner's guide to psychoactive drugs for children and adolescents* (2nd ed.). New York: Plenum Press.

standard doses of Ritalin (Pelham et al., 1999, 2000; Swanson et al., 1999). In a double-blind placebo-controlled study of Adderall, Pelham et al. (2000) compared two doses of Ritalin and Adderall in both recreational and academic settings in a summer day-treatment program. Results revealed that both were superior to placebo in improving academic productivity as well as ratings of behavior. In addition, Adderall was found to be superior to Ritalin on several assessment measures. More important, Adderall was found to be superior to Ritalin where the effects of Ritalin dissipated at midday and in the late afternoon. In addition, a low side-effect profile was similar for both stimulants. This recent investigation by Pelham and associates (Pelham et al., 2000) is important because it suggests that Adderall is at least as effective as Ritalin in the short term in improving behavior and academic productivity for children with ADHD. On the basis of these data, Pelham et al. (2000) recommended the use of Adderall, particularly for children in whom the effects of Ritalin dissipate rapidly.

Antidepressants and Antimanic Drugs

For those children and adolescents who have been refractory to stimulant medication, the tricyclic antidepressants have been demonstrated to be a viable alternative (Geller, Reising, Leonard, Riddle, & Walsh, 1999), although these agents have been consistently less effective than the stimulants (Pliszka, 1991). In addition, the antidepressants have been the drugs of choice for those youngsters with externalizing disorders with remarkable comorbid symptoms of anxiety, depression, lability of mood, and a significant family history of mood disorder, particularly where these youths have been refractory to stimulant medication. Furthermore, where there has been a remarkable personal or family history of tics or where there is a family member at risk for abusing or selling stimulant medication, the use of tricyclic antidepressants is a reasonable alternative (Biederman et al., 1995; Ryan, 1990). In addition, one atypical antidepressant, buproprion

(Wellbutrin), has demonstrated some promise in double-blind clinical trials with children diagnosed with ADHD (Barrickman, Peery, Allen, & Kuperman, 1995).

Buproprion (Wellbutrin) is an antidepressant that has had widespread clinical use with children because it shows some promise in attenuating attentional problems associated with ADHD. Studies suggest that buproprion may reduce symptoms of ADHD (Barrickman et al., 1995) despite its adverse effects that include agitation, confusion, irritability, as well as possible hypertension. Additional controlled trials are needed to further establish the safety and efficacy of buproprion in pediatric populations.

Those antidepressants that have been the most widely investigated include the tricyclics imipramine (Tofranil), nortriptyline (Aventyl, Pamelor), and desipramine (Norpramin, Petrofrane; Barrickman et al., 1995; Conners, Casat, Gualtieri, & Weller, 1996). These particular medications have been most efficacious in reducing overactivity and restlessness, although their effects on attention are less clear (Pliszka, 1987), and they seem to exert no effect on symptoms related to aggression and conduct disturbances. However, use of trazodone (Desyrel), which is an antidepressant chemically unrelated to the tricyclics, does appear to result in demonstrated improvements in impulsivity, emotional lability, temper tantrums, and overt aggression in children with disruptive behavior disorders (Ghaziuddin & Alessi, 1992; Zubieta & Alessi, 1992).

Anticholinergic adverse side effects are frequently associated with tricyclic antidepressant medications, including dry mouth, constipation, nausea, tiredness, and blurred vision. Sedation also is a frequent adverse effect. Finally, tricyclic medications have a major effect on the cardiovascular system, and there have been reports of sudden deaths among children taking desipramine. For this reason, ongoing cardiac monitoring is essential.

There has been some limited investigation of the monoamine oxidase inhibitors (MAOIs) in the management of ADHD, and the data have been generally positive (Trott, Friese, Mengel, & Nissen, 1992; Zametkin, Rapoport, Murphy, Leinnola, & Ismond, 1985). Nonetheless, because of potential deleterious effects with the MAOIs (i.e., they can cause severe hypertension when combined with certain medications, such as the selective serotonin reuptake inhibitors [SSRIs], or when combined with the ingestion of foods such as cheese, chocolate, and yogurt that contain tyramine) and the fact that there are few controlled trials assessing efficacy and safety, it is generally recommended that these agents be used only as a last resort in managing ADHD and associated symptoms. Because of the severe dietary restriction associated with the MAOIs, the use of these medications must be weighed carefully with their adverse effects, and these medications should probably be used only when all other medications have failed and only in very controlled inpatient settings (Viesselman, 1999).

The SSRIs is a class of antidepressants that inhibit the reuptake of serotonin in the presynaptic neuron terminal. They have been widely used in adults with various affective disorders, and their efficacy and safety have been well established for adults. There have been some limited clinical trials with fluoxetine (Prozac) and venlafaxine (Effexor) in pediatric populations, and improvements related to symptoms associated with ADHD, aggression, and mood disturbances have been demonstrated (Olvera, Pliszka, Luh, & Tatum, 1996; Rudolph & Feiger, 1999; Waslick et al., 1999). There have been some isolated reports of memory impairment from fluoxetine, and thus it is recommended that it be used with caution in the management of ADHD (Bangs, Petti, & Janus, 1994; Bradley & Kulik, 1993). The SSRIs have a range of adverse effects on the gastrointestinal system, including nausea, diarrhea, dyspepsia, and weight loss. Adverse behavioral effects also include motor restlessness, social disinhibition, and sleep disturbances (Viesselman, 1999).

Because children and adolescents who are referred for difficulties associated with disruptive behavior disorders frequently evidence explosive and aggressive behavior, there has been some investigation of the antimanic drugs in the management of severe aggression for children and adolescents with disruptive behavior disorders (M. Campbell et al., 1984; DeLong & Aldershof, 1987). However, in the absence of any affective symptoms, the effects of these medications have been minimal. Furthermore, their long-term safety has not yet been demonstrated, and they should be used judiciously with children and adolescents.

Neuroleptics

The neuroleptic medications have been demonstrated to diminish symptoms of impulsivity and overactivity. Because of the risk of tardive dyskinesia (i.e., involuntary motor movements of the mouth, face, tongue, or limbs), the use of these medications is probably limited only to those children and youths who have been refractory to other psychotropic medications.

Because of the high cormorbidity of ADHD with CD (Klein & Mannuzza, 1988), some of the pharmacological effects associated with ADHD are posited to be appropriate for children and adolescents with CD. However, the pharmacotherapy of CD clearly has been underinvestigated. In addition, because many of the earlier studies of children with ADHD also included youths who were comorbid for CD, reported improvements in aggression and noncompliance are quite encouraging (M. Campbell, Gonzalez, & Silva, 1992; Kaplan, Busner, Kupietz, Wassermann, & Segal, 1990). The most widely investigated psychotropic agent for children and adolescents with CD is haloperidol (Haldol), which has been demonstrated to reduce specific types of impulsive aggression (M. Campbell et al., 1992; Kaplan et al., 1990; Teicher & Glod, 1990). Finally, although carbamazepine (Tegretol) has shown some promise for impulsive aggression in an open medication trial (Kafantaris et al., 1992), these findings were not supported in a controlled double-blind trial (Cueva et al., 1996). Finally, there is no evidence of any psychotropic medication in the management of ODD, although when the disorder is comorbid with ADHD, pharmacological management of the ADHD does diminish some of the symptoms associated with the ODD.

The host of adverse effects associated with the neuroleptics, including extrapyramidal symptoms (muscular reactions), tardive dyskinesia, lethargy, cognitive toxicities, and weight gain, mandate their careful and judicious use in pediatric populations. They are considered generally safest when they are used in low doses. The most pervasive short-term adverse effect of antipsychotics is cognitive impairment that may result in learning and academic difficulties. Some research has suggested that cognitive and behavioral toxicities are dose dependent, with lower doses reducing the impact of these adverse effects. Because many children with externalizing behavioral problems also have learning problems and evidence academic delay, their use with these children should only be when all other treatment approaches have failed.

Other Medications

In the last several years a new class of antipsychotic medications have been developed that have fewer adverse effects than the widely used antipsychotic agents such as haloperidol. The clinical efficacy of these new medications has revolutionized the management of specific psychiatric disorders and symptoms in pediatric populations because of the favorable side-effect profile. Most important, the short-term use of these medications is encouraging because no symptoms of tardive dyskinesia have emerged. Resperidone (Risperdal) has been used primarily in the management of psychotic symptoms and impulsive aggression that are sometimes encountered in youth with severe conduct disorders (Werry & Aman, 1999). Unlike most antipsychotic medications, sedation has been found to be minimal with resperidone and its side-effect profile has generally compared favorably to other neuroleptic agents (Armenteros, Whitaker, Welikson, Stedge, & Gorman, 1997). As noted, the most promising aspect of resperidone is that no reports of tardive dyskinesia have been documented, although the long-term safety of resperidone with pediatric populations remains to be demonstrated through future controlled clinical trials.

Clonidine (Catapres) is an antihypertensive drug that reduces symptoms associated with comorbid CD and ADHD, particularly hyperarousal and aggression. Clonidine has been less useful for managing symptoms associated with attention and concentration. Guanfacine (Tenex) is a longer acting medication and has similar effects of clonidine with fewer adverse effects. Hunt, Capper, and O'Connell (1990) noted that clonidine diminished overactivity, impulsivity, aggression, and inattention. They also reported that clonidine increases goal-directed behavior. There had been significant increase of these medications in the management of comorbid CD/ADHD and ODD (oppositional defiant disorder) in the early to mid-1990s, but unfortunately clinical use of these psychotropic medications has far surpassed research demonstrating efficacy and safety (Brown & Sawyer, 1998). Adverse effects of these medications include hypotension, depressive symptoms, and sedation (Werry & Aman, 1999). Table 6.3 presents medications clinically validated in double-blind studies for the treatment of disruptive behavior disorders, and Table 6.4 summarizes psychotropic medications examined in open trials.

Psychosocial Interventions

There are available to the practitioner several empirically validated psychosocial treatments for use with children and adolescents with ADHD, CD, and ODD. We review these therapies and note that some are recommended for only ADHD symptoms and difficulties related to ODD and CD, whereas other treatments have been demonstrated to be effective for all of the disorders.

Behavioral Therapies

There has been an extensive literature on the use of behavioral interventions in an attempt to manage the symptoms associated with disruptive behavioral disorders. Some behavioral interventions have focused on improving peer relationships and social skills, whereas other interventions have devoted their efforts on improving academic functioning and classroom behaviors. Those studies using behavioral approaches designed to improve academic performance have demonstrated increased academic performance and also decreased disruptive behaviors (for a review, see Pelham, 1999). Positive reinforcement has been frequently used whereby a child earns points or tokens that reflect some value (e.g., free time, specific classroom activities), although the child also may lose points for not attending to specific assignments (response cost; for a review, see Pelham, 1999). Thus, a combination of both positive reinforcement and response cost has been found to be superior to either approach used alone. It is important to note that positive reinforcement is frequently used to increase specific behaviors, whereas response cost is often used to decrease undesirable behaviors.

TABLE 6.3

Medications Clinically Validated in Double-Blind Studies for the Treatment of Conduct Disorder (CD) and Oppositional Defiant Disorder (ODD)

Generic Name (Trade Name)	Children mg/kg/day or Daily Dose	Adolescents mg/kg/day or Daily Dose	Treatment Outcome	Adverse Effect
Clonidine (Catapres)	0.3–0.5 mg	0.3–0.5 mg	Effective in symptom reduction of overarousal, aggression, and defiance. It is most often used in cases of comorbidity of ODD/CD and ADHD.	10% reduction in blood pressure requires close monitoring. Sedation and fatigue are common.
Haloperidol (Haldol)	.05–.075 mg/kg 600 mg maximum	.05–.075 mg/kg 600 mg maximum	Reduction in severe aggression.	Cognitive blunting, tardive dyskinesia, neuroleptic malignant syndrome.
Trazodone (Desyrel)			Reduction in impulsivity, emotional liability, temper tantrums, and overt aggression. Frequently used in the treatment of comorbid ODD/CD and ADHD.	Dry mouth, constipation, nausea, and blurred vision.
Venlafaxine (Effexor)	Not yet established	Not yet established	Improvement in ADHD, aggression, and mood disturbances. Frequently used in the treatment of comorbid ODD/CD and ADHD.	Insomnia, nausea, diarrhea, weight loss, restlessness, and social inhibition.

Note. Sources include Campbell, Gonzalez, and Silva (1992); Connor, Barkley, and Davis (2000); Connor, Fletcher, and Swanson (1999); and *Physicians' Desk Reference* (1999).

TABLE 6.4

Medications Clinically Validated in Open Studies for the Treatment of Conduct Disorder (CD) and Oppositional Defiant Disorder (ODD)

Generic Name (Trade Name)	Children mg/kg/day or Daily Dose	Adolescents mg/kg/day or Daily Dose	Treatment Outcome	Adverse Effect
Buspirone (BuSpar)	Not yet established	Not yet established	Reduction in irritability, defiance, anger, and aggression.	Dizziness and drowsiness.
Carbamazepine (Tegretol)	50–600 mg	50–600 mg	Reduction in impulsivity and aggression.	Dizziness, nausea, vomiting, and drowsiness.
Guanfacine (Tenex)	Not yet established	Not yet established	Reduction in overarousal and aggression.	Decrease in blood pressure requires close monitoring. Sedation and fatigue during early stages of treatment.
Pemoline (Cylert)	50–75 mg	50–75 mg	Reduction in aggression, defiance, anger, and irritability.	Appetite reduction, sleep disturbances. Use with extreme caution because of possible acute liver failure.
Risperidone (Risperdal)	Not yet established	Not yet established	Reduction in impulsivity, aggression, overarousal, and defiance.	Weight gain.

Note. Sources include Dunne (1999); Kafantaris et al. (1992); Kewley (1999); *Physicians' Desk Reference* (1999); and Shah, Seese, Abikoff, and Klein (1994).

Child-Based Interventions

Because children with disruptive behavior disorders frequently encounter difficulties interacting with other children in social situations, some treatments have been developed that primarily focus on teaching these children to negotiate social situations with peers. Kazdin and associates (Kazdin, Bass, Siegel, & Thomas, 1989; Kazdin, Siegel, & Bass, 1992) have demonstrated the efficacy of a problem-solving skills training program in reducing aggressive antisocial behaviors in children with CD when combined with behavioral therapy. Older children were found to benefit more than their younger counterparts. Cognitive–behavioral programs also have been evaluated for children with ADHD, and the results of these therapies with this population have not been found to be particularly promising (Abikoff, 1991). Hinshaw (1991) suggested that impulsivity and inattention coupled with poor regulatory skills impede these children from demonstrating the skills offered by these cognitive–behavioral programs.

Family Interventions

The use of family-based therapies have had particular appeal for the treatment of ODD and CD, primarily because their theoretical models underscore the role of parent–child interactions in managing symptoms associated with these disorders. Family therapies that have demonstrated the best success have been behaviorally oriented treatment programs designed to train parents in behavioral management strategies (for a review, see Johnston & Ohan, 1999). The use of family therapies that teach caregivers behavioral management strategies has demonstrated beneficial effects in reducing aggression and noncompliance at least in the short term (Forehand & McMahon, 1981). Similarly, Eyberg (1988) developed a program designed to teach caregivers both behavioral management strategies and problem-solving techniques as well as play skills for the purpose of enhancing parent–child relationships. Data from these family programs have suggested generalization over time, with positive effects sustaining well into adolescence (Forehand & Long, 1988). For ADHD children, the use of parent behavioral management training has been demonstrated to be particularly successful (for reviews, see Anastopoulos, Barkley, & Shelton, 1996; Pelham, 1999). A careful examination of the results of these studies suggests that they are most successful for the associated symptoms of ADHD and comorbid conditions that frequently occur with ADHD during elementary school. These therapies appear to be less promising for ADHD at adolescence (Barkley, Guevremont, Anastopolous, & Fletcher, 1992).

The use of family therapy has been demonstrated to be particularly efficacious for adolescents with ODD and CD. In an investigation comparing the influence of a behavioral parenting intervention, an intervention consisting of a teen-focused self-regulation procedure, a combination of both these approaches, a placebo control group, and a no-treatment condition, Dishion and Andrews (1995) demonstrated the beneficial effects of the parenting intervention, even 1 year following termination of therapy. Of interest is the finding that the group consisting of teenage self-regulation intervention increased in symptoms associated with ODD and CD, which the investigators attributed to a contagion effect of youths with conduct difficulties.

For adolescents with ADHD, behavioral parent training has not been demonstrated to be as successful as for their younger childhood peers with the disorder. Barkley and associates (Barkley et al., 1992) examined behavioral management, communication training, and family interactions and found no differences among the therapies for adolescents ranging from age 12 to 18 years. No clinical changes were revealed for any of the therapies.

School and Community Interventions

One unique program designed to target at-risk children is the FAST (Families and Schools Together) program. Specifically, the program is designed to intervene with children designated by parents and teachers to be at risk because of their aggressive behavior during kindergarten. The program includes behavioral parent training, home–school communication, social skills training for the children, academic tutoring, and classroom interventions. The program is developmentally sensitive as it targets children at critical periods when they are deemed to be most vulnerable (e.g., at school entry and during transition periods such as middle school).

Combined Interventions

Given the potential promise of both the psychotherapies and pharmacotherapies for childhood externalizing disorders, of interest is whether the separate and combined effects of medication therapy and psychotherapy are more effective than either therapy used alone. This issue has been the topic of the largest clinical trial sponsored by the National Institute of Mental Health and is probably one the most definitive long-term studies addressing the issue of multimodal therapies in childhood psychopathology. The investigation consisted of several collaborative sites (Arnold et al., 1997; Greenhill et al., 1996; MTA Cooperative Group, 1999; Richters et al., 1995; Wells et al., 2000).

The Multimodal Treatment Study for ADHD (MTA) is based on the extensive literature documenting the efficacy of behavioral and pharmacological therapies for ADHD. Specifically, the MTA study examined the relative effectiveness of 14 months of four treatments for managing ADHD. Treatments included behavioral treatment (i.e., 35 sessions of behavioral parent training, 10 teacher–school consultations per school year, a classroom aide, and an intensive summer treatment program), medication management (i.e., psychostimulant medication administered 7 days per week), combined behavioral training and medication management, and a community control group of children who received traditional treatments for ADHD. It also should be noted that 67% of the community sample was receiving some type of psychotropic medication, primarily stimulants. Children participating in the investigation included 579 seven- to nine-year-olds, all of whom were diagnosed with ADHD. The participants were assigned randomly to one of the four treatment groups. The children received in-depth evaluations at 9 months and 14 months following treatment.

Findings of the MTA investigation reveal that although all four groups demonstrated remarkable reductions in symptoms over time, pharmacological interventions (i.e., stimulant medication) were more effective than behavioral treatments and that the addition of behavioral treatments to medication resulted in only modest benefit to medication used alone. The data also revealed that behavioral therapies alone did not differ from the community control intervention (i.e., participants who received a variety of nonstandardized treatments from providers in the community). However, for children who had comorbidity of symptoms (including aggression, oppositional behavior, and internalizing symptoms), combined treatments of medication and behavior therapy proved superior to behavioral treatment used alone or to traditional treatments provided in the community. It also should be noted that parents preferred the behavioral therapy condition over the medication-alone treatment.

The MTA study also has received some criticism because of methodological and design issues, including the fact that children were receiving medication at the time of follow-up assessment and that some of the children who were receiving only behavioral management were later placed on stimulant drug therapy (Pelham, 1999). Despite these criticisms, the findings of this investigation are particularly important because it is the largest randomized controlled clinical trial with a child psychiatric population that has examined the combined effects of medication and psychotherapy. For this reason, it is expected to affect clinical practice significantly. It will be important for future studies to compare psychotherapy and pharmacotherapy for children and adolescents with other disorders, including CD and anxiety disorder. In addition, variables that mediate and moderate the beneficial effects of pharmacotherapy and psychotherapy for children with various internalizing and externalizing disorders will be an important next direction for future research.

CONCLUSION

The externalizing disorders (i.e., ADHD, ODD, and CD) comprise the majority of disorders referred for evaluation by clinical and school psychologists. The etiologies for these disorders are varied, although there is compelling evidence to suggest a biological basis for ADHD and that ODD and CD are associated with familial discord and parental interactions. This has implications for pharmacological management of ADHD. Many children and adolescents frequently meet diagnostic criteria for other disorders, including both comorbid externalizing disorders and internalizing disorders (e.g., anxiety-related disorders, depressive disorders). The issue of comorbidity for the externalizing disorders is of prime importance, as it has implication for treatment planning. In addition, the comorbidity of ADHD and ODD or CD suggests a more guarded prognosis than either disorder occurring alone. It also has been suggested that ADHD in the presence of familial risk factors, including marital discord and poor parenting, increases the probability of other externalizing disorders including ODD and CD. Specifically, the presence of attentional problems and impulsivity is posited to drive the onset of behaviors associated with ODD and accelerate some of the severe symptoms that are related to CD.

A host of pharmacotherapies are available for the management of externalizing behavior disorders, although the clinical use of these medications, with the exception of the stimulants, far exceeds the data that are available attesting to their efficacy and safety. The majority of studies in pediatric psychopharmacology have been with the stimulants (Ritalin, Dexadrine, and Adderall), and these investigations have included primarily children diagnosed with ADHD. The evidence regarding the efficacy and safety of these medications has been overwhelming, particularly with regard to the short-term effects of these medications on specific target behaviors associated with ADHD. There is evidence that the stimulants are useful for managing some of the aggressive behaviors that may be associated with CD and ODD. Those studies that have demonstrated efficacy of the stimulants for these target behaviors have found that they are most useful for comorbid groups in which ADHD and CD are present.

The use of antidepressant medications including the tricyclic antidepressants and the specific serotonin reuptake inhibitors have shown particular promise for children with ADHD who have been refractory to stimulant medication and especially for children with ADHD who have comorbidity of anxiety and depressive disorders. The potential of deleterious adverse effects from these medications also must be considered, particularly cardiac arrhythmias resulting in death for some children when the tricyclic antidepressants have been used. The uses of antihypertensive medications also have been somewhat encouraging, although clearly their use has surpassed research studies demonstrating their safety and efficacy.

Regarding psychotherapies for children and adolescents with externalizing behavioral disorders, the behavioral therapies have received the most research attention, demonstrating their success at least in the short term. Child-based interventions, including problem-solving skills in reducing aggressive antisocial behaviors for youths with CD, have shown some promise, although the use of cognitive–behavioral approaches for children with ADHD has not been found to be particularly effective. Family interventions have shown the most promise for managing symptoms associated with ODD and CD because of the theoretical models underlying the role of parent–child interactions in these disorders. Other promising interventions are school and community programs designed to target at-risk children in the preschool and early elementary grades who exhibit aggression. Finally, the use of the comprehensive multimodal program appears to be most promising for disorders in which aggression, oppositional behavior, and internalizing symptoms are comorbid with ADHD.

It is clear that the clinical use of most psychotropics with the exception of the stimulants far outweighs the research studies demonstrating the efficacy and safety of these medications. Additional controlled trials are needed both in the long and short term to demonstrate the efficacy of the antidepressants, particularly the SSRIs, in the management of the externalizing disorders. More studies are needed regarding the safety and efficacy of the antihypertensive medications for the externalizing disorders, particularly on the target behaviors related to aggression. Studies modeled after the MTA trial are needed for other externalizing disorders, including CD and ODD. Also, given the recent evidence of the increase in the use of psychotropic medications for preschool children, additional studies are needed evaluating the efficacy of various pharmacotherapies with this age group as well as the combination of psychotherapy and pharmacotherapy in the management of these children. It is anticipated that the National Institute of Mental Health ADHD preschool study that is currently under way will help address these issues.

In conclusion, collaborative approaches that combine psychosocial programs and carefully monitored psychotropic medication treatment have produced mixed results, with some proving the combined treatment efficacious in the management of childhood and adolescent externalizing disorders and others favoring one treatment approach alone over another or over a combined approach. Much more research needs to be done focusing on the long-term effectiveness of psychotherapy in conjunction with stimulant medication in the treatment of these disorders.

REFERENCES

Abbott Pharmaceuticals. (1996). *Important drug warning* [Letter]. North Chicago: Author.

Abikoff, H. (1991). Cognitive training in ADHD children: Less to it than meets the eye. *Journal of Learning Disabilities, 24,* 205–209.

American Academy of Pediatrics. (2000). Treatment guideline for diagnosis of ADHD. *Pediatrics, 105,* 1158–1170.

American Psychiatric Association. (1994). *Diagnostic and statistical manual of mental disorders* (4th ed.). Washington, DC: Author.

Anastopoulos, A. D., Barkley, R. A., & Shelton, T. L. (1996). Family based treatment: Psychosocial intervention for children and adolescents with attention deficit hyperactivity disorder. In E. D. Hibbs & P. S. Jensen (Eds.), *Psychosocial treatments for children and adolescents with attention deficit hyperactivity disorders: Empirically based strategies for clinical practice* (pp. 267–284). Washington DC: American Psychological Association.

Armenteros, J. L., Whitaker, A. H., Welikson, M., Stedge, D. J., & Gorman, J. (1997). Risperidone in adolescents with schizophrenia: An open pilot study. *Journal of the American Academy of Child and Adolescent Psychiatry, 36,* 694–700.

Arnold, L. E., Abikoff, H. B., Cantwell, D. P., Conners, C. K., Elliott, G., Greenhill, L. L., Hechtman, L., Hinshaw, S. P., Hoza, B., Jensen, P. S., Kraemer, H. C., March, J. S., Newcorn, J. H., Pelham, W. E., Richters, J. E., Schiller, E., Severe, J. B., Swanson, J. M., Vereen, D., & Wells, K. C. (1997). National Institute of Mental Health Collaborative Multimodal Treatment Study of Children With ADHD (the MTA): Design challenges and choices. *Archives of General Psychiatry, 54,* 865–870.

Bangs, M. E., Petti, T. A., & Janus, M. D. (1994). Fluoxetine-induced memory impairment in an adolescent. *Journal of the American Academy of Child and Adolescent Psychiatry, 33,* 1303–1306.

Barkley, R. A., & Cunningham, C. E. (1979). The effects of methylphenidate on the mother–child interactions of hyperactive children. *Archives of General Psychiatry, 36,* 201–208.

Barkley, R. A., Fischer, M., Edelbrock, C. S., & Smallish, L. (1990). The adolescent outcome of hyperactive children diagnosed by research criteria: I. An 8-year prospective follow-up study. *Journal of the American Academy of Child and Adolescent Psychiatry, 29,* 545–547.

Barkley, R. A., Fischer, M., Edelbrock, C. S., & Smallish, L. (1991). The adolescent outcome of hyperactive children diagnosed by research criteria: III. Mother–child interactions, family conflicts and maternal psychopathology. *Journal of Child Psychology and Psychiatry, 32,* 233–253.

Barkley, R. A., Guevremont, D. C., Anastopoulos, A. D., & Fletcher, K. E. (1992). A comparison of three family therapy programs for treating family conflicts in adolescents with attention-deficit hyperactivity disorder. *Journal of Consulting and Clinical Psychology, 60,* 450–462.

Barkley, R. A., Karlsson, J., Strzelecki, E., & Murphy, J. V. (1984). Effects of age and Ritalin dosage on the mother–child interactions of hyperactive children. *Journal of Consulting and Clinical Psychology, 52,* 750–758.

Barkley, R. A., McMurray, M. B., Edelbrock, S. S., & Robbins, K. (1990). Side effects of methylphenidate in children with attention deficit hyperactivity disorder: Systemic, placebo-controlled evaluation. *Pediatrics, 86,* 184–192.

Barrickman, L. L., Peery, P. J., Allen, A. J., & Kuperman, S. (1995). Bupropion versus methylphenidate in the treatment of ADHD. *Journal of the American Academy of Child and Adolescent Psychiatry, 34,* 649–657.

Bennett, F. C., Brown, R. T., Craver, J., & Anderson, D. (1999). Stimulant medication for the child with attention deficit/hyperactivity disorder. *Pediatric Clinics of North America, 46,* 924–944.

Biederman, J., Baldessarini, R. J., Wright, V., & Knee, D. (1989). A double-blind placebo controlled study of desipramine in the treatment of ADHD. *Journal of the American Academy of Child and Adolescent Psychiatry, 28,* 777–784.

Biederman, J., Faraone, S. V., Keenan, K., Knee, D., & Tsuang, M. T. (1990). Family-genetic and psychosocial risk factors in DSM–III attention deficit disorder. *Journal of the American Academy of Child and Adolescent Psychiatry, 29,* 526–533.

Biederman, J., Faraone, S., Mick, E., & Moore, P. (1996). Child Behavior Checklist findings further support comorbidity between ADHD and major depression in a referred sample. *Journal of the American Academy of Child and Adolescent Psychiatry, 35,* 734–742.

Biederman, J., Wilens, T., Mick, E., Milberger, S., Spencer, F. J., & Faraone, S. V. (1995). Psychoactive substance use disorders in adults with attention deficit disorder (ADHD): Effects of ADHD and psychiatric comorbidity. *American Journal of Psychiatry, 152,* 1652–1658.

Bradley, S. J., & Kulik, L. (1993). Fluoxetine and memory impairment. *Journal of the American Academy of Child and Adolescent Psychiatry, 32,* 1078–1079.

Brown, R. T., & Sawyer, M. G. (1998). *Medications for school age children: Effects on learning and behavior.* New York: Guilford Press.

Burhmester, D., Whalen, C. K., Henker, B., MacDonald, V., & Hinshaw, S. P. (1992). Prosocial behavior in hyperactive boys: Effects of stimulant medication and comparison with normal boys. *Journal of Abnormal Child Psychology, 20,* 103–121.

Campbell, M., Gonzalez, N. M., & Silva, R. R. (1992) The pharmacologic treatment of conduct disorders and rage outbursts. *Psychiatric Clinics of North America, 15,* 69–85.

Campbell, M., Small, A. M., Green, W. H., Jennings, S. J., Perry, R., Bennett, W. G., & Anderson, L. (1984). Behavioral efficacy of haloperidol and lithium carbonate: A comparison in hospitalized aggressive children with conduct disorder. *Archives of General Psychiatry, 41,* 650–656.

Campbell, S. B. (1990). *Behavior problems in preschool children.* New York: Guilford Press.

Conners, C. K., Casat, C. D., Gualtieri, C. T., & Weller, E. (1996). Bupropion hydrochloride in attention deficit disorder with hyperactivity. *Journal of the American Academy of Child and Adolescent Psychiatry, 35,* 1314–1321.

Connor, D. F., Barkley, R. A., & Davis, H. T. (2000). A pilot study of methylphenidate, clonidine, or the combination in ADHD comorbid with aggressive oppositional defiant or conduct disorder. *Clinical Pediatrics, 39,* 15–25.

Connor, D. F., Fletcher, K. F., & Swanson, J. M. (1999). A meta-analysis of clonidine for symptoms of ADHD. *Journal of the American Academy of Child and Adolescent Psychiatry, 38,* 1551–1559.

Connors, D. (1996). Bupropion hydrochloride in attention deficit disorder with hyperactivity. *Journal of the American Academy of Child and Adolescent Psychiatry, 35,* 1314–1321.

Cueva, J. E., Overall, J. E., Small, A. M., Armenteros, J. L., Perry, R., & Campbell, M. (1996). Carbamazepine in aggressive children with conduct disorder: A double-blind and placebo controlled study. *Journal of the American Academy of Child and Adolescent Psychiatry, 35,* 480–490.

DeLong, G. R., & Aldershof, A. L. (1987). Long-term experience with lithium treatment in childhood: Correlation with clinical diagnosis. *Journal of the American Academy of Child and Adolescent Psychiatry, 26,* 389–394.

Dishion, T. J., & Andrews, D. W. (1995). Preventing escalation in problem behavior with high-risk young adolescents: Immediate and 1-year outcomes. *Journal of Consulting and Clinical Psychology, 63,* 538–548.

Dunne, J. F. (1999). Buspirone in ODD. *Journal of the American Academy of Child and Adolescent Psychiatry, 38,* 942.

DuPaul, G. J., Anastopoulos, A. D., Kwasnik, D., Barkley, R. A., & McMurray, M. B. (1996). Methylphenidate effects on children with attention deficit hyperactivity disorder: Self-report of symptoms, side effects and self-esteem. *Journal of Attention Disorders, 1,* 3–15.

DuPaul, G. J., Barkley, R. A., & Connor, D. F. (1998). Stimulants. In R. A. Barkley (Ed.), *Attention deficit hyperactivity disorder: A handbook for diagnosis and treatment* (pp. 510–551). New York: Guilford Press.

DuPaul, G. J., & Rapport, M. D. (1993). Does methylphenidate normalize the classroom performance of children with attention deficit disorder? *Journal of the American Academy of Child and Adolescent Psychiatry, 32,* 190–198.

Eyberg, S. M. (1988). Parent–child interaction therapy: Integration of traditional and behavior concerns. *Child and Family Behavior Therapy, 10,* 33–46.

Faraone, S. V., Biederman, J., Keenan, K., & Tsuang, M. T. (1991). Separation of *DSM–III* attention deficit disorder and conduct disorder: Evidence from a family genetic study of American child psychiatric patients. *Psychological Medicine, 21,* 109–121.

Fischer, M., Barkley, R. A., Fletcher, K. E., & Smallish, L. (1993). The adolescent outcome of hyperactive children: Predictors of psychiatric, academic, social, and emotional adjustment. *Journal of the American Academy of Child and Adolescent Psychiatry, 32,* 324–332.

Forehand, R., & Long, N. (1988). Outpatient treatment of the acting out child: Procedures, long-term follow-up data, and clinical problems. *Advances in Behavior Research and Therapy, 10,* 129–177.

Forehand, R., & McMahon, R. J. (1981). *Helping the noncompliant child: A clinician's guide to parent training.* New York: Guilford Press.

Gadow, K. D. (1997). An overview of three decades of research in pediatric psychopharmacoepidemiology. *Journal of Child and Adolescent Psychopharmacology, 7,* 219–236.

Geller, B., Reising, D., Leonard, H. L., Riddle, M. A., & Walsh, B. T. (1999). Critical review of tricyclic antidepressant use in children and adolescents. *Journal of the American Academy of Child and Adolescent Psychiatry, 38,* 513–516.

Ghaziuddin, N., & Alessi, N. E. (1992). An open clinical trial of trazodone in aggressive children. *Journal of Child and Adolescent Psychopharmacology, 2,* 291–297.

Greenhill, L. L., Abikoff, H. B., Arnold, L. E., Cantwell, D. P., Conners, C. K., Elliott, G., Hechtman, L., Hinshaw, S. P., Hoza, B., Jensen, P. S., March, J. S., Newcorn, J., Pelham, W. E., Severe, J. B., Swanson, J. M., Vitiello, B., & Walls, K. (1996). Medication treatment strategies in the MTA study: Relevance to clinicians and researchers. *Journal of the American Academy of Child and Adolescent Psychology, 35,* 1304–1313.

Hinshaw, S. P. (1991). Stimulant medication and the treatment of aggression in children with attentional deficits. *Journal of Clinical Child Psychology, 20,* 301–312.

Hinshaw, S. P. (2000). Family processes and treatment outcomes in the MTA: Negative/ineffective parenting practices in relation to multimodal treatment. *Journal of Abnormal Child Psychology, 28,* 555–568.

Hunt, R. D., Capper, L., & O'Connell, P. (1990). Clonidine in child and adolescent psychiatry. *Journal of Child and Adolescent Psychopharmacology, 1,* 87–102.

Jacobvitz, D., Sroufe, A. L., Stewart, M., & Leffert, N. (1990). Treatment of attention and hyperactivity problems in children with sympathomimetic drugs: A comprehensive review. *Journal of the American Academy of Child and Adolescent Psychiatry, 29,* 677–688.

Jensen, P. S., Kettle, L., Roper, M. T., Sloan, M. T., Dulcan, M. K., Hoven, C., Bird, H. R., Bauermeister, J. J., & Payne, J. D. (1999). Are stimulants overprescribed? Treatment of ADHD in four U.S. communities. *Journal of the American Academy of Child and Adolescent Psychiatry, 38,* 797–804.

Johnston, C., & Ohan, J. L. (1999). Externalizing disorders. In W. K. Silverman & T. H. Ollendick (Eds.), *Developmental issues in the clinical treatment of children* (pp. 279–294). Boston: Allyn & Bacon.

Kafantaris, V., Campbell, M., Pardon-Gayol, M. V., Small, A. M., Locascio, J. J., & Rosenberg, C. R. (1992). Carbamazepine in hospitalized aggressive conduct disorder children: An open pilot study. *Psychopharmacology Bulletin, 28,* 193–199.

Kaplan, S. L., Busner, J., Kupietz, S., Wassermann, E., & Segal, B. (1990). Effects of methylphenidate on adolescents with aggressive conduct disorder and ADHD: A preliminary report. *Journal of the American Academy of Child and Adolescent Psychiatry, 29*, 719–723.

Kazdin, A. E. (1987). Treatment of antisocial behavior in children: Current status and future directions. *Psychological Bulletin, 102*, 187–203.

Kazdin, A. E., Bass, D., Siegel, T., & Thomas, C. (1989). Cognitive–behavioral therapy and relationship therapy in the treatment of children referred for antisocial behavior. *Journal of Consulting and Clinical Psychology, 60*, 733–747.

Kazdin, A. E., Siegel, T. C., & Bass, D. (1992). Cognitive problem-solving skills training in the treatment of antisocial behavior in children. *Journal of Consulting and Clinical Psychology, 60*, 733–747.

Kewley, G. D. (1999). Risperidone in comorbid ADHD and ODD/CD. *Journal of the American Academy of Child and Adolescent Psychiatry, 38*, 1327–1328.

Klein, R. G., & Mannuzza, S. (1988). Hyperactive boys almost grown up: III. Methylphenidate effects on ultimate height. *Archives of General Psychiatry, 45*, 1131–1134.

Lahey, B. B., & Loeber, R. (1994). Framework for a developmental model of oppositional defiant disorder and conduct disorder. In D. K. Routh (Ed.), *Disruptive behavior disorders in childhood* (pp. 139–180). New York: Plenum Press.

Lahey, B. B., Loeber, R., Quay, H. C., Frick, P. J., & Grimm, S. (1992). Oppositional defiant and conduct disorders: Issues to be resolved for *DSM–IV. Journal of the American Academy of Child and Adolescent Psychiatry, 31*, 539–546.

Manos, M. J., Short, E. J., & Findling, R. L. (1999). Differential effectiveness of methylphenidate and Adderall in school-age youths with ADHD. *Journal of the American Academy of Child and Adolescent Psychiatry, 38*, 813–819.

Multimodal Treatment Study for Children With ADHD Cooperative Group. (1999). A 14-month randomized clinical trial of treatment strategies for attention-deficit/hyperactivity disorder. *Archives of General Psychiatry, 56*, 1073–1086.

Olvera, R. L., Pliszka, S. R., Luh, J., & Tatum, R. (1996). An open trial of venlafaxine in the treatment of attention-deficit/hyperactivity disorder in children and adolescents. *Journal of Child and Adolescent Psychopharmacology, 6*, 241–250.

Patterson, G. R. (1982). *Coercive family process.* Eugene, OR: Castalia.

Pelham, W. E., Jr. (1999). The NIMH multimodal treatment study for attention deficit hyperactivity disorder: Just say yes to drugs alone? *Canadian Journal of Psychiatry, 10*, 981–990.

Pelham, W. E., Aronoff, H. R., Midlam, J. K., Shapiro, C. J., Gnagy, E. M., Chronis, A. M., Onyango, A. N., Forehand, G., Nguyen, A., & Waxmonsky, J. (1999). A comparison of Ritalin and Adderall: Efficacy and time-course in children with attention-deficit/hyperactivity disorder. *Pediatrics, 103*, e43.

Pelham, W. E., Gnagy, E. M., Greiner, A. R., Hoza, B., Hinshaw, S. P., Swanson, J. M., Simpson, S., Shapiro, C., Bukstein, O., Baron-Myak, C., & McBurnett,

K. (2000). Behavioral versus behavioral and pharmacological treatment in ADHD children attending a summer treatment program. *Journal of Abnormal Child Psychology, 28*, 507–525.

Pelham, W. E., Greenblade, K. E., & Vodde-Hamilton, M. (1990). Relative efficacy of long-acting stimulants on children with attention deficit hyperactivity disorder: A comparison of standard methylphenidate, sustained released methylphenidate, sustained release dextroamphetamine, and pemoline. *Pediatrics, 86*, 226–237.

Pelham, W. E., Swanson, J. M., Furman, M. B., & Schmidt, H. (1995). Pemoline effects on children with ADHD: A time-response by dose-response analysis on classroom measures. *Journal of the American Academy of Child and Adolescent Psychiatry, 34*, 1504–1513.

Physicians' Desk Reference. (53rd ed.). (1999). Montvale, NJ: Medical Economics.

Pliszka, S. R. (1987). Tricyclic antidepressants in the treatment of children with attention deficit disorder. *Journal of the American Academy of Child and Adolescent Psychiatry, 26*, 127–132.

Pliszka, S. R. (1991). Antidepressants in the treatment of child and adolescent psychopathology. *Journal of Clinical Child Psychology, 20*, 313–320.

Quay, H., & Hogan, A. E. (Eds.). (1999). *Handbook of disruptive behavior disorders.* New York: Plenum.

Rappley, M. D., Mullan, P. B., Alvarez, F. J., Eneli, I. U., Wang, J., & Gardiner, J. C. (1999). Diagnosis of attention-deficit/hyperactivity disorder and use of psychotropic medication in very young children. *Archives of Pediatric and Adolescent Medicine, 153*, 1039–1045.

Richters, J. E., Arnold, L. E., Jensen, P. S., Abikoff, H., Conners, C. K., Greenhill, L. L., Hechtman, L., Hinshaw, S. P., Pelham, W. E., & Swanson, J. M. (1995). NIMH collaborative multisite multimodal treatment study of children with ADHD: I. Background and rationale. *Journal of the American Academy of Child and Adolescent Psychiatry, 34*, 987–1000.

Rudolph, R. L., & Feiger, A. D. (1999). A double-blind, randomized, placebo-controlled trial of once-daily venlafaxine extended release (XR) and fluoxetine for the treatment of depression. *Journal of Affective Disorders, 56*, 227–236.

Ryan, N. D. (1990). Pharmacotherapy of adolescent major depression. Beyond TCAs. *Psychopharmacology Bulletin, 26*, 75–79.

Safer, D. J., & Krager, J. M. (1988). A survey of medication treatment for hyperactive/inattentive students. *Journal of the American Medical Association, 260*, 2256–2258.

Swanson, J., Gupta, S., Guinta, D., Flynn, D., Agler, D., Lerner, M., Williams, L., Shoulson, I., & Wigal, S. (1999). Acute tolerance to methylphenidate in the treatment of ADHD in children. *Clinical Pharmacological Therapy, 66*, 295–305.

Swanson, J., Wigal, S., Greenhill, L., Browne, R., Waslick, B., Lerner, M., & Williams, L. (1998). Objective and subjective measures of the pharmacodynamic effects of Adderall in the treatment of children with ADHD in a controlled laboratory classroom setting. *Psychopharmacology Bulletin, 34,* 55–60.

Teicher, M. H., & Glod, C. A. (1990). Seasonal affective disorder: Rapid resolution by low dose alprazolam. *Psychopharmacology Bulletin, 26,* 197–202.

Thomas, A., & Chess, S. (1977). *Temperament and development.* New York: Brunner/Mazel.

Trott, G. E., Friese, H. J., Mengel, M., & Nissen, G. (1992). Use of moclobemide in children with attention deficit hyperactivity disorder. *Psychopharmacology (Berlin), 106*(Suppl.), 5134–5136.

Viesselman, J. O. (1999). Antidepressants and antimanic drugs. In J. S. Werry & M. G. Aman (Eds.), *Practitioner's guide to psychoactive drugs for children and adolescents* (2nd ed., pp. 239–268). New York: Plenum.

Waslick, B. D., Walsh, B. T., Greenhill, L. L., Eilenberg, M., Capasso, L., & Lieber, D. (1999). Open trial of fluoxetine in children and adolescents with dysthymic disorder or double depression. *Journal of Affective Disorders, 56,* 227–236.

Webster-Stratton, C. (1990). Stress: A potential disruption of parent perceptions and family interactions. *Journal of Clinical Child Psychology, 19,* 303–312.

Webster-Stratton, C., & Dahl, R. W. (1995). Conduct disorder. In M. Hersen & R. T. Ammerman (Eds.), *Advanced abnormal child psychology* (pp. 333–352). Hillsdale, NJ: Erlbaum.

Webster-Stratton, C., & Spitzer, A. (1991). Development, reliability, and validity of the daily telephone discipline interview. *Behavioral Assessment, 13,* 221–239.

Weiss, G., & Hechtman, L. T. (1993). *Hyperactive children grown up.* New York: Guilford Press.

Wells, K., Pelham, W. E., Kotkin, R. A., Hogan, B., Abikoff, H., Arnold, L. E., Abramowitz, A., Cantwell, D. P., Conners, C. K., Del Carmen, R., Elliott, G., Greenhill, L. L., Hechtman, L. T., Hinshaw, S. P., Jensen, P. S., March, J. S., Schiller, E., Severe, J., & Swanson, J. M. (2000). Psychosocial treatment strategies in the MTA study: Rationale, methods, and critical issues in design and implementation. *Journal of Abnormal Child Psychology, 28,* 483–505.

Werry, J. S., & Aman, M. G. (1999). *Practitioner's guide to psychoactive drugs for children and adolescents* (2nd ed.). New York: Plenum Press.

Whalen, C. K., Henker, B., Hinshaw, S. P., & Granger, D. A. (1989). Externalizing behavior disorders, situational generality, and the Type A behavior pattern. *Child Development, 60,* 1453–1462.

Wigal, S. B., Swanson, J. M., Greenhill, L., Waslick, B., Cantwell, D., Clevenger, W., Davies, M., & Lerner, M. (1998). Evaluation of individual subjects in the analog classroom setting: Effects of dose of amphetamine Adderall. *Psychopharmacology Bulletin, 34,* 833–838.

Williams, S., Anderson, J., McGee, R., & Silva, P. A. (1990). Risk factors for behavioral and emotional disorder in preadolescent children. *Journal of the American Academy of Child and Adolescent Psychiatry, 29,* 413–419.

Zametkin, A. J., Nordahl, T. E., Gross, M., King, A. C., Semple, W. E., Rumsey, J., Hamburger, S., & Cohen, R. M. (1990). Cerebral glucose metabolism in adults with hyperactivity of childhood onset. *New England Journal of Medicine, 323,* 1361–1366.

Zametkin, A., Rapoport, J. L., Murphy, D. L., Leinnola, M., & Ismond, D. (1985). Treatment of hyperactive children with monoamine oxidase inhibitors: I. Clinical efficacy. *Archives of General Psychiatry, 42,* 962–966.

Zeiner, P. (1995). Body growth and cardiovascular function after extended (1.75) years with methylphenidate in boys with attention-deficit hyperactivity disorder. *Journal of Child and Adolescent Psychopharmacology, 5,* 129–138.

Zito, J. M., Safer, D. J., dosReis, S., Gardner, J. F., Boles, M., & Lynch, F. (2000). Trends in the prescribing of psychotropic medications to preschoolers. *Journal of the American Medical Association, 283,* 1025–1030.

Zubieta, J. K., & Alessi, N. E. (1992). Acute and chronic administration of trazodone in the treatment of disruptive behavior disorders in children. *Journal of Clinical Psychopharmacology, 12,* 346–351.

7

MENTAL RETARDATION AND
AUTISTIC SPECTRUM DISORDERS

This chapter reviews pharmacological and behavioral approaches for the management of children and adolescents with developmental disabilities. The developmental disabilities considered here are mental retardation and the autistic spectrum disorders. Because many of the approaches for managing the two disorders differ, the pharmacological and behavioral approaches for each of the disorders are reviewed separately, and common research agendas for each of the disorders are developed. (Refer to the *Glossary of Terms* for definitions of medical terminology.)

MENTAL RETARDATION

The struggle to define and classify mental retardation has existed for the past century (King, State, Shah, Davanzo, & Dykens, 1998). The essential elements that define mental retardation are children's or adolescents' capabilities as they relate to the environment in which they live and to functioning in this environment. "Capabilities" consist of intelli-

This chapter was written in part with the assistance of Michelle M. Macias, Department of Pediatrics; Eve. G. Spratt, Departments of Pediatrics and Psychiatry; and Jane M. Charles, Department of Pediatrics, Medical University of South Carolina.

gence and adaptive behavior skills. The understanding of the concept of intelligence has evolved, but intelligence has remained central to the definition of mental retardation (Szymanski & Stark, 1996). However, there has been an expanded focus on functional adaptive components in 10 areas: communication, self-care, home living, social skills, community use, self-direction, health and safety, functional academics, leisure, and work (King et al., 1998; Szymanski & Stark, 1996). The current nomenclature of mental retardation in the fourth edition of the *Diagnostic and Statistical Manual of Mental Disorders* (DSM–IV) has three criteria: (a) significant impairment in current intellectual functioning, defined as an IQ of 70 or below on a standardized, individually administered test of intelligence; (b) impairment in the current adaptive functioning in at least two areas; and (c) onset before age 18 years (American Psychiatric Association, 1994).

The prevalence of behavioral and mood disturbances in children and adults with mental retardation is greater than that in the general population (Borthwick-Duffy, 1994). This includes a higher incidence of behavior problems such as aggression, self-injurious behavior, tantrums, and stereotyped behavior (Harris, Delmolino, & Glasberg, 1996). Both environmental factors and medical factors may contribute to severe disruptive behavior in children and adults with mental retardation.

The concept of dual diagnosis (i.e., the concurrent existence of mental retardation and psychopathology) is a frequently overlooked problem in children and adolescents. Frequently, diagnostic overshadowing occurs, which is the tendency to dismiss symptoms of emotional, behavioral, and thought problems as underlying expressions of mental retardation and not psychiatric disorders (Reiss, Levitan, & Syszko, 1982). Comorbid psychiatric disorders are one of the most important factors influencing adaptation and quality of life for children and adolescents with mental retardation (American Academy of Child and Adolescent Psychiatry [AACAP], 1999). In fact, psychiatric disorders may be one of the primary factors limiting adaptive functioning of children and adolescents with the disorder (Reiss, 1994).

Recent interest has developed concerning valid and reliable instruments to identify psychological disturbances in children and adolescents with mental retardation (Harris et al., 1996). An important component of such instruments is that they be developmentally sensitive, particularly given the developmental delays that children and adolescents experience with mental retardation. The Reiss Scales for Children's Dual Diagnosis was designed for use in children and young adults ages 4–21 years. Reiss and Valenti-Hein (1994) reported good reliability and validity for the presence of a dual diagnosis and for use as a general screening instrument. The Aberrant Behavior Checklist was designed to rate inappropriate and maladaptive behaviors of individuals with mental retardation to monitor the effects of psychotropic medications as well as other treatments that may have an impact on social behavior (Aman & Singh, 1994). Several other functional behavior rating scales have been developed, although reliability and validity have not clearly been established for children and adolescents (Strumey, 1994).

TREATMENT OF MENTAL RETARDATION

The basic principles for treatment of behavioral disturbances for children and adolescents with mental retardation are the same as those without mental retardation, but modification of techniques is necessary to correspond with the child's developmental and communicative level (AACAP, 1999). The overall treatment program should include medical, habilitative, and educational interventions. Treatment for children and adolescents is typically directed at comorbid behavioral disturbances rather than the mental retardation itself. The two most widely used approaches for the management of problem behaviors in children and adolescents with mental retardation are pharmacotherapy and psychosocial interventions.

Medical Interventions

Psychotropic medications are widely used for children and adolescents with mental retardation. Results from a survey of both children and adults with mental retardation ranging in age from 9 to 92 years revealed that nearly one third of residents of group homes were found to be receiving one or more psychotropic drugs for behavior problems (Aman, Sarphare, & Burrow, 1995). Baumeister, Todd, and Sevin (1993) reported that behavior-modifying medications are used in 57% of institutional residents, 41% of community residents, and 23% of special school students. In recent years, the use of medications to change or modify the behavior of people with mental retardation has been closely scrutinized (Bregman, 1996). To reduce unnecessary and inappropriate medication use, agencies that serve children and adolescents with mental retardation have been reassessing medication-prescribing practices and implementing stricter guidelines for usage (Bregman, 1996).

Several caveats exist when using psychopharmaceutical agents with children who have mental retardation. First, consideration should be given not only to symptom suppression but also to the potential negative impact of medication on habilitative function or overall quality of life. The risk/benefit ratio for a medication to be used with children and adolescents needs to be fully considered. Second, medication should always be integrated as part of a comprehensive treatment plan. Third, target symptoms should be carefully considered; medication should be used to address the primary symptoms targeted for change. Fourth, children and adolescents should be monitored carefully for minimum appropriate dose, emergence of adverse effects, efficacy of a particular medication, and drug interactions. Fifth, informed consent should be obtained from a guardian before administration of psychotropic agents (AACAP, 1999). Finally, practitioners always must be cognizant that the majority of research on psychotropic medications with people with mental retardation has been with adult populations rather than with pediatric populations. Thus, there is a scant database in which to guide psychopharmacological treatments with children and adolescents.

Medication effects in children and adolescents with mental retardation are usually the same as the general population, and no hard evidence exists that intellectual functioning changes the mechanism of action of psychotropic drugs in these children (AACAP, 1999). There is some suggestion, however, that the effects of medication may differ for children with mental retardation with comorbid neurological disturbances than their peers without such coexisting conditions. This is evidenced in some of the adverse effects associated with some psychotropic medications that are used for children and adolescents with mental retardation. For example, sensitivity to disinhibiting effects of sedative-hypnotic agents are more likely to occur in some children and adolescents with mental retardation than in the general population, and anticholinergic adverse effects (e.g., delirium, dry mouth, and sedation) may be more prominent in pediatric populations with Down syndrome (AACAP, 1999). Anticholinergic drugs include the antihistamines hydroxyzine (Atarax, Vistril), diphenhydramine (Benadryl), and promethazine (Phenergan). Thus, astute practitioners must be judicious in the use of psychotropic medications that have not previously been evaluated for children and adolescents with mental retardation, particularly when there are comorbid neurological disorders.

Assessment, monitoring, and careful follow-up for adverse effects are important, as children and adolescents with mental retardation may be unable to adequately self-report adverse effects. This is especially important for extrapyramidal symptoms (i.e., adverse neurological effects that may be classified according to the part of the body they affect or whether they occur in the short term or are idiosyncratic), tardive dyskinesia (i.e., abnormal voluntary movements that involve muscles of any part of the body but most frequently affect muscles of the mouth, face, tongue, jaw, or limbs), and akathisia (i.e., motor restlessness, with children or adolescents appearing very agitated and reporting that they feel driven). The use of standardized side-effect rating scales can be helpful, such as the Abnormal Involuntary Movement Scale (Kaplan & Sadock, 1998) and the Stimulant Side Effects Rating Scale (Barkley, 1981). Medications should be used only if there is clear evidence that the benefits of pharmacotherapy outweigh the adverse effects and possible risks. Dose reduction and discontinuation should be gradual, as should be initiation of medication. There is no established optimal rate of drug taper.

Medication Management of Specific Co-occurring Symptoms

Children and adolescents with mental retardation frequently demonstrate associated symptoms, including disturbances in mood, problems with attention and concentration, aggression, and perseverative behaviors. These co-occurring symptoms are likely associated with central nervous system abnormalities and brain dysmorphology that are often characteristic of children and adolescents with mental retardation. For this reason, we review the literature, albeit limited, as it pertains to children and adolescents with coexisting conditions. Table 7.1 presents medications that have been clinically validated in double-blind studies, whereas Table 7.2 lists medications tested in open studies. In Table 7.3, we list the medications that may possibly be dangerous or ineffective for children and adolescents with developmental disabilities.

Mood Disturbances

In recent years, clinicians have been increasingly aware of the high comorbidity of depressive symptoms among children with mental retardation (Bregman, 1996). However, few controlled trials of antidepressant medications have been conducted with children and adolescents with mental retardation. An open trial of fluoxetine (Prozac) at 20–70 mg/day was conducted in 8 children and adolescents with mild to profound mental retardation with coexisting disturbances of mood and impulse control (Cook, Rowlett, Jaselskis, & Leventhal, 1992). Six children were characterized as responders. Venlafaxine (Effexor) and buspirone (BuSpar) also have been demonstrated to be effective for the management of associated mood disturbances, anxiety, and irritability in this population (Botteron & Geller, 1999). Clearly, additional double-blind, placebo-controlled studies are needed, given the relatively frequent occurrence of comorbid symptoms among children and adolescents with developmental disorders.

In several open-label lithium (Eskaloth, Lithane, Lithobid, Lithonate) trials involving children and adolescents with cyclic mood disorders, 50%– 75% of the patients derived significant benefit and relief of symptoms (Linter, 1987; McCracken & Diamond, 1988). Cognitive dulling may occur and may be a rate-limiting adverse effect (Poindexter et al., 1998). Because adverse effects on cognitive functioning are of concern among children and adolescents with mental retardation, particularly in the classroom setting, ongoing monitoring of cognitive effects is imperative.

Valproic acid (Depakote, Depakene) has been successfully used for children and adults with mental retardation and cyclic mood disorders (Poindexter et al., 1998). The target symptoms of irritability and behavioral

TABLE 7.1
Medications Clinically Validated in Double-Blind Studies for the Treatment of Developmental Disorders

Generic Name (Trade Name)	Children mg/kg/day or Daily Dose	Adolescents mg/kg/day or Daily Dose	Treatment Outcome	Adverse Effect
Chlorpromazine (Thorazine)	1/4 mg per lb of body weight	1/4 mg per lb of body weight	Reduction in combativeness, explosive, destructive, and perseverative behaviors.	Lowered seizure threshold, sedation, and impaired cognition and learning. Risk of involuntary dyskinetic movements and other extrapyramidal side effects.
Clomipramine (Anafranil)	1–3 mg/kg	1–3 mg/kg	Reduction of obsessive–compulsive, repetitive stereotyped behaviors, and overactivity. Improved social relatedness.	Drowsiness, dizziness, dry mouth, headaches, and fatigue.
Clonidine (Catapres)	0.3–0.5 mg	0.3–0.5 mg	Reduction of overarousal, aggression, and repetitive behaviors.	10% reduction in blood pressure requires close monitoring. Sedation and fatigue are common.
Haloperidol (Haldol)	0.25–6.0 mg/kg	1.0–1.6 mg/kg	Reduction in self-injurious and perseverative behaviors.	Moderate involuntary dyskinetic movements and other extrapyramidal side effects.
Methylphenidate (Ritalin)	5–20 mg	5–20 mg	Improvement in on-task behavior, academic productivity, attentional skills, and hyperactivity.	Appetite suppressant, insomnia, and irritability.
Pimozide (Orap)	Not yet established	0.5 mg/kg	Reduction in sterotypical behaviors, angry affect, and tics.	Hepatic toxicity, tardive dyskinesia, and neuroleptic malignant syndrome.
Risperidone (Risperdal)	0.25–6 mg	0.5–6 mg	Reduction in aggression, self-injurious behaviors, and temper tantrums. Improvement in social relatedness.	Sedation and involuntary dyskinetic movements and extrapyramidal side effects.
Thioridazine (Mellaril)	10–200 mg	50–600 mg	Reduction in destructive behavior, aggression, perseveration, and agitation.	Sedation and anticholinergic side effects (dry eyes, mouth, and throat; blurred vision). Lowered seizure threshold.

Note. Sources include Aman, White, Vaithianathan, and Teehan (1986); Aman, Marks, Turbott, Wilsher, and Merry (1991a, 1991b); Baumeister, Sevin, and King (1998); Fankhauser, Karumanchi, German, and Yates (1992); Gordon, State, Nelson, and Hamburger (1993); Millichamp and Singh (1987); *Physicians' Desk Reference* (1999); and Vanden-Borre et al. (1993).

TABLE 7.2
Medications Clinically Validated in Open Studies for the Treatment of Developmental Disorders

Generic Name (Trade Name)	Children mg/kg/day or Daily Dose	Adolescents mg/kg/day or Daily Dose	Treatment Outcome	Adverse Effect
Buspirone (BuSpar)	15–45 mg	15–45 mg	Reduction in anxiety and irritability.	Dizziness and drowsiness.
Carbamazepine (Tegretol)	Not yet established	400 mg	Reduction in irritability and explosiveness.	Dizziness, drowsiness, and vomiting.
Clomipramine (Anafranil)	3–5 mg/kg	3–5 mg/kg	Reduction in aggression, impulsivity, and obsessive-compulsive behaviors. Improvement in social relatedness and sleeping.	Dizziness, drowsiness, headaches, and dry mouth.
Fluoxetine (Prozac)	20–80 mg	20–80 mg	Reduction in irritability, lethargy, aggression, and stereotypical compulsive behaviors.	Appetite suppression and restlessness.
Lithium (Eskalith, Lithane, Lithobid, Lithonate)	Blood serum levels at 0.6 to 1.2 mEq/L are desirable		Reduction of comorbid manic and mood cycling symptoms.	Cognitive dulling, diarrhea, nausea, and drowsiness.
Naltrexone (Revia)	1.0 mg/kg	1.0 mg/kg	Modest improvements in hyperactivity, restlessness, and irritability.	Mild, transient drowsiness and crying episodes.
Olanazapine (Zyprexa)	Not yet established	Not yet established	Somewhat effective in reduction of sterotypical and perseverative behaviors.	Sedation and anticholinergic side effects (constipation, blurred vision, and dry eyes, mouth, and throat). Safety with children under 12 years of age not yet established.
Paroxetine (Paxil)	10–20 mg	10–20 mg	Reduction in temper tantrums and self-injurious behaviors. Improvement in sleeping.	Drowsiness.
Sertraline (Zoloft)	Up to 200 mg	Up to 200 mg	Reduction in irritability and mood disturbances.	Nausea, diarrhea, insomnia, reduced appetite, and drowsiness.
Valproic Acid (Depakote)	Not yet established	Up to 750 mg	Reduction in irritability, mood cycling, self-injurious behavior, and aggression.	Nausea, vomiting, and indigestion.
Venlafaxine (Effexor)	12–50 mg	12–50 mg	Reduction in repetitive behaviors, inattention, and hyperactivity. Improvement in social relatedness.	Nausea, headaches, insomnia, dry mouth, and hair loss.

Note. Sources include Brasic, Barnett, Kaplan, and Sheitman (1994); Buitelaar et al. (1998); Fatemi, Realmuto, Khan, and Thuras (1998); Findling, Maxwell, and Wizniter (1997); Hollander, Kaplan, Cartwright, and Reichman (2000); McCracken and Diamond (1988); McDougle et al. (1992); Nicholson, Awad, and Sloman (1998); Perel, Alcami, and Bilaberte (1999); *Physicians' Desk Reference* (1999); Poindexter et al. (1998); Posey, Litwiller, Koburn, and McDougle (1999); and Snead, Boon, and Presberg (1994).

TABLE 7.3
Medications That Are Dangerous or Not Effective for Children and Adolescents With Developmental Disorders

Generic Name (Trade Name)	Adverse Effect and Cautionary Statement
Clomipramine (Anafranil)	There is a significant risk for seizure exacerbation. Clinicians are encouraged to carefully consider its use.
Clozapine (Clozaril)	Significant risk of agranulocytosis and seizures. Not recommended for routine use.
Fenfluramine (Pondimin, Ponderex)	There is a potential risk for long-term irreversible changes in 5HT neurons. Not recommended as a routine treatment for most children and adolescents with autistic disorders. Confirmed reports of pulmonary hypertension and cardiac valvopathy have resulted in removal of this medication from the market.
Quetiapine (Jeroquel)	No improvement in behavior, poorly tolerated, hyperphagia, and weight gain.

Note. Sources include Fisman (1997); Werry and Aman (1999).

cycling seem to be the most responsive to valproic acid, although self-injurious behavior and aggression also have been found to improve in several open clinical trials (Kastner, Finesmith, & Walsh, 1993; Sovner, 1989). Newer antiepileptic drugs, such as gabapentin (Neurontin) and lamotrigine (Lamictal), hold potential promise as treatments for cyclic mood disorders in children and adolescents with mental retardation, although further investigation is necessary, especially with regard to safety and efficacy.

Attention Deficit Hyperactivity Disorder

Children with mental retardation frequently have symptoms associated with attention deficit hyperactivity disorder (ADHD; Gadow, 1985). In an investigation of 12 children whose IQs ranged from 50 to 74 and who also met diagnostic criteria for ADHD, Handen, Breaux, Gosling, Ploof, and Feldman (1990) examined the efficacy of methylphenidate (Ritalin) compared with a placebo. Findings revealed significant improvements for 75% of the children in the areas of on-task behavior, academic productivity, and attention skills. However, consistent with the ADHD literature, improvements were not observed in the areas of learning and social interactions with peers. The data were interpreted to support the notion that stimulant medication exerts similar effects in children who are diagnosed with mental retardation as in their normally developing peers.

Aman, Marks, Turbott, Wilsher, and Merry (1991b) found that for children with comorbid mental retardation and ADHD, stimulant medication reduced teachers' ratings of disruptive and problem behaviors, but parental ratings revealed no improvements as a function of the medication.

Ratings completed by parents and teachers revealed that a more favorable response was associated with children who were of higher intelligence. Children who were lower functioning were found to have more adverse effects associated with the stimulant medication, although other studies by this same research group have not confirmed these findings (Handen et al., 1992; Handen, Janosky, McAuliffe, Breaux, & Feldman, 1994). Similarly, Aman, Kern, McGhee, and Arnold (1993) found that children with intelligence quotients above 45 responded more favorably to stimulant medication than did their peers with IQs below 45. In fact, Aman, Marks, Turbott, Wilsher, and Merry (1991a) found that thioridazine (Mellaril), a low-potency neuroleptic agent used frequently to treat people with mental retardation, produced less absolute change on behavioral ratings of inattention and global ratings of behavior in children with mental retardation than did stimulant medication. These data are important because they suggest that intelligence may be associated with positive response to stimulant medication in children with mental retardation. More important, the data offer an alternative to the neuroleptic medications that frequently have been used with children and adolescents with mental retardation and that have been associated with a host of adverse effects including cognitive toxicities (for a review, see Brown & Sawyer, 1998).

In another double-blind investigation of methylphenidate versus placebo, Handen et al. (1992) examined 14 children whose IQs ranged from 48 to 74. Findings revealed that over half of the sample responded positively to methylphenidate, with significant improvements evidenced with on-task behaviors and attention and concentration. Consistent with the findings of Handen et al. (1990), no improvements on learning and social behavior were observed. Finally, Handen, Feldman, Gosling, Breaux, and McAuliffe (1991) reviewed the incidence of adverse effects of stimulant medication in children with mental retardation. They concluded that children with mental retardation may be at greater risk for developing motor tics and social withdrawal.

Aman and colleagues (1993) studied 28 children who ranged in age from 4 to 13 years in a double-blind, placebo-controlled crossover study comparing methylphenidate (Ritalin) to fenfluramine (Pondimin, Ponderax). Findings revealed that methylphenidate and fenfluramine were superior to placebo, with slightly better performance with methylphenidate on laboratory tests of sustained and selective attention, visual and color matching, and teacher ratings of overactivity and irritability. Again, consistent with the other studies reviewed, none of the children with severe mental retardation evidenced improvement in behavior on either of the active medications when compared with placebos.

In summary, the stimulants generally have demonstrated similar efficacy in children with mental retardation as they have in children diagnosed only with ADHD. There is a significant association between intellectual functioning and positive response to the stimulant medications, with higher functioning children evidencing more positive response. More important, the stimulants offer a viable alternative to the use of other medications where safety has not yet been fully established.

Aggression and Self-Injurious Behaviors

Disruptive behavior is probably the most common reason that psychotropic medication is initiated for children and adolescents with mental retardation. The most concerning disruptive behaviors are aggression and self-injurious behavior; nearly 33%–50% of institutionalized residents exhibit aggression, and 10%–20% exhibit self-injurious behavior (Aman et al., 1993; Baumeister et al., 1993). Between 1% and 6.5% of noninstitutionalized individuals with mental retardation exhibit self-injurious behavior (Baumeister et al., 1993). The pathogenesis of aggression and self-injurious behavior is quite different, and responses to medications are not uniform, particularly for children and adolescents with mental retardation (AACAP, 1999). Frequently, these problems may be symptomatic of a comorbid psychiatric disorder (Bregman, 1996).

The choice of medication can be guided by examining the dopamine, serotonin, and noradrenergic and endogenous opioid systems. Hypersensitivity of D1 dopamine receptors appears to provoke self-injurious behavior in animal and human models (Aman et al., 1993). D1 dopamine antagonists effectively block this self-injurious behavior response. Abnormalities of serotonin metabolism have been associated with impulse control problems and destructive behavior. The endogenous opioid system appears to be involved in the pathogenesis of self-injurious behavior, either by overactivity or by underactivity (Bregman, 1996).

Neuroleptic medications have been the most extensively used and studied in the mental retardation population, particularly for decreasing disruptive and self-injurious behavior in residential settings (Baumeister et al., 1993). However, there is a paucity of well-controlled studies with these agents, particularly with pediatric populations. Symptom suppression appears to be nonspecific; multiple target behaviors often improve simultaneously (Baumeister, Sevin, & King, 1998). However, disruptive, destructive, and repetitive patterns of behavior tend to cluster. Controlled trials involving various neuroleptics, such as chlorpromazine (Thorazine), thioridazine (Mellaril), and risperidone (Risperdal), have revealed significantly decreased destructive behavior in both adolescents and adults (Aman, White, Vaithianathan, & Teehan, 1986; Millichamp & Singh, 1987; Vanden-Borre et al., 1993).

The neuroleptic medications (i.e., chlorpromazine, thioridazine, haloperidol [Haldol], and pimozide [Orap]) have been used most frequently with individuals with mental retardation who have comorbid behavioral disturbances, including self-injurious behavior. However, the majority of studies that have examined the safety and efficacy of these agents have been with adults with mental retardation residing in residential treatment centers (for a review, see Ernst et al., 1999; Gadow, 1999). Few studies have examined the safety and efficacy of the neuroleptics in the management of disruptive behavior in children and adolescents with mental retardation (Aman et al., 1991a; Claghorn, 1992; Goldberg & Kurland, 1974). A chief concern with the prolonged use of neuroleptic medications is the occurrence of possible irreversible adverse effects, including tardive dyskinesia. In addition, some of these agents have been found to lower seizure threshold, cause sedation, and impair cognition and learning.

Millichamp and Singh (1987) conducted a double-blind controlled trial to assess the effects of intermittent neuroleptic drug therapy on stereotyped behaviors in 6 individuals with profound mental retardation who ranged in age from 12 to 37 years. All of the individuals were receiving the neuroleptic medications for a period of 3 years. Upon reduction of the dose of medication, no decrements in functioning were observed. The findings are important because many individuals who reside in residential treatment facilities are administered large doses of neuroleptic medications on a long-term basis. The findings by Millichamp and Singh would suggest that the dose may be tapered without losing the therapeutic effects of the medication. Despite these encouraging results, the data are limited to the treatment of stereotyped behavior, and whether the findings are generalizable for self-injurious behavior is not certain. Much more research will need to be conducted regarding the safety and efficacy of neuroleptic agents, particularly over the course of time for children and adolescents. There is a dearth of well-controlled studies, and hence little information is available to guide pharmacological management.

Perseverative Behavior and Stereotyped Behavior

Neuroleptics have also been used to manage stereotyped and perseverative behaviors, and stereotyped behaviors are generally decreased with neuroleptics (Aman, Teehan, White, Turbott, & Vaithianathan, 1989). Chlorpromazine, thioridazine, and haloperidol have been reported to reduce stereotyped behaviors (Baumeister et al., 1998). As neuroleptics have significant adverse effects in children and adolescents, including cognitive toxicities, potential alternative agents are being explored. The atypical antipsychotics, such as risperidone (Risperdal) and olanzapine (Zyprexa), hold some promise, although no controlled studies in either children or adults with mental retardation have been completed to date. Clinical and anecdotal evidence suggests that these newer agents have fewer cognitive toxicities and adverse effects (Werry & Aman, 1999).

Because of their relatively benign side-effect profile, the selective serotonin reuptake inhibitors (SSRIs) have been investigated for stereotyped and perseverative behavior. Fluoxetine (Prozac) was found to be of benefit in decreasing perseverative, compulsive, and stereotyped behavior in several open clinical trials (Cook et al., 1992; Ricketts, Goza, Ellis, Singh, & Singh, 1993) in children and adolescents with developmental disorders. Although these data are encouraging, controlled trials are needed to further evaluate the efficacy and safety of the specific serotonin reuptake inhibitors for children and adolescents with developmental disabilities, particularly in the long term.

Psychosocial Interventions

It is well accepted that mental retardation is a multidisciplinary problem and that optimal treatment and management is multimodal in nature. Treatment strategies in the area of mental retardation focus mainly on decreasing associated complications, such as treating behavioral and mood disorders (King et al., 1998). As with any behavioral problems, concrete target goals should be established, with the overall aim of achieving a feasible improvement in the quality of life of these children and adolescents. When disruptive behavior is encountered, the goal should not only be to suppress the child's behavior but also to replace it with constructive, adaptive behaviors (AACAP, 1999). Functional analysis of behavior is increasingly used as part of the behavioral treatment plan for children with mental retardation and behavior problems. This analysis involves a detailed examination of antecedent events, behavioral consequences, and the function that maladaptive behavior serves to the child (King et al., 1998). Four possible functions of maladaptive behavior are (a) avoid or escape tasks, (b) acquire adult or peer attention, (c) gain access to a privilege or object, and (d) acquire sensory stimulation (Horner, 1994). To determine the appropriate intervention for an individual, one must understand the function of behavior. If the function of behavior is to avoid work demands, an appropriate strategy may be to eliminate opportunities for negative reinforcement through task avoidance, to make the work more exciting and novel, and to provide positive reinforcement for task initiation and persistence. If the function of behavior is to gain peer attention, an effective strategy may be to reduce opportunities for acquiring peer attention for maladaptive behavior and to increase opportunities for peer attention through prosocial behaviors (Northup et al., 1995). Punishment through the use of response cost (i.e., privilege removal) and timeout procedures can be effective in reducing opportunities to gain positive reinforcement for unwanted behaviors. The use of more aversive punishment techniques, such as seclusion procedures, is generally not recommended.

Parent training as well as school-based treatment programming also has been demonstrated to be important treatment adjuncts for children and adolescents with mental retardation who have comorbid behavioral disturbances. In particular, close collaboration with school authorities becomes increasingly important as the child becomes involved in a greater range of settings within the school program and as tasks become increasingly more complex, which may result in a great deal of frustration and potentially disruptive behavior (for a review, see Kobe & Mulick, 1995). Finally, the use of social skills training, and staff and peer training has been efficacious in enhancing generalization of skills and behaviors across settings and domains (Matson & Coe, 1992).

AUTISTIC SPECTRUM DISORDERS

Autistic spectrum disorders, or the pervasive developmental disorders, are lifelong neuropsychiatric syndromes of childhood. Autistic disorder, Asperger's disorder, Rett's disorder, childhood disintegrative disorder, and pervasive developmental disorder not otherwise specified are part of a spectrum of pervasive developmental disorders. The most important clinical manifestation of autism is markedly abnormal or impaired development in communication and social interaction. Autistic spectrum disorders are also characterized by a markedly restrictive repertoire of activities and interests (American Psychiatric Association, 1994). These symptoms may be manifested differently at various chronological ages. Autistic disorder is typically the severe end of a spectrum of difficulties and is the primary focus of this discussion.

Autism is typically considered a disorder of childhood; however, most people with autism have significant functional impairment throughout the life span. Long-term outcome studies reveal that only 5%–10% are independent as adults, 25% make progress but still require close supervision, and the remainder are severely impaired and require intensive intervention and care (Kaplan & Sadock, 1998).

Cognitive competence and adequacy of social skills and relationships are major determinants of outcome in adult life. Approximately 70%–75% of people with autism have intelligence scores below 70 with uneven skill development (Gillberg, 1993). Deficits are usually more marked in verbal skills, especially in the area of language comprehension. Likewise, children with autism may show hyperactivity and impulsivity and have a short attention span. They may have a high threshold for pain, oversensitivity to sound and touch, and preoccupation with the smell or feel of objects. There may be abnormalities of mood or affect and inappropriate (excessive or lack of) reaction to perceived dangers. Finally, children with autism may demonstrate temper tantrums, aggression, and a variety of self-injurious behaviors, including head banging, self-biting, or poking of various body orifices.

The precise etiology of autism remains unknown, although biological factors related to brain structure (primarily cerebellum) and neurochemical dysfunction (primarily in the serotonergic system) have been suggested (Hollander, Kaplan, et al., 2000). Neuroanatomical studies involving autopsied brain samples from patients with autism have revealed structural alterations, including a loss of purkinje cells in the hippocampus, amygdala, and cerebellum. Immunological, prenatal, postnatal, and genetic factors are also believed to play a role in the pathophysiological mechanisms of autistic spectrum disorders (Hollander, Cartwright, et al., 1998). Frontal lobe dysfunction has been strongly implicated in the pathophysiology of autism by functional imaging, autopsy findings, and neuropsychological evidence. In summary, findings associated with brain morphology in autism have been reported in various brain regions. This neuroanatomical heterogeneity most likely reflects etiological heterogeneity.

An interdisciplinary assessment is required for a comprehensive diagnostic evaluation and treatment of individuals suspected of having autistic spectrum disorders. This includes an etiological work-up, an assessment of communicative and social skills, functional assessments of behavioral strengths and weaknesses, and an individualized treatment plan that includes educational, behavioral, pharmacological, social, and other indicated medical interventions.

A detailed history should be obtained, with particular emphasis on specific symptoms typical of autism and on associated features, early development, course of development, and progress. A mental status examination should attempt to assess (a) the child's relatedness to and interest in the professional, caregiver, siblings, peers, and other people in the child's environment; (b) the quality of reciprocal social exchange in verbal and nonverbal communication (e.g., eye contact, gestures, facial expression, stereotyped speech, echolalia, and pronominal reversal); (c) the child's ability to engage in reciprocal imaginative play with representational toys; (d) presence of perseverative, stereotyped, and ritualistic behavior; and (e) presence of problematic behaviors. The child's adaptive functioning should be assessed to determine the ability to adapt to environmental demands.

TREATMENT OF AUTISTIC SPECTRUM DISORDERS

Medical Interventions

Pharmacological interventions to reduce or eliminate maladaptive and injurious behaviors often have an important place in the treatment of autism. A survey of 838 care providers of children and adolescents with autism revealed that over one third (34%) of the sample received psychotropic drugs or vitamin supplements (Aman, Van Bourgondien, Wolford,

& Sarphare, 1995). It is imperative that pharmacotherapy be instituted only in conjunction with a comprehensive individualized behavioral and family treatment program. Pharmacological intervention may increase the ability of children and adolescents with autism to benefit to a greater extent from educational and other interventions (McDougle, 1997). It is important to note that there are no medications that specifically address the core symptoms of autism; rather they manage associated behavioral disturbances associated with autism.

Even though a specific etiology has not been identified for autism and research points to a multifactorial cause of the disorder, certain neurochemical systems may be particularly relevant to the treatment of autism and have been the basis of much psychopharmacological research. For clinical purposes, pharmacological intervention in autism is usually designed to address specific target symptoms, with emphasis placed on addressing attention problems, aggression, ritualistic or stereotyped behaviors, self-injurious behaviors, and seizures. As with other medications, extreme care should be taken in the selection and administration of psychotropic medications (AACAP, 1999). Children and adolescents with autism are often nonverbal, and therefore reliance on caregiver reports and observations of specific behaviors is common. Close follow-up is recommended to assess the efficacy of medication, side-effect profiles, and continued need for medication. No clear end point of medication administration exists because of the lifelong nature of the disorder. Often, long-term medication administration is needed.

Disorders of Impulse Control

The most common reason for starting medication in people with autism is hyperarousal and disruptive behavior, including aggression, hyperactivity, self-injurious behaviors, and stereotyped behaviors. Symptom suppression may be nonspecific as improvement in multiple target behaviors is often seen. Dopamine antagonists have been the most frequently used psychopharmacological agents in the treatment of autism to address disruptive behavior. Most recent studies have been with risperidone (Risperdal), an atypical antipsychotic that is a potent dopamine D2/serotonin (5HT) receptor antagonist with powerful antipsychotic properties (Remington, 1993). In an open clinical trial, risperidone showed clinical efficacy in the reduction of aggression and other behavioral problems for 13 of 20 children, ages 8–17 years, who were previously refractory to other psychotropic medications. Adverse effects included weight gain (in 3 patients) and galactorrhea (production of breast milk) in 2 adolescent girls (Hardan, Johnson, Johnson, & Hrecznyj, 1996). A 12-week, prospective, systematic, open-label trial of risperidone in 18 adult participants (15 male and 3 female) with pervasive developmental disorder, 14 of whom had comorbid mental retardation, demonstrated significant improvement in aggression, impulsivity, and some elements of impaired social relatedness. Two thirds of the participants (n = 12) were considered responders, with 50% of participants described as much improved. Risperidone helped reduce repetitive behavior, aggression, and impulsivity at clinically significant levels despite the small sample size (McDougle et al., 1998). In another study, Horrigan and Barnhill (1997) found substantial clinical improvement in aggression, self-injury, explosivity, and poor sleep hygiene in males with autism (n = 11) with mental retardation using risperidone. An open clinical trial of risperidone monotherapy in 6 children (ages 5–9 years) resulted in improved symptomatology for all participants on a mean dose of 1.1 mg. Optimal dosages in the studies ranged from 1 to 4 mg/day. All studies revealed weight gain to be the most significant adverse effect, with a few patients experiencing sedation. Risperidone was generally quite well-tolerated. No clinically significant difficulties with blood pressure, heart rate, respiratory rate, acute extrapyramidal symptoms, seizures, or cardiac events were evident. There have been case reports of possible tardive dyskinesia and neuroleptic malignant syndrome (Horrigan & Barnhill, 1997), but at low doses these serious adverse effects are uncommon.

There are currently few studies in this population of treatment of hyperarousal and disruptive behavior with other atypical antipsychotics. Olanzapine (Zyprexa) at doses up to 20 mg daily successfully reduced aggressive and disruptive behavior in 2 children with autism, mental retardation, and bipolar disorder (Horrigan, Barnhill, & Courvoisie, 1997). Olanzapine also was effective in reducing hyperactivity and aggressive behavior in an 8-year-old with autism (Malek-Ahmadi & Simonds, 1998). An open-label clinical trial of quetiapine (Jeroquel), another atypical antipsychotic, was conducted in 6 children and adolescents with autism (Martin, Koenig, Scahill, & Bregman, 1999). After the 16-week trial, it was concluded that the group as a whole displayed no statistically significant improvement between baseline and follow-up; additionally, quetiapine was poorly tolerated and associated with serious adverse effects (behavioral activation, hyperphagia, weight gain, as well as 1 participant with a seizure; Martin et al., 1999). Clozapine (Clozaril) has a significant associated risk of agranulocytosis and seizures and is therefore not recommended for routine use (Fisman, 1997). In general, the newer atypical antipsychotic medications appear to pose less long-term risk of undesired adverse effects than the older neuroleptics and show promise in the treatment of children and adolescents with autism. A frequent adverse effect is marked weight gain with use of risperidone and olanzapine.

The D2 antagonists haloperidol (Haldol) at 0.25–4 mg/day (Anderson et al., 1989; Campbell et al., 1978; Joshi, Capozzoli, & Coyle, 1988) and pimozide (Orap) at 1–9 mg/day (Naruse et al., 1982) have been demonstrated to decrease symptoms of withdrawal, stereotyped behaviors, hyperactivity, fidgetiness, negativism, and angry affect. Haloperidol (Haldol) has been the most extensively studied and in the past has been potentially the most useful medication for symptoms of autism. Thioridazine (Mellaril) is the most useful of the low-potency traditional neuroleptics in decreasing aggression and agitation (Fisman, 1997). These medications have also been shown to increase relatedness and facilitate discrimination learning due to their effects on attention mechanisms. However, traditional neuroleptics should be used with caution and preferably limited to short-term acute management because of many adverse and potentially irreversible long-term side effects, such as tardive dyskinesia, neuroleptic malignant syndrome, and cognitive suppression that may seriously impede learning. It appears that greater cumulative haloperidol doses or longer exposure to haloperidol may increase the risk of dyskinesias (Campbell et al., 1997).

Opiate-blocking agents have been postulated to reduce self-injurious, stereotyped, and aggressive behaviors and to increase prosocial behaviors for children with autism. Several studies have explored the efficacy of naltrexone (Revia), an opiate blocker, in children ranging from ages 3 to 7 years to address symptoms of stereotyped behaviors and aggression (Campbell et al., 1989; Kolmen, Feldman, Handen, & Janosky, 1995, Willemsen-Swinkels, Buitelaar, & van Engeland, 1996). Naltrexone, 1.0 mg/kg, was administered daily in a randomized, double-blind, placebo-controlled cross-over design trial in 13 children with autism who ranged in age from 3 to 8 years. Modest improvements in hyperactivity, restlessness, and communication were noted, with only mild, transient adverse effects (drowsiness, brief episodes of crying, and possibly increased aggressiveness in 2 children; Kolmen et al., 1995). In a double-blind, placebo-controlled crossover study of 23 children diagnosed with autism who ranged in age from 3 to 7 years, teachers significantly favored naltrexone over a placebo because of a noted decrease in hyperactivity and irritability (Willemsen-Swinkels et al., 1996). No significant improvements for the children receiving naltrexone were revealed in parents' ratings of social behavior and on analyses of playroom data.

Hyperactivity and inattention are common problems in individuals with autism. Stimulant medication use in children and adolescents with autism is frequent, despite few studies that have systematically evaluated their efficacy in the autistic population (Aman, Van Bourgondien et al., 1995; Campbell, Shopler, Cueva, & Hallin, 1996). Earlier studies found an increase in stereotyped behaviors and irritability as a function of stimulant medication in children with autism (Campbell et al., 1978). A double-blind crossover study evaluating efficacy of methylphenidate (Ritalin) in children with autism found statistically significant improvement of methylphenidate compared with a placebo on ratings of over-activity. No significant adverse effects occurred on medication (Quintana et al., 1995). Other studies have examined the effect of methylphenidate in the management of overactivity and inattention in children with autism (Aman et al., 1986; Strayhorn, 1989; Strayhorn, Rapp, Donina, & Strain, 1988), and findings have generally revealed that stimulants can be helpful for short attention span, hyperactivity, and impulsivity in some children; however, close follow-up is needed as stimulants may potentially worsen the behavior and stereotypies in some children and adolescents with autism.

The hyperarousal behaviors (e.g., stereotyped body movements, self-stimulation, hypervigilance, and hyperactivity) evidenced in many children with autism have been successfully managed with clonidine (Catapres), an alpha$_2$ adrenergic receptor agonist, in two small double-blind, placebo-controlled studies using oral and transdermal clonidine with both children and adults ranging in age from 5 to 33 years. Sedation and fatigue were noted adverse effects (Fankhauser et al., 1992). Tolerance may develop to the therapeutic, but not sedative, effects of clonidine. Guanfacine (Tenex), another alpha$_2$ agonist, has less sedative side effects, but this medication has not been studied in children with autism.

Uncontrolled rage outbursts are sometimes present in individuals with autism. Valproic acid (Depakote, Depakene), carbamazepine (Tegretol), and propranolol (Inderal) have been found to be effective in such aggressive behaviors (Fisman, 1997; Mattes, Rosenberg, & Mayus, 1984). In individuals with autism, the use of beta blockers have been used with some success (Ratey, Bemporad, & Sorgi, 1987), but conclusions cannot be drawn because of the limited data available.

Obsessive–Compulsive Behaviors

Perseverative, compulsive, and ritualistic behaviors and other symptoms similar with those of obsessive–compulsive disorders are frequently noted in individuals with autism. In this population, it is sometimes difficult to differentiate between perseverative behavior and obsessive–compulsive behavior. The SSRIs inhibit serotonin transport and were initially of interest because of the relatively consistent finding of high peripheral serotonin levels in autism (AACAP, 1999). Potent 5HT reuptake inhibitors—clomipramine (Anafranil), fluoxetine (Prozac), fluvoxamine (Luvox), and sertraline (Zoloft)—have been studied in autism. Clomipramine at 90–170 mg/day in children (Gordon, State, Nelson, & Hamburger, 1993) and fluoxetine at 20 mg every other day to 80 mg/day in children and adults (Cook et al., 1992; DeLong, Teague, & Kamran, 1998; Fatemi, Realmuto, Khan, & Thuras, 1998) have been shown to improve repetitive behaviors, obsessive–compulsive symptomatology, and aggression in children with autism.

Fluoxetine (Prozac) has been evaluated in several open-label and case report studies. Cook et al. (1992) found that fluoxetine was associated with improved level of functioning for children with autism or mental retardation. Fatemi et al. (1998) noted improvement in irritability, lethargy, stereotypy, and inappropriate speech. DeLong et al. (1998) studied 37 children with autism ranging in age from 2 to 7 years; 22 of 37 children had a beneficial treatment response to fluoxetine in behavioral, language, cognitive, affective, and social domains. It also was noted that response to fluoxetine was positively associated with a family history of affective disorder.

Fluvoxamine (Luvox) may be effective in decreasing obsessive–compulsive behaviors. A double-blind, placebo controlled study was completed in adults with autism. About half of this group responded positively with decreased obsessive–compulsive symptomatology (McDougle, 1997).

Clomipramine (Anafranil) is also a potent inhibitor of the serotonin transporter. In a randomized, crossover study of children with autism, clomipramine was found to be superior to desipramine in decreasing overactivity and obsessive–compulsive symptomatology (Gordon, Rapoport, Hamburger, State, & Mannheim, 1992). In a series of case reports, McDougle et al. (1992) found that 4 of 5 adolescents and young adults with autism ranging in age from 13 to 33 years showed significant improvement in social relatedness, obsessive–compulsive symptoms, and aggressive and impulsive behavior. Adverse effects include irritability, aggression, seizures, and electrocardiographic changes (Gordon et al., 1992; McDougle et al., 1997). The potential for seizure exacerbation is clearly a significant risk factor that needs to be carefully considered.

Mood Disorders and Anger Control

Affective symptoms, including affective lability, inappropriate affective responses, anxiety, and depressive symptoms, are frequently seen in individuals with autism. Individuals with higher functioning autism or Asperger's disorder may be at particular risk for depression (Ghaziuddin & Tsai, 1991). The depression observed may respond to antidepressants (Klin & Volkmar, 1997). Rage attacks and cyclical changes in behavior may suggest bipolar illness symptomatology.

Minimal information and studies are available concerning the use of lithium (Eskalith, Lithane, Lithobid, Lithonate) in children with autism, and even less information is available concerning other mood stabilizers. When there is cyclic irritability and explosiveness, with or without aggression, a trial of lithium or the anticonvulsant mood stabilizers such as valproic acid (Depakene, Depakote) or carbamazepine (Tegretol) can decrease symptomatology (Fisman, 1997). In general, lithium has not been shown to have beneficial effects in the core symptoms of autism (Campbell, Anderson, & Small, 1990). However, if clinical features suggest that bipolar disorder may exist comorbidly with autism, lithium may be of benefit, especially if there is a strong family history of bipolar disorder (Steingard & Biederman, 1987). Olanzapine (Zyprexa) at doses up to 20 mg daily successfully reduced aggressive and disruptive behavior in two children with autism, mental retardation, and bipolar disorder (Horrigan et al., 1997). Anticonvulsants are used to treat seizures, mood lability, and aggression in children with autism in the same manner as in children without autism. The disadvantage of all these medications is the need for routine serum drug level monitoring, as well as thyroid and renal function tests with lithium, white blood cell counts with carbamazepine, and liver function tests with valproic acid.

Contraindicated Medications

Based on the findings of dysregulation in 5HT function in some children with autism, several drugs affecting this system have been studied. Fenfluramine (Pondimin, Ponderex) is an indirect 5HT agonist that releases 5HT presynaptically and blocks its reuptake from 5HT neurons. Ongoing administration has been reported to result in a reduction of brain 5HT (Schuster, Lewis, & Seiden, 1986). In an initial double-blind, placebo crossover study with fenfluramine, there was a decrease in whole-blood serotonin concentrations along with an improvement in scales measuring social and sensory functioning and a decrease in abnormal motor movements (Ritvo, Freeman, Geller, & Yiwiler, 1983). Subsequent studies with fenfluramine with children and adolescents have not shown consistent clinical improvement in stereotyped behaviors or in the core symptoms of autism as compared with placebo, and many adverse effects such as weight loss, excessive sedation, loose stools, and irritability have been reported (Campbell et al., 1988). Because of the potential risk of long-term, possibly irreversible changes in 5HT neurons, and the preponderance of studies that have yielded few results, fenfluramine cannot be recommended as a routine treatment for most children and adolescents with autistic disorder (Campbell et al., 1988). Recent confirmed reports of pulmonary hypertension and cardiac valvulopathy in patients exposed to fenfluramine or dexfenfluramine have resulted in removal of this medication from the market (Morbidity and Mortality Weekly Report, 1997; Simonneau et al., 1998).

Psychosocial Interventions

Rutter (1985) advocated the following goals of treatment in children and adolescents with autism: fostering normal development; promoting cognitive, language, and social learning; reducing rigidity and stereotypy; eliminating nonspecific maladaptive behaviors; and alleviating family distress. Treatment programs used in the United States vary widely in philosophy, from the very strict, environmentally structured program of the

TEACCH Program (Treatment and Education of Autistic and Communication-related Handicapped Children; Lord & Schopler, 1994) to the Young Autism Program's use of 40 hours a week of individualized, discrete trial training to teach new skills (Lovaas, Smith, & McEachin, 1989). All of the programs include a structured curriculum teaching attention to environmental stimuli and other people, motor and verbal imitation, comprehension of language, appropriate play with toys, and appropriate interaction with others.

Behavioral approaches are the mainstay of treatment to reduce rigidity, stereotypy, and perseveration and to eliminate maladaptive behaviors such as tantrums, aggression, and self-injurious behavior in children and adolescents with autism (for a review, see Harris, 1995). Antecedents and consequences of disruptive behavior must be examined in the context of a functional assessment of behavior to eliminate potential positive or negative reinforcements increasing the likelihood that the behavior will increase. In some cases, adaptive behavior can be promoted by simply modifying the environment. Stereotyped behaviors tend to increase in unstimulating environments and unstructured situations; hence, structured environments that provide children with meaningful stimulation help encourage more socially accepted behavior. Clinicians should avoid using aversive techniques whenever possible (Elder, 1996).

Gresham, Beebe-Frankenberger, and MacMillan (1999) meticulously reviewed the available treatment programs for children with autism. Conclusions are that there are no well-established empirically supported treatment programs for autism, although nearly all of the programs have documented developmental gains for the children, particularly in the area of intellectual functioning.

CONCLUSION

The use of psychotropic medication for children and adolescents with autism and mental retardation must be recommended on the basis of specific target symptoms for the individual. Nonetheless, it is clear that prescribing practices for these agents far exceed the empirical data that are available for children and adolescents. In particular, little is known about many of the psychotropic agents used with these populations. More important, there are few data regarding long-term efficacy and safety. Particularly, with the neuroleptic agents, there is concern about cognitive toxicities and tardive dyskinesia. Although the newer neuroleptic agents and the stimulants, in some instances, offer a safer alternative to other psychotropic agents for both children and adolescents with mental retardation and autism, more research is needed regarding their long-term efficacy and safety.

The behavioral and psychosocial approaches have been the gold standard in the management of children and adolescents with autism and mental retardation, and there is an array of specialized programs from which practitioners may choose. Additional investigation is needed regarding the relative efficacy of pharmacological approaches compared with behavioral and educational interventions. In particular, studies are needed that evaluate the relative efficacy of behavioral and pharmacological approaches used alone in comparison with combined or multimodal pharmacological and behavioral therapies. It is posited that collaborative approaches to management of these disorders that include behavioral programs and carefully monitored psychotropic medication will prove most efficacious in the management of these children. Likewise, it is anticipated that collaborative approaches will result in therapies that are both effective and safe, and at the same time empirically valid for children and adolescents with developmental disorders. No matter what treatment methods are utilized, clear monitoring of target symptoms during interventions is needed to help these children and adolescents achieve their maximum potential.

REFERENCES

Aman, M. G., Kern, R. A., McGhee, D. E., & Arnold, L. E. (1993). Fenfluramine and methylphenidate in children with mental retardation and ADHD: Clinical and side effects. *Journal of the American Academy of Child and Adolescent Psychiatry, 32,* 851–859.

Aman, M. G., Marks, R. E., Turbott, S. H., Wilsher, C. P., & Merry, S. N. (1991a). Clinical effects of methylphenidate and thioridazine in intellectually subaverage children. *Journal of the American Academy of Child and Adolescent Psychiatry, 30,* 246–256.

Aman, M. G., Marks, R. E., Turbott, S. H., Wilsher, C. P., & Merry, S. N. (1991b). Methylphenidate and thioridazine in the treatment of intellectually subaverage children: Effects on cognitive–motor performance. *Journal of the American Academy of Child and Adolescent Psychiatry, 30,* 816–824.

Aman, M. G., Sarphare, G., & Burrow, W. H. (1995). Psychotropic drugs in group homes: Prevalence and relation to demographic/psychiatric variables. *American Journal of Mental Retardation, 99,* 500–509.

Aman, M. G., & Singh, N. N. (1994). *The Aberrant Behavior Checklist.* East Aurora, NY: Slosson Educational.

Aman, M. G., Teehan C. J., White, A. J., Turbott, S. H., & Vaithianathan, C. (1989). Halperiodal treatment with chronically medicated residents: Dose effects on clinical behavior and reinforcement contingencies. *American Journal of Mental Retardation, 93,* 452–460.

Aman, M. G., Van Bourgondien, M. E., Wolford, P. L., & Sarphare, G. (1995). Psychotropic and anticonvulsant drugs in subjects with autism: Prevalence and patterns of use. *Journal of the American Academy of Child and Adolescent Psychiatry, 34,* 1672–1681.

Aman, M. G., White, A. J., Vaithianathan, C., & Teehan, C. J. (1986). Preliminary study of imipramine in profoundly retarded residents. *Journal of Autism and Developmental Disorder, 16,* 263–273.

American Academy of Child and Adolescent Psychiatry. (1999). Practice parameters for the assessment and treatment of children, adolescents, and adults with mental retardation and comorbid mental disorders. *Journal of the American Academy of Child and Adolescent Psychiatry, 38*(Suppl. 1), 5–31.

American Psychiatric Association. (1994). *Diagnostic and statistical manual of mental disorders* (4th ed.). Washington, DC: Author.

Anderson, L. T., Campbell, M., Adams, P., Small, A. M., Perry, R., & Shell, J. (1989). The effects of haloperidol discrimination learning and behavioral symptoms in autistic children. *Journal of Autism and Developmental Disorders, 19,* 227–239.

Barkley, R. A. (1981). *Hyperactive children: A handbook for diagnosis and treatment.* New York: Guilford Press.

Baumeister, A. A., Sevin, J. A., & King, B. H. (1998). Neuroleptics. In S. Reiss & M. G. Aman (Eds.), *Psychotropic medications and developmental disabilities: The international consensus handbook* (pp. 133–150). Columbus: Ohio State University, Nisonger Center.

Baumeister, A. A., Todd, M. E., & Sevin, J. A. (1993). Efficacy and specificity of pharmacological therapies for behavioral disorders in persons with mental retardation. *Clinical Neuropharmacology, 16,* 271–194.

Borthwick-Duffy, S. A. (1994). Epidemiology and prevalence of psychopathology in people with mental retardation. *Journal of Consulting and Clinical Psychology, 62,* 17–27.

Botteron, K., & Geller, G. (1999). Disorders, symptoms, and their pharmacotherapy. In J. S. Werry & M. G. Aman (Eds.), *Practitioner's guide to psychoactive drugs for children and adolescents* (2nd ed., pp. 183–209). New York: Plenum.

Brasic, J. R., Barnett, J. Y., Kaplan, D., & Sheitman, B. B. (1994). Clomipramine ameliorates adventitous movement and compulsions in prepubertal boys with autistic disorder and severe mental retardation. *Neurology, 44,* 1309–1312.

Bregman, J. D. (1996). Pharmacologic interventions. *Child and Adolescent Psychiatric Clinics of North America, 5,* 853–880.

Brown, R. T., & Sawyer, M. G. (1998). *Medications for school-age children: Effects on learning and behavior.* New York: Guilford Press.

Buitelaar, J. K., Willemsen-Swinkels, S., Van Engeland, H., Kolmen, B. K., Felman, H. M., Handen, B. I., & Janosky, J. E. (1998). Naltrexone in children with autism. *Journal of the American Academy of Child and Adolescent Psychiatry, 37,* 800–802.

Campbell, M., Adams, P., Small, A., Curren E. L., Overall, J. E., Anderson, L. T., Lynch, N., & Perry, R. (1988). Efficacy and safety of fenfluramine in autistic children. *Journal of the American Academy of Child and Adolescent Psychiatry*, *27*, 434–439.

Campbell, M., Anderson, L. T., Meier, M., Cohen, I. L., Small, A. M., Samit C., & Sachar, E. J. (1978). A comparison of haloperidol, behavior therapy and their interaction in autistic children. *Journal of the American Academy of Child Psychiatry*, *17*, 640–655.

Campbell, M., Anderson, L. T., & Small, A. M. (1990). Pharmacotherapy in autism: A summary of research at Bellevue/New York University. *Brain Dysfunction*, *3*, 299–307.

Campbell, M., Armenteros, J. L., Malone, R. P., Adams, P. B., Eisenberg, Z. W., & Overall, J. E. (1997). Neuroleptic-related dyskinesias in autistic children: A prospective, longitudinal study. *Journal of the American Academy of Child and Adolescent Psychiatry*, *36*, 835–843.

Campbell, M., Overall, J. E., Small, A. M., Sokol, M. S., Spencer, E. K., Adams, P., Foltz, R. L., Monti, K. M., Perry R., & Nobler, M. (1989). Naltrexone in autistic children: An acute open dose range tolerance trial. *Journal of the American Academy of Child and Adolescent Psychiatry*, *28*, 200–206.

Campbell, M., Shopler, E., Cueva, J. E., & Hallin, A. (1996). Treatment of autistic disorder. *Journal of the American Academy of Child and Adolescent Psychiatry*, *35*, 134–143.

Claghorn, J. L. (1992). A double-blind comparison of haloperidol (Haldol) and thioridazine (Mellanil) in outpatient children. *Current Therapeutic Research Clinical and Experimental Journal*, *14*, 785–789.

Cook, E. H., Rowlett, R., Jaselskis, C., & Leventhal, B. L. (1992). Fluoxetine treatment of children and adults with autistic disorder and mental retardation. *Journal of the American Academy of Child and Adolescent Psychiatry*, *31*, 739–745.

DeLong, G. R., Teague, L. A., & Kamran, M. M. (1998). Effects of fluoxetine treatment in young children with idiopathic autism. *Developmental Medicine and Child Neurology*, *40*, 551–562.

Elder, J. H. (1996). Behavioral treatment of children with autism, mental retardation, and related disabilities: Ethics and efficacy. *Journal of Child and Adolescent Nursing*, *9*, 28–38.

Ernst, M., Malone, R. P., Rowan, A. B., George, R., Gonzalez, N. M., & Silva, R. R. (1999). Antipsychotics (neuroleptics). In J. S. Werry & M. G. Aman (Eds.), *Practitioner's guide to psychoactive drugs for children and adolescents* (2nd ed., pp. 297–320). New York: Plenum.

Fankhauser, M. P., Karumanchi, V. C., German, M. K., & Yates, A. (1992). A double-blind placebo-controlled study of the efficacy of transdermal clonidine in autism. *Journal of Clinical Psychiatry*, *53*, 77–82.

Fatemi, S. H., Realmuto, G. M., Khan, L., & Thuras, P. (1998). Fluoxetine in the treatment of adolescent patients with autism: A longitudinal open trial. *Journal of Autism and Developmental Disorders*, *28*, 303–307.

Findling, R. L., Maxwell, K., & Wizniter, M. (1997). An open clinical trial of risperidone monotherapy in young children with autistic disorder. *Psychopharmacology Bulletin, 33,* 155–159.

Fisman, S. (1997). Pharmacotherapy of the pervasive developmental disorders: A practical approach. *Child and Adolescent Psychopharmacology News, 2*(4), 1–4.

Gadow, K. D. (1985). Relative efficacy of pharmacological, behavioral, and combination treatments for enhancing academic performance. *Clinical Psychology Review, 5,* 513–533.

Gadow, K. D. (1999). Prevalence of drug therapy. In J. S. Werry & M. G. Aman (Eds.), *Practitioner's guide to psychoactive drugs for children and adolescents* (2nd ed., pp. 51–69). New York: Plenum.

Ghaziuddin, M., & Tsai, L. (1991). Depression in autistic disorder. *British Journal of Psychiatry, 159,* 721–723.

Gillberg, C. (1993). Autism and related behaviors. *Journal of Intellectual Disabilities Research, 37,* 343–372.

Goldberg, J. B., & Kurland, A. A. (1974). Pinozide in the treatment of behavioral disorders of hospitalized adolescents. *Journal of Clinical Pharmacology, 14,* 134–139.

Gordon, C. T., Rapoport, J. L., Hamburger, S. D., State, R. C., & Mannheim, G. B. (1992). Differential response of seven subjects with autistic disorder to clomipramine and desipramine. *American Journal of Psychiatry, 149,* 363–366.

Gordon, C. T., State, R. C., Nelson, J. E., & Hamburger, S. D. (1993). A double-blind comparison of clomipramine, desipramine, and placebo in the treatment of autistic disorder. *Archives of General Psychiatry, 50,* 441–447.

Gresham, F. M., Beebe-Frankenberger, M. E., & MacMillan, D. L. (1999). A selective review of treatment for children with autism: Description and methodological considerations. *School Psychology Review, 28,* 559–575.

Handen, B. L., Breaux, A. M., Gosling, A., Ploof, D. L., & Feldman, H. (1990). Efficacy of methylphenidate among mentally retarded children with attention deficit hyperactivity disorder. *Pediatrics, 86,* 922–930.

Handen, B. L., Breaux, A. M., Jonosky, J., McAuliffe, S., Feldman, H., & Gosling, A. (1992). Effects and noneffects of methylphenidate in children with mental retardation and ADHD. *Journal of the American Academy of Child and Adolescent Psychiatry, 31,* 455–561.

Handen, B. L., Feldman, H., Gosling, A., Breaux, A. M., & McAuliffe, S. (1991). Averse side effects of methylphenidate among mentally retarded children with ADHD. *Journal of the American Academy of Child and Adolescent Psychiatry, 30,* 241–245.

Handen, B. L., Janosky, J., McAuliffe, S., Breaux, A. M., & Feldman, H. (1994). Prediction of response of methylphenidate among children with ADHD and mental retardation. *Journal of the American Academy of Child and Adolescent Psychiatry, 33,* 1185–1193.

Hardan, A., Johnson, K., Johnson, C., & Hrecznyj, B. (1996). Case study: Risperidone treatment of children and adolescents with developmental disorders.

Journal of the American Academy of Child and Adolescent Psychiatry, 35, 1551–1556.

Harris, S. L. (1995). Educational strategies in autism. In E. Schopler & G. B. Mesibor (Eds.), *Learning and cognition in autism: Current issues in autism* (pp. 293–309). New York: Plenum.

Harris, S. L., Delmolino, L., & Glasberg, B. A. (1996). Psychological and behavioral assessment in mental retardation. *Child and Adolescent Psychiatric Clinics of North America, 5,* 797–808.

Hollander, E., Cartwright, C., Wong, C. M., DeCaria, C. M., DelGiudice-Asch, G., Buchsbaum, M. S., & Aronowitz, B. R. (1998). A dimensional approach to the autism spectrum. *CNS Spectrums, 3,* 22–39.

Hollander, E., Kaplan, A., Cartwright, C., & Reichman, D. (2000). Venlafaxine in children, adolescents, and young adults with autism spectrum disorders: An open retrospective report. *Journal of Child Neurology, 15,* 132–135.

Horner, R. H. (1994). Functional assessment: Contributions and future directions. *Journal of Applied Behavior Analysis, 27,* 401–404.

Horrigan, J. P., & Barnhill, L. J. (1997). Risperidone and explosive aggressive autism. *Journal of Autism and Developmental Disorders, 27,* 313–323.

Horrigan, J. P., Barnhill, L. J., & Courvoisie, H. E. (1997). Olanzapine in PDD. *Journal of the American Academy of Child and Adolescent Psychiatry, 36,* 1166–1167.

Joshi, P. T., Capozzoli, J. A., & Coyle, J. T. (1988). Low dose neuroleptic therapy for children with childhood onset pervasive developmental disorder. *American Journal of Psychiatry, 145,* 335–338.

Kaplan, H. I., & Sadock, B. J. (1998). *Kaplan and Sadock's synopsis of psychiatry: Behavioral sciences/clinical psychiatry* (8th ed.). Baltimore: Williams & Wilkins.

Kastner, T., Finesmith, R., & Walsh, K. (1993). Long-term administration of valproic acid in the treatment of affective symptoms in people with mental retardation. *Journal of Clinical Psychopharmacology, 13,* 448–451.

King, B. H., State, M. W., Shah, B., Davanzo, P., & Dykens, E. (1998). Mental retardation: A review of the past 10 years. Part I. *Reviews in Child and Adolescent Psychiatry, 36,* 126–133.

Klin, A., & Volkmar, F. R. (1997). Asperger syndrome. In D. J. Cohen & F. R. Volkmar (Eds.), *Handbook of autism and pervasive developmental disorders* (2nd ed., pp. 94–122). New York: Wiley.

Kobe, F. H., & Mulick, J. A. (1995). Mental retardation. In R. T. Ammerman & M. Hersen (Eds.), *Handbook of child behavior therapy in the psychiatric setting: Wiley series on personality processes* (pp. 153–180). New York: Wiley.

Kolmen, B. K., Feldman, H. M., Handen, B. L., & Janosky, J. E. (1995). Naltroxene in young autistic children: Replication study and learning measures. *Journal of the American Academy of Child and Adolescent Psychiatry, 34,* 223–231.

Linter, C. M. (1987). Short-cycle manic-depressive psychosis in a mentally handicapped child without family history. *British Journal of Psychiatry, 152,* 554–555.

Lord, C., & Schopler, E. (1994). TEACCH services for preschool children. In S. Harris & J. Handleman (Eds.), *Preschool education programs for children with autism* (pp. 176–189). Austin, TX: Pro-Ed.

Lovaas, O. I., Smith, T., & McEachin, J. J. (1989). A comprehensive behavioral theory of autistic children: Paradigm for research and treatment. *Journal of Behavior Therapy and Experimental Psychiatry, 20,* 17–29.

Malek-Ahmadi, P., & Simonds, J. F. (1998). Olanzapine for autistic disorder with hyperactivity. *Journal of the American Academy of Child and Adolescent Psychiatry, 37,* 902–903.

Martin, A., Koenig, K., Scahill, L., & Bregman, J. (1999). Open-label quetiapine in the treatment of children and adolescents with autistic disorder. *Journal of Child and Adolescent Psychopharmacology, 9,* 99–107.

Matson, J. L., & Coe, D. A. (1992). Applied behavior analysis: Its impact on the treatment of mentally retarded emotionally disturbed people. *Research in Developmental Disabilities, 13,* 171–189.

Mattes, J. A., Rosenberg, J., & Mayus, D. (1984). Carbamzepine versus propranolol in patients with uncontrolled rage outburst: A random assignment study. *Psychopharmacology Bulletin, 20,* 98–100.

McCracken, J. T., & Diamond, R. P. (1988). Bipolar disorder in mentally retarded adolescents. *Journal of the American Academy of Child and Adolescent Psychiatry, 27,* 494–499.

McDougle, C. J. (1997). Psychopharmacology. In D. J. Cohen & F. R. Volkmar (Eds.), *Handbook of autism and pervasive developmental disorders* (2nd ed., pp. 169–194). New York: Wiley.

McDougle, C. J., Holmes J. P., Bronson, M. R., Anderson, G. M., Volkmar, F. R., Price, L. H., & Cohen, D. J. (1997). Risperidone treatment of children and adolescents with pervasive developmental disorders: A prospective, open-label study. *Journal of the American Academy of Child and Adolescent Psychiatry, 36,* 685–693.

McDougle, C. J., Holmes, J. P., Carleson, D. C., Pelton, G. H., Cohen, D. J., & Price, L. H. (1998). A double-bind, placebo controlled study of risperidone in adults with autistic disorder and other pervasive developmental disorders. *Archives of General Psychiatry, 55,* 633–644.

McDougle, C. J., Price, L. H., Volkmar, F. R., Goodman, W. K., Ward-O'Brien, D., Nielsen, J., Bregman, J., & Cohen, J. (1992). Clomipramine in autism: Preliminary evidence of efficacy. *Journal of the American Academy of Child and Adolescent Psychiatry, 31,* 746–750.

Millichamp, C. J., & Singh, N. N. (1987). The effects of intermittent drug therapy on stereotypy and collateral behaviors of mentally retarded persons. *Research in Developmental Disabilities, 8,* 213–227.

Morbidity and Mortality Weekly Report. (1997). Cardiac valvulopathy associated with exposure to fenfluramine or dexfenfluramine: U.S. Department of Health and Human Services interim public health recommendations. *Morbidity and Mortality Weekly Report, 45,* 1061–1066.

Naruse, H., Nagahata, M., Nakane, Y., Shirahashi, K., Takesada, M., & Yamazaki, K. (1982). A multi-center double-blind trial of pimozide (Orap), haloperidol and placebo in children with behavior disorders, using cross-over design. *Acta Paedopsychiatrica, 48*, 173–184.

Nicholson, R., Awad, G., & Sloman, L. (1998). An open trial of risperidone in young autistic children. *Journal of the American Academy of Child and Adolescent Psychiatry, 37*, 372–376.

Northup, J., Broussard, C., Jones, K., George, T., Vallmer, T., & Herring, M. (1995). The differential effects of teacher and peer attention on the disruptive behavior of three children with attention deficit hyperactivity disorder. *Journal of Applied Behavior Analysis, 28*, 277–282.

Perel, M., Alcami, M., & Bilaberte, I. (1999). Fluoxetine in children with autism. *Journal of the American Academy of Child and Adolescent Psychiatry, 38*, 1472–1473.

Physicians' Desk Reference. (53rd ed.). (1999). Montvale, NJ: Medical Economics.

Poindexter, A. R., Cain, N., Clarke, D. J., Cook, E. H., Corbett, J. A., & Levitas, A. (1998). Mood stabilizers. In S. Reiss & M. G. Aman (Eds.), *Psychotropic medications and developmental disabilities: The international consensus handbook* (pp. 215–228). Columbus: Ohio State University, Nisonger Center.

Posey, D. J., Litwiller, M., Koburn, A., & McDougle, C. J. (1999). Paroxetine in autism. *Journal of the American Academy of Child and Adolescent Psychiatry, 38*, 111–112.

Quintana, H., Birmaker, B., Stedge, D., Lennon, S., Freed, J., Bridge, J., & Greenhill, L. (1995). Use of methylphenidate in the treatment of children with autistic disorder. *Journal of Autism and Developmental Disorders, 25*, 283–294.

Ratey, J. J., Bemporad, J., & Sorgi, P. (1987). Open trial effects of beta-blockers on speech and social behaviors in 8 autistic adults. *Journal of Autism and Developmental Disorders, 17*, 439–446.

Reiss, S. (1994). *Handbook of challenging behavior: Mental health aspects of mental retardation.* Worthington, OH: IDS.

Reiss, S., Levitan, G. W., & Syszko, J. (1982). Emotional disturbance and mental retardation: Diagnostic overshadowing. *American Journal of Mental Deficiency, 86*, 567–574.

Reiss, S., & Valenti-Hein, D. (1994). Development of a psychopathology rating scale for children with mental retardation. *Journal of Consulting Clinical Psychology, 62*, 28.

Remington, G. I. (1993). Clinical consideration in the use of risperidone. *Canadian Journal of Psychiatry, 38*, S96–S100.

Ricketts, R. W., Goza, A. B., Ellis, C. R., Singh, Y. N., & Singh, N. N. (1993). Fluoxetine treatment of severe self-injury in young adults with mental retardation. *Journal of the American Academy of Child and Adolescent Psychiatry, 32*, 865–869.

Ritvo, E., Freeman, B., Geller, E., & Yiwiler, A. (1983). Effects of fenfluramine on 14 outpatients with the syndrome of autism. *Journal of the American Academy of Child Psychiatry, 22,* 549–558.

Rutter M. (1985). Infantile autism. In D. Shaffer, A. A. Ehrhardt, & L. L. Greenhill (Eds.), *The clinical guide to child psychiatry* (pp. 48–78). New York: Free Press.

Schuster, C., Lewis, M., & Seiden, L. (1986). Fenfluramine: Neurotoxicity. *Psychopharmacology Bulletin, 22,* 148–151.

Simonneau, G., Fartoukh, M., Sitbon, O., Humbert, M., Jagot, J. L., & Herve, P. (1998). Primary pulmonary hypertension associated with the use of fenfluramine derivatives. *Chest, 114,* 195–199.

Snead, R. W., Boon, F., & Presberg, J. (1994). Paroxetine for self-injurious behavior. *Journal of the American Academy of Child and Adolescent Psychiatry, 33,* 909–910.

Sovner, R. (1989). The use of valproate in the treatment of mentally retarded persons with typical and atypical bipolar disorders. *Journal of Clinical Psychiatry, 50,* 40–43.

Steingard, R., & Biederman, J. (1987). Lithium responsive manic-like symptoms in two individuals with autism and mental retardation. *Journal of the American Academy of Child and Adolescent Psychiatry, 26,* 932–935.

Strayhorn, J. (1989). More on methylphenidate in autism. *Journal of the American Academy of Child and Adolescent Psychiatry, 28,* 299.

Strayhorn, J. M., Jr., Rapp, N., Donina, W., & Strain, P. S. (1988). Randomized trial of methylphenidate for an autistic child. *Journal of the American Academy of Child and Adolescent Psychiatry, 27,* 244–247.

Strumey, P. (1994). Assessing the functions of aberrant behaviors: A review of psychometric instruments. *Journal of Autism and Developmental Disorders, 24,* 293.

Szymanski, L. S., & Stark, J. (1996). Mental retardation past, present, and future. *Child and Adolescent Psychiatric Clinics of North America, 5,* 769–780.

Vanden-Borre, R., Vermote, R., Buttiens, M., Thiry, P., Dierick G., Geutiens, J., Sieben, G., & Heylen, S. (1993). Risperidone as add-on therapy in behavioral disturbances in mental retardation: A double-blind placebo-controlled crossover study. *Acta Psychiatrica Scandanavia, 87,* 167–171.

Werry, J. S., & Aman, M. G. (Eds.). (1999). *Practitioner's guide to psychoactive drugs for children and adolescents* (2nd ed.). New York: Plenum.

Willemsen-Swinkels, S. H. N., Buitelaar, J. K., & van Engeland, H. (1996). The effects of chronic naltrexone treatment in youth autistic children: A double-blind placebo-controlled crossover study. *Biological Psychiatry, 39,* 1023–1031.

8

MOOD DISORDERS

Mood disorders have typically been conceptualized into three classifications: depressive disorders, bipolar disorders, and medically related or induced disorders (i.e., mood disorder due to a medical condition and substance-induced mood disorder). Such a classification scheme is reflected in the criteria presented in the fourth edition of the *Diagnostic and Statistical Manual of Mental Disorders* (DSM–IV; American Psychiatric Association, 1994). Within the classification of depressive disorders is major depressive disorder (characterized by one or more distinct depressive episodes) and dysthymic disorder (defined as a more generalized and pervasive depressed mood that lasts at least 1 year in children or adolescents; American Psychiatric Association, 1994). The bipolar classification is divided into Bipolar I (manic or mixed episodes), Bipolar II (depressive episodes accompanied by hypomania [mild mania]), and cyclothymia (chronic mood disturbance that fluctuates between hypomania and depressive symptoms; American Psychiatric Association, 1994).

Because pharmacological and psychosocial intervention data are not quantified to this degree of specificity, this chapter focused on two primary areas: depressive disorders (a combination of both major depressive disorder and dysthymia) and bipolar disorders (a compilation of Bipolar I, Bipolar II, and cyclothymia).

DEPRESSIVE DISORDERS

Unlike adults, major depressive disorder and dysthymia in children may be difficult to discern readily. The symptomatology varies considerably across different developmental stages and diverse ethnic groups (American Academy of Child and Adolescent Psychiatry [AACAP], 1998). Irritability, changes in appetite or weight, anxiety, somatic complaints, decreased energy levels, altered sleep patterns, and difficulty with schoolwork are common symptoms (Birmaher, Ryan, Williamson, Brent, & Kaufman, 1996). Seldom do children verbalize their feelings of melancholy or depression; rather, temper tantrums, mood swings, a low frustration tolerance, peer difficulties, and behavioral problems often signal the onset of depression (AACAP, 1998).

Epidemiological studies place the occurrence of depression in the pediatric population at approximately 2% of children (2–12 years) and 8% of adolescents (13–18 years; Fleming & Offord, 1990; Lewinsohn, Clarke, Seeley, & Rohde, 1994). In childhood, the male-to-female prevalence ratio is equal. Yet in adolescence, the male-to-female ratio transforms to 1:2 (Kessler et al., 1994; Lewinsohn et al., 1994). This notable change in adolescence may be due to culturally determined gender role wherein girls are encouraged to be passive, to be dependent, and to focus on the depressed feelings rather than take action (McGrath, Keita, Strickland, & Russo, 1990; Nolen-Hoeksema & Girgus, 1994; Overaschel, Beeferman, & Kabacoff, 1997). Other factors that have been considered include biological changes associated with puberty and increased genetic loading (Birmaher, Ryan, Williamson, Brent, Kaufman, Dahl, et al., 1996; Kovacs, Devlin, Pollock, Richards, & Mukerji, 1997; Thapar & NcGuffin, 1996).

There are numerous studies documenting the interplay of nature and nurture in the development of depression. First, twin and adoptions studies with adult samples have indicated that genetic factors account for approximately 50% of the variance in the diagnosis of depressive disorders (Cox, Reich, Rice, & Elston, 1989). Although far fewer studies have been completed with a pediatric cohort, the data do support a genetic presence. For example, Thapar and McGuffin (1996) conducted a population-based study of twins ages 8 to 16 years and analyzed the influence of genetic factors and age on the development of depression. Results indicated depressive symptoms in adolescents were highly correlated with genetic heritability. In addition, children with a high loading of genetic factors exhibited self-deprecating behaviors and low self-esteem. Likewise, Warner, Weissman, Mufson, and Wickramaratne (1999) reported notable evidence for multigenerational risk status when studying the incidence of depression in biological grandparents, parents, and grandchildren. These researchers concluded that prepubertal onset of anxiety disorders was a notable risk factor for the later development of clinically significant and life-long reoccurrences of depression.

Yet such a model does not account for the development of a gender differential when girls enter puberty. A study by Silberg et al. (1999) evaluated the impact of life events, pubertal status, and sex in the development of depression in male and female child and adolescent twin pairs from the Virginia Twin Study of Adolescent Twin Pairs. Their findings indicated that increased genetic loading among adolescent girls was largely responsible for the onset and long-term maintenance of depression. Nonetheless, far more studies are necessary before the causal pathway of child and adolescent onset of depression is evident.

BIPOLAR DISORDERS

Bipolar disorders have long been underdiagnosed in the pediatric population (Weller, Weller, & Fristad, 1995). Until recently, there was a commonly held belief that children and adolescents were unlikely to exhibit these disorders. Hence, clinicians resorted to alternative diagnoses such as schizophrenia to account for the symptomatology presented (Faedda et al., 1995). As with depressive disorders, bipolar disorders are often difficult to discern in children and adolescents. Many times juveniles present with an agitated depressed mood instead of the typical acute manic episode common in the adult population (Weller et al., 1995). Possible indicators pointing to an emerging bipolar disorder are a familial history of bipolar disorder as well as the onset of hypomania with the administration of antidepressant medications (Geller et al., 1998).

Pediatric bipolar disorders frequently present as psychomotor agitation, elevated or expansive mood, increased verbalizations, distractibility, inflated self-esteem, and a decreased need for sleep (Lewinsohn, Klein, & Seeley, 1995; Steele & Fisman, 1997). Unlike adults, children and adolescents seldom present with irritable mood, flight of ideas, or excessive engagement in pleasurable activities that have a high potential for painful consequences (Lewinsohn et al., 1995). Rapid cycling between mania and depression is often viewed as a hallmark of child and adolescent bipolarity (Bowring & Kovacs, 1992). The age of onset varies from study to study but is generally around puberty (Geller & Luby, 1997; Lewinsohn et al., 1995; Strober et al., 1995).

Large-scale epidemiological studies have indicated a prevalence rate of approximately 1% of adolescents (Carlson & Kashani, 1988; Lewinsohn et al., 1995), a percentage comparable with adult rates. Unlike the depressive disorders, the male-to-female prevalence ratio of bipolar disorder is 1:1 and remains so throughout the life span (American Psychiatric Association, 1994).

There is substantial evidence for a significant genetic contribution to the etiology of bipolar disorders. Recent genetic linkage studies suggest bipolar and schizophrenia share similar genetic susceptibility (Torrey, 1999; Wildenauer, Schwab, Maier, & Detera-Wadleigh, 1999). Because there is not a complete concordance for bipolar symptoms in monozygotic twins, it is evident that the transmission does not follow a simple Mendelian approach (Klar, 1999). That is, Gregor Mendel identified traits that are expressed whenever a dominant gene is present. This dominant gene may be inherited from either parent, and only one copy is necessary for the disorder to be evident. By comparison, a recessive gene is never expressed when in combination with a dominant gene. Alternative hypotheses include multifactorial origins such as transmission through multiple genes or a single recessive gene that is evidenced because of an interaction with environmental risk factors (Meltzer, 2000). Numerous researchers are investigating various locations on chromosomes X, 4, 12, 13, 18, 21, and 22 as the probable site for genetic transmission of bipolar disorder (Berrettini, 2000; Ewald, Degn, Mors, & Kruse, 1998).

MEDICAL INTERVENTIONS

Although the utilization of tricyclic antidepressants (TCAs) and selective serotonin re-uptake inhibitors (SSRIs) have proved effective in the adult population (Potter, Rudorfer, & Manji, 1991; Tollefson, 1995), such pharmacological interventions appear to be more limited in their effectiveness in the juvenile population (Birmaher, 1998). Comparatively few double-blind studies have been conducted with the pediatric population, and extrapolating pharmacological strategies from adult efficacy data is precarious at best (AACAP, 1998). Furthermore, many psychotropic agents prescribed for children are not specifically approved for pediatric use by the U.S. Food and Drug Administration.

Although medication may be deemed necessary in pediatric cases that have proved refractory to psychological interventions, the indiscriminate use of psychotropic agents as a first line of treatment and without validated efficacy in the pediatric population is difficult to justify (AACAP, 1998; Birmaher, Ryan, Williamson, Brent, & Kaufman, 1996; Birmaher, Ryan, Williamson, Brent, Kaufman, Dahl, et al., 1996). It is advised, therefore, that treatment of pediatric depressive disorders always incorporate psychological (e.g., cognitive–behavioral and interpersonal) intervention components and that medication be viewed as a possible augmentation. Tables 8.1 and 8.2 provide, respectively, a summary of the antidepressant medications clinically validated in double-blind and open studies for use with children and adolescents. Given the number of medications that are *not* efficacious with the pediatric population, Table 8.3 contains a listing of

TABLE 8.1
Medications Clinically Validated in Double-Blind Studies for Use With Children and Adolescents With Mood Disorders

Generic Name (Trade Name)	Children mg/kg/day or Daily Dose	Adolescents mg/kg/day or Daily Dose	Treatment Outcome	Adverse Effect
Clomipramine (Anafranil)	1–3 mg/kg	1–3 mg/kg	Reduction of depression when compared with placebo double-blind crossover comparisons.	Risk of seizure onset with prolonged use (>1 year) and high dosage (300 mg/day), drowsiness, dizziness, tremors, headaches, dry mouth, and fatigue.
Fluoxetine (Prozac)	10–20 mg	10–20 mg	Reduction of depression when compared with placebo double-blind, randomized trials.	Effects usually mild and transient. Nausea, decreased appetite, and insomnia.
Lithium (Eskalith, Lithane, Lithobid, Lithonate)	Blood serum levels at 0.6 to 1.2 mEq/L are desirable		Reduction of manic and rapid cycling symptoms.	Diarrhea, nausea, and drowsiness.

Note. Sources include DeLong and Nieman (1983); Emslie et al. (1997); Geller et al. (1997); McKnew et al. (1981); *Physicians' Desk Reference* (1999); Sallee, Hilial, Dougherty, Beach, and Nesbitt (1998); and Sallee, Vrindavanam, Deas-Nesmith, Carson, and Sethuraman (1997).

TABLE 8.2
Medications Clinically Validated in Open Studies for Use With Children and Adolescents With Mood Disorders

Generic Name (Trade Name)	Children mg/kg/day or Daily Dose	Adolescents mg/kg/day or Daily Dose	Treatment Outcome	Adverse Effect
Carbamazepine (Tegretol)	50–400 mg	50–400 mg	Decrease in manic symptoms in bipolar adolescents.	Dizziness, drowsiness, nausea, and vomiting.
Clozapine (Clozaril)	—	100–900 mg	Decrease in bipolar symptoms in adolescents.	Cognitive sedation and extrapyramidal side effects.
Fluvoxamine (Luvox)	50–200 mg	50–200 mg	Decline in severity of depressive symptoms.	Nausea, drowsiness, insomnia, headaches, hyperactivity, weight loss, and dermatitis.
Nefazodone (Serzone)	Not yet established	Not yet established	Decline in severity of depressive symptoms.	Headaches, dry mouth, nausea, and drowsiness.
Paroxetine (Paxil)	Not yet established	Not yet established	Decline in severity of depressive symptoms.	Drowsiness, vomiting, anxiety, nervousness, and abdominal pain. Safety with pediatric population has yet to be established.
Risperidone (Risperdal)	Not yet established	2–10 mg	Decrease in manic symptoms in bipolar adolescents.	Cognitive sedation and extrapyramidal side effects.
Sertraline (Zoloft)	Up to 200 mg	Up to 200 mg	Decline in severity of depressive symptoms.	Nausea, diarrhea, insomnia, reduced appetite, and drowsiness.
Valproic Acid (Depakote)		Up to 750 mg	Decrease in manic symptoms in bipolar adolescents.	Nausea, vomiting, and indigestion.

Note. Sources include Alderman, Wolkow, Chung, and Johnston (1998); Ambrosini et al. (1999); Apter et al. (1994); Cosgrove (1994); Deltito, Levitan, Damore, Hajal, and Zambenedetti (1997); Papatheodorou and Kutcher (1993); Papatheodorou, Kutcher, Katic, and Szalai (1995); *Physicians' Desk Reference* (1999); Sallee, Hilial, Dougherty, Beach, and Nesbitt (1998); West, Keck, and McElroy (1995); and Woolston (1999).

TABLE 8.3
Medication With No Documented Efficacy for Use With Children and Adolescents With Mood Disorders

Generic Name (Trade Name)	Adverse Effect and Cautionary Statement
Amitriptyline (Elavil, Etrafon, Limbitrol, Triavil)	Double-blind studies found no significant differences between medication and placebo. In addition, adverse effect profile includes cardiotoxicity.
Desipramine (Norpramin)	Double-blind studies found no significant differences between medication and placebo. In addition, adverse effect profile includes cardiotoxicity and reports of sudden deaths in children. Clinicians should use it cautiously, if at all, in the management of depression in children and adolescents.
Imipramine (Tofranil)	Double-blind studies found no significant differences between medication and placebo. In addition, adverse effect profile includes cardiotoxicity and reports of sudden deaths in children. It should only be considered for use when other appropriate medications are not effective.
Nortriptyline (Pamelor)	Double-blind studies found medication no more effective than placebo. Adverse effect profile includes cardiac complications, low blood pressure, and drowsiness. It is not recommended for this pediatric population.
Venlafaxine (Effexor)	A single double-blind study found no significant differences between medication and placebo. More research is necessary.

Note. Sources include Birmaher et al. (1998); Boulos et al. (1991); Geller, Cooper, Graham, Marsteller, and Bryant (1990); Geller, Fox, Cooper, and Garrity (1992); Hughes, Preskorn, Wrona, Hassanein, and Tucker (1990); Kutcher et al. (1994); Kye et al. (1996); *Physicians' Desk Reference* (1999); and Puig-Antich et al. (1987).

medications not recommended for use with children. A synopsis of the pharmacological options is now provided with the listing in alphabetical order to facilitate reader ease. (Refer to the *Glossary of Terms* at the end of the book for definitions of medical terms.)

Amitriptyline

Amitriptyline (Elavil, Etrafon, Limbitrol, and Triavil), a TCA that is commonly prescribed for adults, has no documented efficacy over a placebo with children and adolescents. For example, Kye et al. (1996) conducted a double-blind, placebo-controlled trial of amitriptyline with 31 adolescents diagnosed with acute major depression. Although both groups improved with treatment, there were no significant differences between amitriptyline and the placebo. Similar findings were reported for a 10-week randomized double-blind placebo trial involving 27 adolescents diagnosed with severe depression (Birmaher et al., 1998). Although youngsters in both the placebo and amitriptyline groups showed a decrease in depressive symptomatology, there was no significant difference between treatment types. In addition, amitriptyline has an adverse effect profile that includes cardiotoxicity.

Clomipramine

Clomipramine (Anafranil) is a TCA that is approved for use in children older than age 10 years (*Physicians' Desk Reference*, 1999). Although its primary use is in the management of obsessive–compulsive disorder (see this volume, chapter 4), it appears to have potential in the treatment of pediatric depression. For example, Sallee, Vrindavanam, Deas-Nesmith, Carson, and Sethuraman (1997) conducted a randomized double-blind, crossover trial involving 16 outpatient adolescents diagnosed with depression. Treatment consisted of saline solution or 200 mg clomipramine administered intravenously. Results indicated a significant reduction in depressive symptoms in the experimental group (as measured by the Hamilton Depression Rating Scale) over the placebo condition at 6 days postadministration. These results were replicated in Sallee, Hilial, Dougherty, Beach, and Nesbitt (1998). On the basis of these findings, it appears that clomipramine may have a place in the treatment of acute depression in adolescents. More replication studies, however, are necessary before any firm conclusions can be reached.

Desipramine

Desipramine (Norpramin) is another compound in the class of TCAs that has been used to treat adult depression. Yet its efficacy with children and adolescents is lacking. For example, Boulos et al. (1991) reported no significant differences between desipramine and placebo treatment in a 6-week double-blind trial involving 30 adolescents with depressive symptoms. Likewise, Kutcher et al. (1994) completed a 6-week double-blind trial with 60 adolescents diagnosed with depression. Again, no significant differences were found between groups, with 40% of both groups reporting a decrease in symptomatology. Unfortunately, because of cardiac toxicities and reports of sudden deaths in children treated with desipramine (Riddle, Geller, & Ryan, 1993; Varley & McClellan, 1997; Werry, 1995), it is recommended it be used cautiously, if at all, in the management of depression in children and adolescents.

Fluoxetine

Fluoxetine (Prozac) is an SSRI that appears to have efficacy in the treatment of pediatric depression. In the largest study to date, Emslie et al.

(1997) completed an 8-week double-blind, placebo-controlled trial with 96 children and adolescents (ages 7–17) treated at an outpatient clinic. Results showed that 56% of those receiving fluoxetine and 33% receiving the placebo showed significant decreases in depressive symptomatology. The results indicated both statistical (p = .02) and clinical superiority of fluoxetine over the placebo condition. A 1-year follow-up study continued to support the efficacy of fluoxetine treatment, with twice as many participants who received fluoxetine showing full remission of symptoms as compared with the placebo group (Emslie et al., 1998). Likewise, an open trial of fluoxetine with 8 adolescents who were comorbid for depression, conduct disorder, and substance use disorder found marked improvement in mood following a 7-week trial (Riggs, Mikulich, Coffman, & Crowley, 1997). Three other open trials of fluoxetine reported positive response rates between 70% and 90% in adolescents (Boulos, Kutcher, Gardner, & Young, 1992; Colle, Belair, DiFeo, Weiss, & LaRoache, 1994; Jain, Birmaher, Garcia, Al-Shabbout, & Ryan, 1992). In all these studies, adverse effects were mild and transient. In conclusion, these data suggest that fluoxetine is safe and efficacious for the treatment of depression in children and adolescents. However, more double-blind studies are warranted.

Fluvoxamine

A SSRI, fluvoxamine (Luvox) has not been well researched in the treatment of juvenile mood disorders. Open trials with children and adolescent participants have indicated the medication resulted in symptom relief (Apter et al., 1994; Cosgrove, 1994). Reported minor adverse effects included hyperactivity, insomnia, nausea, dermatitis, and weight loss. Because no randomized double-blind trials have yet been published, far more data are needed before fluvoxamine can be considered a mainstay in the treatment of juvenile mood disorders.

Imipramine

Imipramine (Tofranil) is another TCA commonly prescribed for the treatment of depression in adults. Yet its efficacy with children has yet to be demonstrated by double-blind studies. Two early open trials (Ryan et al., 1986; Strober, Freeman, & Rigali, 1990) reported significant response rates in adolescents. Unfortunately, subsequent placebo-controlled studies failed to demonstrate the effectiveness of this treatment in the juvenile population (Hughes, Preskorn, Wrona, Hassanein, & Tucker, 1990; Puig-Antich et al., 1987). Only one double-blind placebo-controlled trial (Preskorn, Weller, Hughes, Weller, & Bolte, 1987) involving 22 children younger than age 13 years found statistically significant (but clinically minimal) reductions in depressive symptomatology. As with desipramine, sudden deaths involving cardiac complications in children being treated with imipramine have been reported (e.g., Varley & McClellan, 1997). Given these mixed results, far more supportive documentation is necessary before imipramine could be viewed as an appropriate pharmacological alternative with children and adolescents. It is recommended, therefore, that it be considered for use only when other more appropriate medications (i.e., the SSRIs) have not achieved treatment efficacy.

Lithium Carbonate

Lithium carbonate (Eskalith, Lithane, Lithobid, and Lithonate) is commonly prescribed in the treatment of bipolar disorders in adults. Several randomized controlled trials of lithium with juvenile samples indicate that lithium is efficacious for this population as well. For example, Geller et al. (1998) completed a 6-week double-blind, placebo-controlled study with adolescents (ages 12–18) who were diagnosed with bipolar disorder and secondary substance abuse dependency. The patients in the treatment condition showed statistically significant improvements when compared with control patients. Two earlier double-blind crossover studies reported similar results (DeLong & Nieman, 1983; McKnew et al., 1981). Although these trials indicate support for lithium with adolescents who are diagnosed with bipolar disorder, no double-blind studies evaluating efficacy and safety have been conducted with younger children and are sorely needed.

Nefazodone

Only one study (Wilens, Spencer, Biederman, & Schleifer, 1997) has evaluated nefazodone (Serzone), an SSRI, for use with pediatric clients evidencing depression. In an open trial, the researchers evaluated 7 treatment-resistant children and adolescents who were diagnosed with either unipolar or bipolar mood disorders as well as an array of other co-morbid conditions. Four participants showed improvement with the trial of nefazodone. Given these results, it appears that nefazodone should be more closely examined for use in the management of juvenile mood disorders.

Nortriptyline

Extensive double-blind, placebo-controlled trials with the tricyclic nortriptyline (Pamelor) have indicated that it is no more effective than placebos in the management of childhood or adolescent depressions (Geller, Cooper, Graham, & Fetner, 1992; Geller et al., 1990; Geller et al., 1992). Given the adverse side-effect profile of nortriptyline (cardiac complications, low blood pressure, and drowsiness; *Physicians' Desk Refer-*

ence, 1999), there appears to be no justification for using this medication with the juvenile population.

Paroxetine

Scant evidence is available supporting the use of the SSRI paroxetine (Paxil) in the treatment of juvenile depression. One open trial by Rey-Sanchez and Gutierrez-Casares (1997) demonstrated the effectiveness of paroxetine in children younger than age 14 years. Adverse effects included vomiting, anxiety, nervousness, and abdominal pain. All symptoms were, however, manageable and transient. Nonetheless, further studies are clearly warranted before this medication is used as a mainstay in the treatment of child and adolescent mood disorders.

Sertraline

A SSRI, sertraline (Zoloft) is commonly used in the treatment of depression in adults. Efficacy and safety data for the juvenile population are still forthcoming. Four open trials with child and adolescent clients indicated that the medication was efficacious in treating individuals seen in outpatient (Alderman, Wolkow, Chung, & Johnston, 1998; Ambrosini et al., 1999; Sallee et al., 1998) and inpatient (McConville et al., 1996) settings. Adverse effects (insomnia, drowsiness, reduction in appetite) were mild and transient. These data indicate that double-blind studies using sertraline are warranted.

Venlafaxine

Venlafaxine (Effexor), a selective serotonin-norepinephrine reuptake inhibitor, has received scant attention for use with pediatric cases of depression. In the only double-blind study to date, Mandoki, Tapia, Tapia, Sumner, and Parker (1997) completed a 6-week trial placebo-controlled study with 33 children and adolescents (ages 8–17 years). Both the treatment and placebo group showed symptom improvement, with no significant differences between the two conditions. Therefore, far more research is necessary before venlafaxine should be routinely used for the treatment of mood disorders in this population.

Anticonvulsant and Antipsychotic Medications

Because bipolar disorders in the pediatric population are often resistant to treatment, numerous researchers have attempted open trials with anticonvulsant and antipsychotic medications. For example, four open trials found valproic acid (Depakote) to reduce manic symptoms in adolescents (Deltito, Levitan, Damore, Hajal, & Zambenedetti, 1997; Papatheodorou & Kutcher, 1993; Papatheodorou, Kutcher, Katic, & Szalai, 1995; West, Keck, & McElroy, 1995). Likewise, carbamazepine (Tegretol) has been used in an open trial to treat adolescent bipolar disorders (Woolston, 1999). Risperidone (Risperdal) and clozapine (Clozaril) also have been evaluated (Frazier et al., 1999; Fuchs, 1994; Kowatch, Suppes, Gilifillan, & Fuentes, 1995). Given the significant cognitive sedation and possible extrapyramidal side effects associated with these drugs, particularly the antipsychotic medications, it is recommended that they be considered as possible alternatives only when the other more typical psychosocial and pharmacological interventions have failed to achieve success.

PSYCHOSOCIAL INTERVENTIONS

As noted earlier, the treatment of pediatric depressive disorders should always incorporate psychological (e.g., cognitive–behavioral and interpersonal) intervention components with medication as a possible augmentation. Regardless of therapeutic approach, it is important that family members be included in developing the treatment plan. Seldom does a child or adolescent function solely without direction and input from significant adults in her or his environment. Such adults may significantly facilitate treatment success by identifying and reducing psychosocial stressors, reinforcing treatment compliance, and facilitating cooperation and participation.

Cognitive–Behavioral Approaches

Cognitive–behavioral therapy (CBT) focuses on the identification and alterations of negative thought patterns, beliefs, and actions that contribute to the maintenance of depressive disorders (Southam-Gerow, Henin, Chu, Marrs, & Kendall, 1997). The intent is to remedy the mood problems by altering beliefs and perceptions and focusing on the learning and practicing of new, more effective, coping skills. The techniques of replacing "faulty" cognitive processes with more adaptive thinking is referred to as *cognitive restructuring* (Kendall, Panichelli-Mindel, & Gerow, 1995). By training the child or adolescent to replace maladaptive depressed thoughts ("No one will sit with me at lunch because they don't like me") to adaptive thoughts ("I'll ask Ricardo if I may sit with him") and to engage in positive verbalizations ("I am a good friend"), the treatment enhances constructive behavior change.

Numerous studies within the past decade have validated the efficacy of CBT when compared with wait list, comparison controls, or other therapeutic conditions in the treatment of pediatric depression (e.g., Clarke et al., 1995; Clarke, Rohde, Lewinsohn, Hops, & Seeley, 1999; Gillham, Reivich, Jaycox, & Seligman 1995; Jaycox, Reivich, Gillham, & Seligman, 1994; Kroll, Harrington, Jayson, Fraser, & Gowers, 1996; Lewinsohn, Clarke, Rohde, & Hops, 1996; Stark, Rouse, & Livingston 1991; Vostanis, Feehan, & Grattan, 1998; Vostanis, Feehan, Grattan, & Bickerton 1996; Weisz, Thurber, Sweeney, Proffitt, & LeGagnoux, 1997; Wood, Harrington, & Moore, 1996). In a meta-analysis of CBT studies, Reinecke, Ryan, and Dubois (1998) reported a treatment effect size of 1.02 standard deviation immediately following treatment and 0.61 standard deviation at later 1- to 2-year follow-ups.

One important issue with any treatment is that of relapse. Several research teams have conducted long-term follow-up studies to determine if the beneficial effects of CBT intervention persist after the active intervention has been completed. Lewinsohn, Clarke, Hops, and Andrews (1990) and Gillham et al. (1995) both found that improvements in depressive symptoms were maintained for up to 2 years after initial treatment with CBT. However, a later study by Lewinsohn et al. (1996) found no differences between treatment and the placebo condition at the 2-year follow-up. Two more recent studies have evaluated the effectiveness of booster sessions to reduce or prevent relapse (Clark et al., 1999; Kroll et al., 1996). Results revealed that relapse rates for the monthly booster group were much lower than the groups that received either quarterly follow-up sessions or no follow-up sessions at all.

Although the efficacy of CBT for the treatment of depression with children and adolescents is well established, no controlled trials have been published on its use for the management of bipolar disorders for this population. Scott (1996) provided an informative overview of CBT in the treatment of adults with bipolar disorder. In addition, Basco and Rush (1996) developed a comprehensive CBT manual for the treatment of adults with bipolar disorder. No comparable strategies, however, have been created for children or adolescents.

Interpersonal Therapy

Interpersonal therapy (IPT) is designed to allow depressed individuals an opportunity to (a) focus on resolving areas of grief, (b) improve interpersonal relationships by reducing conflict, and (c) identify and rectify personal difficulties (Moreau & Mufson, 1997). Moreau, Mufson, Weissman, and Klerman (1991) developed a manualized version of IPT to be used with adolescents with depressive symptoms. Key areas targeted by this program are role transitions, role disputes, interpersonal skill deficits, and grief resolution.

A 12-week IPT open trial involving 14 adolescents resulted in a significant decrease in depressive symptoms after participation (Mufson et al.,

1994). In a 1-year follow-up study involving 10 of the 14 initial participants, Mufson and Fairbanks (1996) reported that treatment gains had
been maintained. Furthermore, Mufson, Weissman, Moreau, and Garfinkel
(1999) conducted a 12-week randomized treatment/wait-list trial with adolescents who were diagnosed as having a depressive disorder and reported
that 75% of the treatment group as compared with 46% of the wait-list
participants evidenced positive outcomes. These preliminary findings are
encouraging and suggest that IPT may be an effective treatment for depression in the adolescent population.

CONCLUSION

Although pharmacological treatments for unipolar depression are
quite successful in the adult population, they do not appear as effective in
children and adolescents. TCAs have generally not demonstrated significant reduction in depressive symptoms, and concerns about serious adverse
effects have dampened the interest in this medication class for treating this
population. Newer SSRIs appear to be safer than TCAs, but their efficacy,
albeit encouraging, awaits further investigation. However, psychosocial interventions, such as CBT and IPT, appear to yield significant improvements
for children and adolescents with depression. By comparison, combined
pharmacological and psychosocial interventions for the management of juvenile bipolar disorders are largely understudied. In conclusion, data indicate that the treatment of pediatric mood disorders always incorporate psychological (e.g., cognitive–behavioral and interpersonal) intervention
components and that medication be viewed as a possible augmentation.

REFERENCES

Alderman, J., Wolkow, R., Chung, M., & Johnston, H. (1998). Sertraline treat-
    ment of children and adolescents with obsessive–compulsive disorder or de-
    pression: Pharmacokinetics, tolerability and efficacy. *Journal of the American
    Academy of Child and Adolescent Psychiatry, 37*, 386–394.

Ambrosini, P., Wagner, K., Biederman, J., Glick, I., Tan, C., Elia, J., Hebeler, J.,
    Rabinovich, H., Lock, J., & Geller, D. (1999). Multicenter open-label sertra-
    line study in adolescent outpatients with major depression. *Journal of the
    American Academy of Child and Adolescent Psychiatry, 38*, 566–572.

American Academy of Child and Adolescent Psychiatry. (1998). Practice param-
    eters for the assessment and treatment of children and adolescents with de-
    pressive disorders. *Journal of the American Academy of Child and Adolescent
    Psychiatry, 37*, 63S–83S.

American Psychiatric Association. (1994). *Diagnostic and statistical manual of mental disorders* (4th ed.). Washington, DC: Author.

Apter, A., Ratzoni, G., King, R., Weizman, A., Iancu, I., Binder, M., & Riddle, M. (1994). Fluvoxamine open-label treatment of adolescent inpatients with obsessive–compulsive disorder or depression. *Journal of the American Academy of Child and Adolescent Psychiatry, 33*, 342–348.

Basco, M., & Rush, A. J. (1996). *Cognitive–behavioral therapy for bipolar disorder.* New York: Guilford Press.

Berrettini, W. H. (2000). Susceptibility loci for bipolar disorder: Overlap with inherited vulnerability to schizophrenia. *Biological Psychiatry, 17*, 245–251.

Birmaher, B. (1998). Should we use antidepressant medication for children and adolescents with depressive disorders? *Psychopharmacology Bulletin, 34*, 35–39.

Birmaher, B., Ryan, N., Williamson, D., Brent, D., & Kaufman, J. (1996). Childhood and adolescent depression: Part II. A review of the past 10 years. *Journal of the American Academy of Child and Adolescent Psychiatry, 35*, 1577–1583.

Birmaher, B., Ryan, N., Williamson, D., Brent, D., Kaufman, J., Dahl, R., Perel, J., & Nelson, B. (1996). Childhood and adolescent depression: Part I. A review of the past 10 years. *Journal of the American Academy of Child and Adolescent Psychiatry, 35*, 1427–1439.

Birmaher, B., Waterman, G. S., Ryan, N. D., Perel, J., McNabb, J., & Balach, L. (1998). A randomized controlled trial of amitriptyline versus placebo for adolescents with "treatment resistant" major depression. *Journal of the American Academy of Child and Adolescent Psychiatry, 37*, 527–535.

Boulos, C., Kutcher, S., Gardner, D., & Young, E. (1992). An open naturalistic trial of fluoxetine in adolescents and young adults with treatment-resistant major depression. *Journal of Child and Adolescent Psychopharmacology, 2*, 103–111.

Boulos, C., Kutcher, S., Marton, P., Simeon J., Ferguson, B., Roberts, N., & Young, E. (1991). Response to desipramine treatment in adolescent major depression. *Psychopharmacology Bulletin, 27*, 60–65.

Bowring, M. A., & Kovacs, M. (1992). Difficulties in diagnosing manic disorders in children and adolescents. *Journal of the American Academy of Child and Adolescent Psychiatry, 31*, 611–614.

Carlson, G. A., & Kashani, J. H. (1988). Manic symptoms in a non-referred adolescent population. *Journal of Affective Disorders, 15*, 219–226.

Clarke, G. N., Hawkins, W., Murphy, M., Sheeber L., Lewinsohn, P., & Seeley, J. (1995). Targeted prevention of unipolar depressive disorder in an at-risk sample of high school adolescents: A randomized trial of a group cognitive intervention. *Journal of the American Academy of Child and Adolescent Psychiatry, 34*, 312–321.

Clarke, G., Rohde, P., Lewinsohn, P., Hops, H., & Seeley, J. (1999). Cognitive–behavioral treatment of adolescent depression: Efficacy of acute group treatment and booster sessions. *Journal of the American Academy of Child and Adolescent Psychiatry, 38*, 272–279.

Colle, L., Belair, J., DiFeo, M., Weiss, J., & LaRoache, C. (1994). Extended open-label fluoxetine treatment of adolescents with major depression. *Journal of Child and Adolescent Psychopharmacology, 4*, 225–232.

Cosgrove, P. V. F. (1994). Fluvoxamine in the treatment of depressive illness in children and adolescents. *Journal of Psychopharmacology, 8*, 118–123.

Cox, N., Reich, T., Rice, J., & Elston, R. C. (1989). Segregation and linkage analyses of bipolar and major depressive illness in multigenerational pedigrees. *Journal of Psychiatric Research, 23*, 109–123.

DeLong, G. R., & Nieman, G. W. (1983). Lithium-induced behavior changes in children with symptoms suggesting manic–depressive illness. *Psychopharmacology Bulletin, 19*, 258–265.

Deltito, J., Levitan, D., Damore, J., Hajal, F., & Zambenedetti, M. (1997). Naturalistic experience with the use of divalproex sodium on an in-patient unit for adolescent psychiatric patients. *Acta Psychiatrica Scandinavica, 97*, 236–240.

Emslie, G. J., Rush, A. J., Weinberg, W. A., Kowatch, R. A., Carmody, R., & Mayes, T. L. (1998). Fluoxetine in child and adolescent depression: Acute and maintenance treatment. *Depression and Anxiety, 7*, 32–39.

Emslie, G. J., Rush, A. J., Weinberg, W. A., Kowatch, R. A., Hughes, C., Carmody, T., & Rintelmann, J. (1997). A double-blind, randomized placebo-controlled trial of fluoxetine in depressed children and adolescents. *Archives of General Psychiatry, 54*, 1031–1037.

Ewald, H., Degn, M. O., Mors, O., & Kruse, T. A. (1998). Significant linkage between bipolar affective disorder and chromosome 12q24. *Psychiatric Genetics, 8*, 131–140.

Faedda, G., Baldessarini, R., Suppes, T., Tondo, L., Becker, I., & Lipschitz, D. (1995). Pediatric-onset bipolar disorder: A neglected clinical and public health problem. *Harvard Review of Psychiatry, 3*, 171–195.

Fleming, J. D., & Offord, D. R. (1990). Epidemiology of childhood depressive disorders: A critical review. *Journal of the American Academy of Child and Adolescent Psychiatry, 29*, 571–580.

Frazier, J., Meyer, M., Biederman, J., Woznik, J., Wilens, T., Spencer, T., Kim, G., & Shapiro, S. (1999). Risperidone treatment for juvenile bipolar disorder: A retrospective chart review. *Journal of the American Academy of Child and Adolescent Psychiatry, 38*, 960–965.

Fuchs, C. (1994). Clozapine treatment of bipolar disorder in a young adolescent. *Journal of the American Academy of Child and Adolescent Psychiatry, 33*, 1299–1302.

Geller, B., Cooper, T. B., Graham, D. L., & Fetner, H. H. (1992). Pharmacokinetically designed double-blind placebo-controlled study of nortriptyline in 6- to 12-year-olds with major depressive disorder. *American Academy of Child and Adolescent Psychiatry, 31*, 34–44.

Geller, B., Cooper, T. B., Graham, D. L., Marsteller, F., & Bryant, D. (1990). Double-blind placebo-controlled study of nortriptyline in depressed adolescents using a "fixed plasma level" design. *Psychopharmacology Bulletin, 26*, 85–90.

Geller, B., Cooper, T., Sun, K., Zimmerman, B., Frazier, J., Williams, M., & Heath, J. (1998). Double-blind and placebo-controlled study of lithium for adolescent bipolar disorders with secondary substance dependency. *Journal of the American Academy of Child and Adolescent Psychiatry, 37*, 171–178.

Geller, B., Fox, K., Cooper, T., & Garrity, K. (1992). Baseline and 2- to 3-year follow-up characteristics of placebo-washout responders from the nortriptyline study of depressed 6- to 12-year olds. *Journal of the American Academy of Child and Adolescent Psychiatry, 31*, 622–628.

Geller, B., & Luby, J. (1997). Child and adolescent bipolar disorder: A review of the past 10 years. *Journal of the American Academy of Child and Adolescent Psychiatry, 36*, 1168–1177.

Gillham, J., Reivich, K., Jaycox, L., & Seligman, M. (1995). Prevention of depressive symptoms in schoolchildren: Two-year follow-up. *Psychological Science, 6*, 343–351.

Hughes, C., Preskorn, S., Wrona, M., Hassanein, R., & Tucker, S. (1990). Follow-up of adolescents initially treated for prepubertal-onset major depressive disorder with imipramine. *Psychopharmacology Bulletin, 26*, 244–248.

Jain, U., Birmaher, B., Garcia, M., Al-Shabbout, M., & Ryan, N. (1992). Fluoxetine in children and adolescents with mood disorders: A chart review of efficacy and adverse effects. *Journal of Child and Adolescent Psychopharmacology, 2*, 259–265.

Jaycox, L. H., Reivich, K. J., Gillham, J., & Seligman, M. (1994). Prevention of depressive symptoms in school children. *Behavior Research and Therapy, 32*, 801–816.

Kendall, P. C., Panichelli-Mindel, S. M., & Gerow, M. A. (1995). Cognitive–behavioral therapies with children and adolescents: An integrative overview. In H. P. van Bilsen, P. C. Kendall, & J. H. Slavenburg (Eds.), *Behavioral approaches for children and adolescents: Challenges for the next century* (pp. 1–18). New York: Plenum Press.

Kessler, R. C., McGonagle, K. A., Nelson, C. B., Hughes, M., Swartz, M., & Blazer, D. G. (1994). Sex and depression in the national comorbidity survey: II. Cohort effects. *Journal of Affective Disorders, 30*, 15–26.

Klar, A. J. S. (1999). Genetic models for handedness, brain lateralization, schizophrenia, and manic-depression. *Schizophrenia Research, 39*, 207–218.

Kovacs, M., Devlin, B., Pollock, M., Richards, C., & Mukerji, P. (1997). A controlled family history study of childhood-onset depressive disorder. *Archives of General Psychiatry, 54*, 613–623.

Kowatch, R. A., Suppes, T., Gilifillan, S. K., & Fuentes, R. M. (1995). Clozapine treatment of children and adolescents with bipolar disorder and schizophrenia: A clinical case series. *Journal of Child and Adolescent Psychopharmacology, 5*, 241–253.

Kroll, L., Harrington, R., Jayson, D., Fraser, J., & Gowers, S. (1996). Pilot study of continuation cognitive–behavioral therapy for major depression in adolescent psychiatric patients. *Journal of the American Academy of Child and Adolescent Psychiatry, 36,* 1156–1161.

Kutcher, S., Boulos, C., Ward, B., Marton, P., Simeon, J., Ferguson, B., Szalai, J., Katic, M., Roberts, N., Dubois, C., & Reed, K. (1994). Response to desipramine treatment in adolescent depression: A fixed-dose, placebo-controlled trial. *Journal of the American Academy of Child and Adolescent Psychiatry, 33,* 686–694.

Kye, C., Waterman, G., Ryan, N., Birmaher, B., Williamson, D. I., Iyengar, S., & Dachille, S. (1996). A randomized, controlled trial of amitriptyline in the acute treatment of adolescent major depression. *Journal of the American Academy of Child and Adolescent Psychiatry, 35,* 1139–1144.

Lewinsohn, P. M., Clarke, G., Hops, H., & Andrews, J. A. (1990). Cognitive–behavioral treatment for depressed adolescents. *Behavior Therapy, 21,* 385–401.

Lewinsohn, P. M., Clarke, G., Rohde, P., & Hops, H. (1996). A course in coping: A cognitive–behavioral approach to the treatment of adolescent depression. In E. D. Hibbs & P. E. Jensen (Eds.), *Psychosocial treatments for child and adolescent disorders: Empirically based strategies for clinical practice* (pp. 109–135). Washington, DC: American Psychological Association.

Lewinsohn, P. M., Clarke, G., Seeley, J., & Rohde, P. (1994). Major depression in community adolescents: Age at onset, episode duration and time to recurrence. *Journal of the American Academy of Child and Adolescent Psychiatry, 33,* 809–818.

Lewinsohn, P. M., Klein, D. N., & Seeley, J. (1995). Bipolar disorders in a community sample of older adolescents: Prevalence, phenomenology, comorbidity, and course. *Journal of the American Academy of Child and Adolescent Psychiatry, 34,* 454–464.

Mandoki, M., Tapia, M., Tapia, M. A., Sumner, G., & Parker, J. (1997). Venlafaxine in the treatment of children and adolescents with major depression. *Psychopharmacology Bulletin, 33,* 149–154.

McConville, R., Minnery, K., Sorter, M., West, S., Friedman, L., & Christian, K. (1996). An open study of the effects of sertraline on adolescent major depression. *Journal of Child and Adolescent Psychopharmacology, 6,* 41–51.

McGrath, E., Keita, G. P., Strickland, B. R., & Russo, N. F. (Eds.). (1990). *Women and depression: Risk factors and treatment issues.* Washington, DC: American Psychological Association.

McKnew, D. H., Cytryn, L., Buchsbaum, M., Hamovit, J., Lamour, M., Rapoport, J., & Gershon, E. (1981). Lithium in children of lithium-responding parents. *Psychiatry Research, 4,* 171–180.

Meltzer, H. Y. (2000). Genetics and etiology of schizophrenia and bipolar disorder. *Biological Psychiatry, 47,* 171–173.

Moreau, D., & Mufson, L. (1997). Interpersonal psychotherapy for depressed adolescents. *Child and Adolescent Psychiatric Clinics of North America, 6,* 97–110.

Moreau, D., Mufson, L., Weissman, M., & Klerman, G. (1991). Interpersonal psychotherapy for adolescent depression: Description of modification and preliminary application. *Journal of the American Academy of Child and Adolescent Psychiatry, 30*, 642–651.

Mufson, L., & Fairbanks, J. (1996). Interpersonal psychotherapy for depressed adolescents: One-year naturalistic follow-up study. *Journal of the American Academy of Child and Adolescent Psychiatry, 35*, 1145–1155.

Mufson, L., Moreau, D., Weissman, M., Wickramaratne, P., Martin, J., & Samoilov, A. (1994). Modification of interpersonal psychotherapy with depressed adolescents (IPT-A): Phase I and II studies. *Journal of the American Academy of Child and Adolescent Psychiatry, 33*, 695–705.

Mufson, L., Weissman, M., Moreau, D., & Garfinkel, R. (1999). Efficacy of interpersonal psychotherapy for depressed adolescents. *Archives of General Psychiatry, 56*, 573–579.

Nolen-Hoeksema, S., & Girgus, J. (1994). The emergence of gender differences in depression during adolescence. *Psychological Bulletin, 115*, 424–443.

Overaschel, H., Beeferman, D., & Kabacoff, R. (1997). Depression, self-esteem, sex, and age in a child and adolescent clinical sample. *Journal of Clinical Child Psychology, 26*, 285–289.

Papatheodorou, G., & Kutcher, S. (1993). Divalproex sodium treatment in late adolescent and young adult acute mania. *Psychopharmacology Bulletin, 29*, 213–219.

Papatheodorou, G., Kutcher, S., Katic, M., & Szalai, J. P. (1995). The efficacy and safety of divalproex sodium in the treatment of acute mania in adolescents and young adults: An open clinical trial. *Journal of Clinical Psychopharmacology, 15*, 110–116.

Physicians' Desk Reference. (53rd ed.). (1999). Montvale, NJ: Medical Economics.

Potter, W. Z., Rudorfer, M. V., & Manji, H. K. (1991). The pharmacologic treatment of depression. *New England Journal of Medicine, 325*, 633–642.

Preskorn, S., Weller, E., Hughes, C., Weller, R., & Bolte, K. (1987). Depression in prepubertal children: Dexamethasone nonsuppression predicts differential response to imipramine vs placebo. *Psychopharmacology Bulletin, 23*, 128–133.

Puig-Antich, J., Perel, J., Lupatkin, W., Chambers, W., Tabrizi, M., King, J., Goetz, R., Davies, M., & Stiller, R. (1987). Imipramine in prepubertal major depressive disorders. *Archives of General Psychiatry, 44*, 81–89.

Reinecke, M., Ryan, N., & Dubois, D. (1998). Cognitive–behavioral therapy of depression and depressive symptoms during adolescence: A review and meta-analysis. *Journal of the American Academy of Child and Adolescent Psychiatry, 37*, 26–34.

Rey-Sanchez, F., & Gutierrez-Casares, J. (1997). Paroxetine in children with major depressive disorder: An open trial. *Journal of the American Academy of Child and Adolescent Psychiatry, 36*, 1443–1447.

Riddle, M., Geller, B., & Ryan, N. (1993). Another sudden death in a child treated with desipramine. *Journal of the American Academy of Child and Adolescent Psychiatry, 32,* 792- 797.

Riggs, P. D., Mikulich, S. K., Coffman, L. M., & Crowley, T. J. (1997). Fluoxetine in drug-dependent delinquents with major depression: An open trial. *Journal of Child and Adolescent Psychopharmacology, 7,* 87–95.

Ryan, N., Puig-Antich, J., Cooper, T., Rabinovich, H., Ambrosini, P., Davies, M., King, J., Torres, D., & Fried, J. (1986). Imipramine in adolescent major depression: Plasma level and clinical response. *Acta Psychiatrica Scandinavica, 73,* 275–288.

Sallee, F., Hilial, R., Dougherty, D., Beach, K., & Nesbitt, L. (1998). Platelet serotonin transporter in depressed children and adolescents: 3H-paroxetine platelet binding before and after sertraline. *Journal of the American Academy of Child and Adolescent Psychiatry, 37,* 777–784.

Sallee, F., Vrindavanam, N., Deas-Nesmith, D., Carson, S., & Sethuraman, G. (1997). Pulse intravenous clomipramine for depressed adolescents: Double-blind controlled trial. *American Journal of Psychiatry, 154,* 668–673.

Scott, J. (1996). Cognitive therapy for clients with bipolar disorder. *Cognitive and Behavioral Practice, 3,* 29–51.

Silberg, J., Pickles, A., Rutter, M., Hewitt, J., Simonoff, E., Maes, H., Carbonneau, R., Murrelle, L., Foley, D., & Eaves, L. (1999). The influence of genetic factors and life stress on depression among adolescent girls. *Archives of General Psychiatry, 56,* 225–232.

Southam-Gerow, M. A., Henin, A., Chu, B., Marrs, A., & Kendall, P. C. (1997). Cognitive–behavioral therapy with children and adolescents. *Child and Adolescent Psychiatric Clinics of North America, 6,* 111–135.

Stark, K. D., Rouse, L., & Livingston, R. (1991). Treatment of depression during childhood and adolescence: Cognitive behavioral procedures for the individual and family. In P. Kendall (Ed.), *Child and adolescent therapy* (pp. 165–206). New York: Guilford Press.

Steele, M., & Fisman, S. (1997). Bipolar disorder in children and adolescents: Current challenges. *Canadian Journal of Psychiatry, 42,* 632–636.

Strober, M., Freeman, R., & Rigali, J. (1990). The pharmacotherapy of depressive illness in adolescence: I. An open label trial of imipramine. *Psychopharmacology Bulletin, 26,* 80–84.

Strober, M., Schmidt-Lackner, S., Freeman, R., Bower, S. Lampert, C., & DeAntonio, M. (1995). Recovery and relapse in adolescents with bipolar affective illness: A five-year naturalistic, prospective follow-up. *Journal of the American Academy of Child and Adolescent Psychiatry, 34,* 724–731.

Thapar, A., & McGuffin, P. (1996). The genetic etiology of childhood depressive symptoms: A developmental perspective. *Development and Psychopathology, 8,* 751–760.

Tollefson, G. (1995). Selective serotonin reuptake inhibitors. In A. Schatzberg & C. B. Nemeroff (Eds.), *American Psychiatric Press textbook of psychopharmacology* (pp. 141–160). Washington, DC: American Psychiatric Press.

Torrey, E. F. (1999). Epidemiological comparison of schizophrenia and bipolar disorder. *Schizophrenia Research, 39,* 101–106.

Varley, C., & McClellan, J. (1997). Case study: Two additional sudden deaths with tricyclic antidepressants *Journal of the American Academy of Child and Adolescent Psychiatry, 34,* 390–395.

Vostanis, P., Feehan, C., & Grattan, E. (1998). Two-year outcome for depression. *European Child and Adolescent Psychiatry, 7,* 12–18.

Vostanis, P., Feehan, C., Grattan, E., & Bickerton, W. L. (1996). A randomized controlled out-patient trial of cognitive–behavioral treatment for children and adolescents with depression: Nine-month follow-up. *Journal of Affective Disorders, 40,* 105–116.

Warner, V., Weissman, M. M., Mufson, L., & Wickramaratne, P. J. (1999). Grandparents, parents, and grandchildren at high risk for depression: A three generation study. *Journal of the American Academy of Child and Adolescent Psychiatry, 38,* 289–296.

Weisz, J. R., Thurber, C. A., Sweeney, L., Proffitt, V., & LeGagnoux, G. (1997). Brief treatment of mild-to-moderate child depression using primary and secondary control enhancement training. *Journal of Consulting and Clinical Psychology, 65,* 703–707.

Weller, E., Weller, R., & Fristad, M. (1995). Bipolar disorder in children: Misdiagnosis, underdiagnosis, and future directions. *Journal of the American Academy of Child and Adolescent Psychiatry, 34,* 709–714.

Werry, J. (1995). Resolved: Cardiac arrhythmias make desipramine an unacceptable choice in children. *Journal of the American Academy of Child and Adolescent Psychiatry, 34,* 1239–1243.

West, S., Keck, P., & McElroy, S. (1995). Oral loading doses in the valproate treatment of adolescents with mixed bipolar disorder. *Journal of Child and Adolescent Psychopharmacology, 5,* 225–231.

Wildenauer, D. B., Schwab, S. G., Maier, W., & Detera-Wadleigh, S. D. (1999). Do schizophrenia and affective disorders share susceptibility genes? *Schizophrenia Research, 39,* 107–111.

Wilens, T., Spencer, T., Biederman, J., & Schleifer, D. (1997). Case study: Nefazodone for juvenile mood disorders. *Journal of the American Academy of Child and Adolescent Psychiatry, 36,* 481–485.

Wood, A., Harrington, R., & Moore, A. (1996). Controlled trial of a brief cognitive–behavioral intervention in adolescent patients with depressive disorders. *Journal of Child Psychology and Psychiatry, 37,* 737–746.

Woolston, J. (1999). Case study: Carbamazepine treatment of juvenile-onset bipolar disorder. *Journal of the American Academy of Child and Adolescent Psychiatry, 36,* 335–338.

9

PSYCHOTIC DISORDERS

Although childhood psychosis has been recognized since the early 20th century, its definition has been subject to change (Campbell & Armenteros, 1996). Because early researchers concluded that all childhood maladies resulting in severe functional impairment eventually developed into adult schizophrenia, early definitions were overly inclusive and included the pervasive developmental disorders (e.g., autism) and even less obvious cases of mental retardation (McClellan & Werry, 1994). Research conducted in this area prior to the 1970s, therefore, is difficult to interpret in light of our current understanding (Tolbert, 1996).

The fourth edition of the *Diagnostic and Statistical Manual of Mental Disorders* (*DSM–IV*; American Psychiatric Association, 1994) identifies schizophrenia as the primary category within the broad spectrum of psychotic disorders. Other diagnoses within this *DSM–IV* classification include schizophreniform disorders (i.e., schizophrenic symptoms that last longer than 1 month), schizoaffective disorder (i.e., schizophrenic symptoms coupled with a mood disorder), delusional disorder (i.e., nonbizarre delusions without other symptoms), shared psychotic disorder (i.e., the individual is influenced by someone else who is exhibiting similar impairment), psychotic disorder due to a general medical condition, substance-induced psychotic disorder, and psychotic disorder not otherwise specified.

DIAGNOSTIC CRITERIA

In adults, the term *psychotic* refers to prominent delusions or hallucinations, impairment in reality testing, and incoherent or disorganized speech (American Psychiatric Association, 1994). Because abstract reasoning, language, and more complex emotions such as empathy and remorse are still in the process of developing in children, the clinical assessment of reality testing, absence of insight into behavior, and idiosyncratic speech or behavior is difficult with this age group (Caplan, 1994; Tolbert, 1996). Thus the Schizophrenia and Other Psychotic Disorders Work Group for the *DSM–IV* concluded that age 7 years should be used as a lower limit for diagnosing thought disorders in children (American Psychiatric Association, 1994). Yet separate diagnostic criteria for children were not viewed as necessary because the symptoms are analogous to those evidenced in adults (Campbell & Armenteros, 1996; Eggers & Bunk, 1997).

To better facilitate an understanding of the classic presentation of schizophrenia in both children and adults, researchers have divided the symptoms into two groupings: (a) present or positive characteristics and (b) absent or negative characteristics (American Psychiatric Association, 1994). Positive symptoms include delusions (i.e., misinterpretation of perceptions or experiences); prominent hallucinations (i.e., auditory [most common], visual, olfactory, gustatory, or tactile perceptions of stimuli that are not actually present); disorganized speech (i.e., incoherent language, tangential speech, or substantial impairment in communication); and disorganized or catatonic behavior (i.e., impaired situational awareness and goal-directed actions). In contrast, negative symptoms include blunted affect (e.g., unresponsiveness, poor eye contact, or reduced body language); alogia (i.e., poverty of expressive speech); and avolition (e.g., apathy and little interest in activities). To meet the *DSM–IV* diagnostic criteria, at least two out of the five categories (i.e., delusions, hallucinations, disorganized speech, disorganized behavior, and negative symptoms) must be present during a 1-month period.

Childhood maladies that may share symptomatology with the psychotic disorders include severe speech/language impairment, the pervasive developmental disorders (e.g., autism, Rett's disorder, and Asperger's disorder), attention deficit hyperactivity disorder, and stereotypic movement disorder (American Psychiatric Association, 1994; Eggers & Bunk, 1997). Because symptom onset is usually between the late teens and the mid-30s, childhood diagnosis of psychosis (younger than age 12 years) is rare, with current prevalence data indicating an approximate ratio of 1.4 per 10,000 (McKenna, Gordon, & Rapoport, 1994). Fewer than 1% of all psychotic disorders are manifested prior to age 10, and only 4% appear before age 15 (Remschmidt, Schulz, Martin, Warnke, & Trott, 1994).

ETIOLOGY

There is overwhelming evidence for a significant genetic contribution to the etiology of schizophrenia (Cloninger et al., 1998; van Os & Marcelis, 1998). To facilitate the identification of specific genetic markers, the National Institute of Mental Health established the Schizophrenia Genetics Initiative in 1996 to fund collaborative research in molecular genetic analyses (http://zork.wustl.edu/nimh/sz.html). Because there is not a complete concordance for psychotic symptoms in monozygotic twins, it is evident that transmission does not follow a simple Mendelian approach. Alternative hypotheses include multifactorial origins such as transmission via multiple genes or a single recessive gene that is evidenced because of an interaction with environmental risk factors (Freedman, Adler, & Leonard, 1999; Gershon et al., 1998; Guidry & Kent, 1999). Numerous researchers are investigating various locations on chromosomes 2, 6, 8, 9, 10, 11, 13, 15, 16, and 18 as the probable site for genetic transmission of schizophrenia (e.g., Chen, Shih, Wang-Wuu, Tai, & Wuu, 1998; Curtis et al., 1999; Schwab et al., 1998; Shaw et al., 1998; Wildenauer & Schwab, 1999).

Childhood onset of psychosis is generally assumed to be associated with increased genetic loading because of the earlier development and severity of symptoms (Eggers & Bunk, 1997; Ross et al., 1999). Whatever the genetic mode of transportation, childhood schizophrenia is related to a gradual decrease in cerebral volume coupled with a progressive increase in ventricular enlargement (Jacobsen et al., 1997; Rapoport et al., 1999). Specific areas of the brain to evidence malfunction or neuronal damage include the hippocampus, prefrontal cortex, and temporal lobe structures (Bertolino et al., 1998; Eastwood & Harrison, 1998; Jacobsen et al., 1998). The alterations manifested in the brain tissue of children with schizophrenia are similar in magnitude to that of patients with adult onset of the disorder, suggesting a biological continuum between childhood and adult onset (Frazier et al., 1996; Zahn et al., 1997). Likewise, the neurodevelopmental models indicate that the more severe the brain anomalies, the earlier the onset of psychotic symptoms (Alaghband-Rad, Hamburger, Giedd, Frazier, & Rapoport, 1997; Nopoulos, Giedd, Andreasen, & Rapoport, 1998).

LONG-TERM PROGNOSIS

Until recently, there were few satisfactory long-term prospective studies regarding the outcomes of childhood-onset psychotic disorders. Three excellent studies that do provide such data indicate that early onset is an extremely disabling and chronic condition with a generally worse prognosis than when onset is during adulthood (Cawthron, James, Dell, & Seagrott, 1994; Eggers & Bunk, 1997; Maziade et al., 1996).

Eggers and Bunk (1997) concluded that the date of first inpatient admission was not a reliable indicator of the timing of initial symptoms because relatives often tolerated the child's behavioral abnormalities for some time. This is particularly true given the heavy genetic loading of childhood onset; that is, it is likely that other first-degree relatives evidence some degree of mental instability. Unfortunately, the longer the psychosis continues untreated, the worse the long-term prognosis (Birchwood, McGorry, & Jackson, 1997).

MEDICAL INTERVENTIONS

Because of the debilitating nature of florid psychotic episodes, the first line of treatment is the administration of medications, in particular, the neuroleptics. Although the efficacy of antipsychotic drugs has been well established with adults, there is a paucity of data regarding such medications with the pediatric population. Nonetheless, there are enough empirically supported outcomes as to inform psychosocial and behavioral clinicians regarding psychotropic options, expected treatment outcomes, and possible adverse effects. It should be noted that all neuroleptic medications are intended to reduce psychotic symptoms by blocking the D2 dopamine receptors in the brain (Carlson, 1995).

Tables 9.1 and 9.2 provide, respectively, a summary of the antipsychotic medications clinically validated in double-blind and open studies for use with children and adolescents. The tables list recommended dosage, expected positive treatment outcomes, and possible adverse effects. Refer to the *Glossary of Terms* at the end of the book for definitions of medical terms.

Clozapine

Clozapine (Clozaril) is intended for the management of psychotic symptoms that cannot be controlled by standard antipsychotic medications (*Physicians' Desk Reference*, 1999). Approved by the U.S. Food and Drug Administration (FDA) in 1990, it is referred to as an atypical antipsychotic because it does not produce the significant extrapyramidal side effects (i.e., involuntary dyskinetic movements, tremors, muscle spasms, and balance difficulties) common in the more traditional neuroleptics. Lack of these symptoms is likely due to low D2 dopamine receptor affinity (Lewis, 1998). Nonetheless, clozapine has the significant drawback of causing agranulocytosis (i.e., bone marrow and white blood cell depletion; Meltzer & Fatemi, 1998). Agranulocytosis can be fatal if not detected early and treat-

TABLE 9.1
Antipsychotic Medications Clinically Validated in Double-Blind Studies for Use With Children and Adolescents With Psychotic Disorders

Generic Name (Trade Name)	Children mg/kg/day or Daily Dose	Adolescents mg/kg/day or Daily Dose	Treatment Outcome	Adverse Effect
Clozapine (Clozaril)	Not yet established	Not yet established	Highly effective with children who have not responded adequately to conventional neuroleptics.	Possibility of extreme drops in bone marrow and white blood cell count, which can be fatal if not detected early. Requires very close monitoring.
Haloperidol (Haldol)	0.25–6.0 mg/kg	1.0–16 mg/kg	Very effective in symptom reduction of schizophrenia.	Moderate involuntary dyskinetic movements and other extrapyramidal side effects (tremors, muscle spasms, balance difficulty).
Loxapine (Daxlin, Loxitane)	Not yet established	25–200 mg	Effective in symptom reduction of schizophrenia.	Less involuntary dyskinetic movements and other extrapyramidal side effects, but excessive sedative effects.
Thioridazine (Mellaril)	10–200 mg	50–600 mg	Effective in symptom reduction of schizophrenia.	Sedation and anticholinergic side effects (dry eyes, mouth, and throat; blurred vision; constipation).
Thiothixene (Navane)	Not yet established	5.0–45 mg/kg	Effective in symptom reduction of schizophrenia.	Sedation and involuntary dyskinetic movements and other extrapyramidal side effects. Safety with children under 12 years of age not yet established.

Note. Sources include McClellan and Werry (1994); *Physicians' Desk Reference* (1999); Remschmidt, Schulz, and Herpertz-Dahlmann (1996); and Spencer and Campbell (1994).

TABLE 9.2

Antipsychotic Medications Clinically Validated in Open Studies for Use With Children and Adolescents With Psychotic Disorders

Generic Name (Trade Name)	Children mg/kg/day or Daily Dose	Adolescents mg/kg/day or Daily Dose	Treatment Outcome	Adverse Effect
Olanzapine (Zyprexa)	Not yet established	Not yet established	Somewhat effective in symptom reduction of schizophrenia.	Sedation and anticholinergic side effects (constipation, blurred vision, and dry eyes, mouth, and throat). Safety with children under 12 years of age not yet established.
Risperidone (Risperdal)	Not yet established	2–10 mg	Effective in symptom reduction of schizophrenia.	Sedation and involuntary dyskinetic movements and extrapyramidal side effects. Safety with children under 12 years of age not yet established.

Note. Sources include Kumra, Jacobsen, Lenane, Karp, et al. (1998); *Physicians' Desk Reference* (1999); and Remschmidt, Schulz, and Martin (1994).

ment discontinued (*Physicians' Desk Reference*, 1999). Thus, the medication requires very close blood plasma monitoring by the prescribing physician.

Numerous open and double-blind studies have documented the efficacy of clozapine with treatment-refractory childhood onset cases (e.g., Birmaher, Baker, Kapur, Quintana, & Ganguli, 1992; Fleischhaker, Schulz, & Remschmidt, 1998; Jacobsen, Walker, Edwards, Chappell, & Woolston, 1994; Kumra, Jacobsen, Lenane, Smith, et al., 1998; Mozes et al. 1994; Remschmidt, Schulz, & Martin, 1994; Towbin, Dykens, & Pugliese, 1994; Turetz et al., 1997). In a double-blind parallel comparison of clozapine with haloperidol (Haldol; Kumra et al., 1996) and another open-trial study that made the same comparison (Frazier et al., 1994), clozapine proved superior to haloperidol in reducing psychotic symptomatology. Thus, clozapine has very positive outcomes yet significant treatment side effects.

In conclusion, clozapine is considered an acceptable alternative only when other antipsychotic medication trials have failed to achieve success. Because of the life-threatening adverse effects, the *Physicians' Desk Reference* (1999) recommends completion of at least *two* trials each with at least *two* different traditional neuroleptic medications before the administration of clozapine.

Haloperidol

First synthesized in the 1960s for use with the adult population, haloperidol (Haldol) quickly became a mainstay in the treatment of childhood-onset schizophrenia. Numerous double-blind, placebo-controlled studies have verified that this medication is superior to placebos in treating children and adolescents who are presenting with active psychotic symptoms (e.g., Piscitelli et al., 1995; Spencer & Campbell, 1994; Spencer, Kanfantaris, Padron-Gayol, Rosenberg, & Campbell, 1992). An advantage of haloperidol is its relatively low level of sedation in comparison with other neuroleptic agents (Campbell & Armenteros, 1996). Youngsters taking this medication, however, have a relatively high incidence of developing extrapyramidal symptoms (i.e., involuntary dyskinetic movements, tremors, muscle spasms, balance difficulties) that occur because of the action on the D2 dopamine receptors. Nonetheless, it is the most commonly prescribed neuroleptic medication with the pediatric population (Lewis, 1998).

Loxapine

Loxapine (Daxlin, Loxitane) is chemically related to clozapine and is considered to be between haloperidol and clozapine in terms of its affinity for dopamine D2 receptors. As a result, there is less likelihood of extrapyramidal side effects than with haloperidol but still a higher probability than with clozapine (Ereshefsky, 1999; Kapra et al., 1997). Current data indicate that loxapine is useful in treating cases of schizophrenia that have not responded to traditional neuroleptic medications (Meltzer & Jayathilake, 1999). Yet most studies have been completed on the adult population. In one of the earliest pediatric studies, Pool, Bloom, Mielke, Roniger, and Gallant (1976) completed a double-blind study that compared loxapine with haloperidol with 75 adolescent patients diagnosed with schizophrenia and concluded that both agents were effective in symptom reduction. The drawback to loxapine, however, is its excessive sedative effects (Campbell & Armenteros, 1996). As a result, researchers suggest loxapine be viewed as an option only when other traditional (e.g., haloperidol) and atypical (e.g., clozapine) neuroleptics have failed (Mowerman & Siris, 1996; *Physicians' Desk Reference*, 1999; Stahl, 1999).

Olanzapine

Approved by the FDA in 1996, efficacy studies with olanzapine (Zyprexa) are few. Similar in D2 dopamine receptor affinity to clozapine, it is viewed as an atypical neuroleptic with significantly fewer extrapyramidal adverse effects than haloperidol (Stahl, 1999). Adverse effects are few but do include sedation, constipation, and dry eyes, mouth, and throat (*Physicians' Desk Reference*, 1999). In a review of all published open and double-blind studies that compared olanzapine with placebos or haloperidol, Kando et al. (1997) concluded that olanzapine was superior to both in symptom reduction. In one of the few published pediatric studies, Kumra, Jacobsen, Lenane, Karp, et al. (1998) conducted an open-trial comparison study of this medication to clozapine on 8 children and adolescents diagnosed with schizophrenia. Overall ratings of symptom reduction indicated that clozapine is more effective than olanzapine. Many more carefully controlled double-blind research studies are clearly necessary before the efficacy and safety of olanzapine with the pediatric population can be established.

Risperidone

Approved by the FDA in 1994, no well-designed double-blind studies exist regarding the use of risperidone (Risperdal) in children and adolescents exhibiting schizophrenic symptoms. Yet numerous open trials indicate that risperidone substantially improves target psychotic behaviors (Armenteros, Whitaker, Welikson, Stedge, & Gorman, 1997; Cozza & Edison, 1994; Grcevich, Findling, Rowane, Friedman, & Schulz, 1996; Mandoki, 1995; Quintana & Keshavan, 1995; Simeon, Carey, Wiggins, Milin, & Hosenbocus, 1995; Zuddas, Pintor, & Cianchetti, 1996). Unfortunately, negative extrapyramidal side effects are evident in pediatric samples at a rate greater than would be expected based on adult studies (Edelman, 1996; Lewis, 1998). Substantially more data are necessary, therefore, to establish the efficacy and safety of this agent with the pediatric population (*Physicians' Desk Reference*, 1999).

Thioridazine and Thiothixene

Although these traditional neuroleptic medications have been available for some time, neither one has been found very effective in the treatment of childhood-onset psychosis. For example, Realmuto, Erickson, Yellin, Hopwood, and Greenberg (1984) compared the effectiveness of both medications in a single-blind study of 21 adolescents diagnosed with schizophrenia. The researchers reported that heavy sedation followed the use of both agents and required dose reductions that limited therapeutic responsiveness. In addition, the adolescents treated with thiothixene (Navane) experienced extrapyramidal symptoms. Although thioridazine (Mellaril) did not result in involuntary dyskinetic movements, it did cause anticholinergic side effects (constipation, blurred vision, and dry eyes, mouth, and throat). In a follow-up study, Erickson, Yellin, Hogwood, Realmuto, and Greenberg (1984) reported similar findings. Overall, the lack of demonstrated efficacy and notable adverse effects limit the use of thioridazine or thiothixene as first-line treatments for psychotic disorders with children.

PSYCHOSOCIAL INTERVENTIONS

Treatment with any child or adolescent displaying psychotic symptoms is best if it is multimodal and incorporates family support services, psychoeducational assistance, and individual interventions (Lange & Julien, 1997). It is recommended that treatment be implemented by a full multidisciplinary team that includes educational, mental health, and psychiatric specialists. Facilitation of family–professional partnerships must go beyond diagnosis and the provision of medical services for these children; instead, endorsed efforts include (a) assistance to the families so that they are an integral part of the child's interdisciplinary care, (b) incorporation of family strengths and cultural values into service planning, (c) encouragement of parent-to-parent support groups, and (d) provision of all services in a manner that is flexible, accessible, and responsive to family needs (de Jesus Mari & Streiner, 1994; Dixon & Lehman, 1995).

Early identification and primary prevention, if possible, are key components to successful treatment. Yet prospective studies of children and adolescents diagnosed with early onset schizophrenia indicate that symptoms often go unrecognized and untreated for a considerable length of time (Eggers & Bunk, 1997; Werry, McClellan, Andrews, & Ham, 1994). Although there are no data to support the efficacy of primary prevention with children who because of a strong family history for mental disorders are at significant risk, the likely long-term benefits of early monitoring and support services would seem to outweigh the traditional pattern of waiting until full-blown symptoms are evident.

Family Support Services

The effectiveness of incorporating family members in the treatment of adults who are displaying psychotic symptoms is well established (Frances, Docherty, & Kahn, 1996; Schulz, Findling, Wise, Friedman, & Kenny, 1998). Such family support services have often included practical support, reduction of stress, and an opportunity to "vent" negative emotions such as anger and frustration (Dixon & Lehman, 1995). There is a clear body of evidence that these strategies do reduce subsequent relapse of psychotic symptoms as well as promote better social functioning for both the adult client and her or his family (de Jesus Mari & Streiner, 1994; Penn & Mueser, 1996). Yet the efficacy of such services with families of pediatric patients has not been evaluated.

Nonetheless, there are interventions that have proved beneficial in our own clinical experience. First, parents may require significant emotional advocacy as they struggle to come to terms with their child's illness and treatment recommendations. Allowing parents an opportunity to express their frustrations is advantageous. In some cases, delaying pharmacological interventions may be necessary until the parents are accepting of the diagnosis and have been thoroughly informed of the possible adverse effects of the selected neuroleptic medication (Dulcan, Bergman, Weller, & Weller, 1998). Second, because psychotic disorders have an indeterminate course, the child and family must be educated about the importance of medication compliance. Third, it is important to inform family members of the symptoms associated with antipsychotic medications such that they can seek appropriate treatment if necessary (Tolbert, 1996). Finally, family members may notice behavioral and socioemotional changes in the youngster before such symptoms are apparent to the treatment team. Thus, family members can assist in treatment management by informing the service providers about fluctuations in the child's functioning and ensure that appropriate alterations are implemented when warranted.

Psychoeducational Assistance

Schools are an ideal place for early symptom identification. However, the early signs of social withdrawal, apathy, and deteriorating academic performance are often misinterpreted as laziness, poor achievement motivation, or naughtiness (Eggers & Bunk, 1997). Nonetheless, childhood-onset psychoses almost always begin with a relatively broad spectrum of behavioral disorders before the emergence of unmistakable psychotic symptoms (Eggers & Bunk, 1997; Werry et al., 1994). Thus, monitoring children who are at significant risk for mental health problems is appropriate. We are not hesitant to add, however, that such a child warrants extra attention but not professional overreaction. When the social and emotional functioning of the child and the situational responses of the family are found wanting, early intervention and specialized assistance may be necessary. But specific interventions with these children and their families should be based on their needs and not on their mental health at-risk status. Within such services, pejorative labeling is best assiduously avoided.

More in-depth individualized psychoeducational services are necessary when the child or adolescent is displaying acute or chronic psychotic symptoms. During an active phase, hospitalization may be required. This may become less necessary as schools adapt a more comprehensive full-service intervention model. For most children, placement in a self-contained classroom or day-school program is a viable option. Such services are implemented by means of the Individuals With Disabilities Education Act of 1997 under the disability category of "Emotionally Disturbed." Likewise the youngster may be eligible for protection under Section 504 of the Vocational Rehabilitation Act of 1973 (Rehabilitation Act, 1973). Regardless of the educational placement, the psychoeducational goal of managing this life-long illness is to allow the child to grow and develop in the least restrictive environment possible while ensuring that her or his psychological, social, and educational needs are being met (Kumra, Jacobsen, Lenane, Smith, et al., 1998; McClellan & Werry, 1994).

Finally, there abounds considerable misinformation among teachers, administrators, and educational support staff regarding psychotic disorders. In-service training with such professionals designed to facilitate a better understanding of the etiology, symptoms, and treatment approaches of schizophrenia and related disorders is recommended. Such instruction will, it is hoped, reduce negative opinions while improving professional commitment to these youngsters.

Individual Interventions

Individual strategies that have been used successfully with adult cases have included social skills training, cognitive–behavioral interventions, and vocational rehabilitation (Penn & Mueser, 1996). Similar interventions, with a substitution of life-skills training (e.g., how to approach someone for directions, decipher a bus schedule, make a store purchase, or seek assistance if lost) for vocational rehabilitation, would seem reasonable with older children and adolescents. Yet such services have yet to be empirically validated with the pediatric population.

In one of the few multimodal intervention studies that has been completed with adolescents diagnosed with schizophrenia, de Haan, Linszen and Gorsira (1998) reported that a combination of life-skills training, medication, and family services improved social functioning and reduced rates of relapse over a 1-year period. Generally, individual interventions should facilitate the child's or adolescent's coping skills with such age-appropriate issues as developing and maintaining positive peer relations, improving social awareness and competencies, recognizing personal strengths and weaknesses, developing decision-making skills, and, if possible, restoring the youngster's functioning to a premorbid level (McClellan & Werry, 1994).

CONCLUSION

Childhood psychosis is a rare and usually chronic disorder likely caused by a combination of genes inherited from one or both of the biological parents. The illness is related to documented neurological alterations that result in a gradual decrease in cerebral tissue coupled with an increase in ventricular enlargement. Unfortunately, the long-term prognosis is poor, with very few children being symptom free as adults. Neuroleptic medications are the mainstay of treatment in spite of a paucity of double-blind efficacy studies with the pediatric population.

Pharmacological treatments that have some support with children and adolescents include clozapine, haloperidol, loxapine, and risperidone. It is advocated that multimodal treatments provided by a full multidisciplinary team be implemented for this population. Family involvement, early identification and treatment, educational support services, and child advocacy are essential components to facilitating a positive long-term prognosis.

REFERENCES

Alaghband-Rad, J., Hamburger, S. D., Giedd, J. N., Frazier, J. A., & Rapoport, J. L. (1997). Childhood-onset schizophrenia: Biological markers in relation to clinical characteristics. *American Journal of Psychiatry, 154,* 64–68.

American Psychiatric Association. (1994). *Diagnostic and statistical manual of mental disorders* (4th ed.). Washington, DC: Author.

Armenteros, J., Whitaker, A., Welikson, M., Stedge, D., & Gorman, J. (1997). Risperidone in adolescents with schizophrenia: An open pilot study. *Journal of the American Academy of Child and Adolescent Psychiatry, 36,* 694–700.

Bertolino, A., Kumra, S., Cellicott, J. H., Mattay, V. S., Lestz, R. M., Jacobsen, L., Barnett, I. S., Duyn, J. H., Frank, J. A., Rapoport, J. L., & Weinberger, D. R. (1998). Common pattern of cortical pathology in childhood-onset and adult-onset schizophrenia as identified by proton magnetic resonance spectro-scopic imaging. *American Journal of Psychiatry, 155,* 1376–1383.

Birchwood, M., McGorry, P., & Jackson, H. (1997). Early intervention in schizo-phrenia. *British Journal of Psychiatry, 170,* 2–5.

Birmaher, B., Baker, R., Kapur, S., Quintana, H., & Ganguli, R. (1992). Clozapine for the treatment of adolescents with schizophrenia. *Journal of the American Academy of Child and Adolescent Psychiatry, 31,* 160–164.

Campbell, M., & Armenteros, J. (1996) Schizophrenia and other psychotic dis-orders. In J. Weiner (Ed.), *Diagnosis and psychopharmacology of childhood and adolescent disorders* (2nd ed., pp. 193–227). New York: Wiley.

Caplan, R. (1994). Communication deficits in childhood schizophrenia spectrum disorders. *Schizophrenia Bulletin, 20,* 671–683.

Carlson, N. (1995). *Foundations of physiological psychology* (3rd ed.). Boston: Allyn & Bacon.

Cawthron, P., James, A., Dell, J., & Seagrott, V. (1994). Adolescent onset psy-chosis: A clinical and outcome study. *Journal of Child Psychology and Psychiatry, 35,* 1321–1332.

Chen, C. H., Shih, H. H., Wang-Wuu, S., Tai, J. J., & Wuu, K. D. (1998). Chromosomal fragile site expression in lymphocytes from patients with schizo-phrenia. *Human Genetics, 103,* 702–706.

Cloninger, C. R., Kaufman, C. A., Paraone, S. V., Malaspina, D., Svrakic, D. M., & Harkavy-Friedman, J. (1998). Genome-wide search for schizophrenia sus-ceptibility loci: The NIMH Genetics Initiative and Millennium Consortium. *American Journal of Medical Genetics, 81,* 275–281.

Cozza, S., & Edison, D. (1994). Risperidone in adolescents. *Journal of the American Academy of Child and Adolescent Psychiatry, 33,* 1211.

Curtis, L., Blouin, J. L., Radhjakrishna, U., Gehrig, C., Lasseter, V. K., Wolyniec, P., Nestadt, G., Dombroski, B., Kazarian, H. H., Pulver, A. E., Houusman, D., Bertrand, D., & Antonarskis, E. D. (1999). No evidence for linkage be-tween schizophrenia and markers at chromosome 15q13–14. *American Journal of Medical Genetics, 88,* 109–112.

de Hann, L., Linszen, D. H., & Gorsira, R. (1998). Early intervention, social functioning, and psychotic relapse of patients with recent-onset schizophrenic disorders. *International Clinical Psychopharmacology, 13*(Suppl. 1), S63–S66.

de Jesus Mari, J., & Streiner, D. L. (1994). An overview of family interventions and relapse on schizophrenia. *Psychological Medicine, 24,* 565–578.

Dixon, L. B., & Lehman, A. F. (1995). Family intervention for schizophrenia. *Schizophrenia Bulletin, 21,* 631–643.

Dulcan, M., Bergman, J., Weller, E., & Weller, R. (1998). Treatment of childhood and adolescent disorders. In A. Schatzberg & C. Nemeroff (Eds.), *The Amer-ican Psychiatric Press textbook of psychopharmacology* (2nd ed., pp. 803–850). Washington, DC: American Psychiatric Press.

Eastwood, S. L., & Harrison, P. J. (1998). Hippocampal and cortical growth-associated protein-43 messenger RNA in schizophrenia. *Neuroscience, 86,* 437–448.

Edelman, R. (1996). Risperidone side effects. *Journal of the American Academy of Child and Adolescent Psychiatry, 35,* 4–5.

Eggers, C., & Bunk, D. (1997). The long-term course of childhood-onset schizophrenia: A 42-year followup. *Schizophrenia Bulletin, 23,* 105–117.

Ereshefsky, L. (1999). Pharmacologic and pharmacokinetic considerations in choosing an antipsychotic. *Journal of Clinical Psychiatry, 60*(Suppl. 10), 20–30.

Erickson, W. D., Yellin, A. M., Hogwood, J. H., Realmuto, G. M., & Greenberg, L. M. (1984). The effects of neuroleptics on attention in adolescent schizophrenics. *Biological Psychiatry, 19,* 745–753

Fleischhaker, C., Schulz, E., & Remschmidt, H. (1998). Biogenic amines as predictors of response to clozapine treatment in early-onset schizophrenia. *Journal of Psychiatric Research, 32,* 325–333.

Frances, A., Docherty, J. P., & Kahn, D. A. (1996). Expert consensus guideline series: Treatment of schizophrenia. *Journal of Clinical Psychiatry, 57*(Suppl. 12B), 34–39.

Frazier, J., Giedd, J. N., Hamburger, S. D., Albus, K. E., Kaysen, D., Vaituzis, A. D., Rajapakse, J. D., Lenane, M. C., McKenna, K., Jacobsen, L. K., Gordon, C. T., Breier, A., & Rapoport, J. L. (1996). Brain anatomic magnetic resonance imaging in childhood-onset schizophrenia. *Archives of General Psychiatry, 53,* 617–624.

Frazier, J., Gordon, C., McKenna, K., Lenane, M., Jih, D., & Rapoport, J. (1994). An open trial of clozapine in 11 adolescents with childhood-onset schizophrenia. *Journal of the American Academy of Child and Adolescent Psychiatry, 33,* 658–663.

Freedman, R., Adler, L. E., & Leonard, S. (1999). Alternative phenotypes for the complex genetics of schizophrenia. *Biological Psychiatry, 45,* 551–558.

Gershon, E. S., Badner, J. A., Goldin, L. R., Sanders, A. R., Cravchik, A., & Detera-Wadleigh, S. D. (1998). Closing in on genes for manic-depressive illness and schizophrenia. *Neuropsychopharmacology, 18,* 233–242.

Grcevich, S., Findling, R., Rowane, W., Friedman, L., & Schulz, S. (1996). Risperidone in the treatment of children and adolescents with schizophrenia: A retrospective study. *Journal of Child and Adolescent Psychopharmacology, 6,* 251–257.

Guidry, J., & Kent, T. A. (1999). New genetic hypothesis of schizophrenia. *Medical Hypotheses, 52,* 69–75.

Individuals With Disabilities Act of 1997, 20 U.S.C § 1400 *et seq.*

Jacobsen, L. K., Giedd, J. N., Berquin, P. C., Krain, A. L., Hamburger, S. D., Kumra, S., & Rapoport, J. L. (1997). Quantitative morphology of the cerebellum and fourth ventricle in childhood-onset schizophrenia. *American Journal of Psychiatry, 154,* 1663–1669.

Jacobsen, L. K., Giedd, J. N., Castellanos, F. X., Valuzis, A. C., Hamburger, S. D.,

Kumra, S., Lenane, M. C., & Rapoport, J. L. (1998). Progressive reduction of temporal lobe structure in childhood-onset schizophrenia. *American Journal of Psychiatry, 155,* 678–685.

Jacobsen, L., Walker, M., Edwards, J., Chappell, P., & Woolston, J. (1994). Clozapine in the treatment of a young adolescent with schizophrenia. *Journal of the American Academy of Child and Adolescent Psychiatry, 33,* 645–650.

Kando, J. D., Shepski, J. C., Satterlee, W., Patel, J. K., Reams, S. G., & Green, A. I. (1997). Olanzapine: A new antipsychotic agent with efficacy in the management of schizophrenia. *Annals of Pharmacotherapy, 31,* 1325–1334.

Kapra, S., Zipursky, R., Remington, G., Jones, C., McKay, G., & Noule, S. (1997). PET evidence that loxapine is an equipotent blocker of 5-HT2 and D2 receptors: Implications for the therapeutics of schizophrenia. *American Journal of Psychiatry, 154,* 1525–1529.

Kumra, S., Frazier, J., Jacobsen, L., McKenna, K., Gordon, C., Lenane, M., Hamburger, S., Smith, A., Albus, K., Alaghband-Rad, J., & Rapoport, J. (1996). Childhood-onset schizophrenia. A double-blind clozapine-haloperidol comparison. *Archives of General Psychiatry, 53,* 1090–1097.

Kumra, S., Jacobsen, L., Lenane, M., Karp, B., Frazier, J., Smith, A., Bedwell, J., Lee, P., Malanga, C., Hamburger, S., & Rapoport, J. (1998). Childhood-onset schizophrenia: An open-label study of olanzapine in adolescents. *Journal of the American Academy of Child and Adolescent Psychiatry, 37,* 377–386.

Kumra, S., Jacobsen, L. K., Lenane, M., Smith, A., Lee, P., Malanga, C. J., Karp, B. I., Hamburger, S., & Rapoport, J. L. (1998). Case series: Spectrum of neuroleptic-induced movement disorders and extrapyramidal side effects in childhood-onset schizophrenia. *Journal of the American Academy of Child and Adolescent Psychiatry, 37,* 221–227.

Lange, D., & Julien, R. (1997). Integration of drugs and psychological therapies in treating mental and behavior disorders. In R. Julien (Ed.), *A primer of drug action: A concise, nontechnical guide to the actions, uses, and side effects of psychoactive drugs* (8th ed., pp. 429– 461). Portland, OR: Freeman.

Lewis, R. (1998). Typical and atypical antipsychotics in adolescent schizophrenia: Efficacy, tolerability, and differential sensitivity to extrapyramidal symptoms. *Canadian Journal of Psychiatry, 43,* 596–604.

Mandoki, M. (1995). Risperidone treatment of children and adolescents: Increased risk of extrapyramidal side effects? *Journal of Child and Adolescent Psychopharmacology, 5,* 49–67.

Maziade, M., Gingras, N., Rodrigue, C., Bouchard, S., Cardinal, A., & Garthier, B. (1996). Long-term stability of diagnosis and symptom dimensions in a systematic sample of patients with onset of schizophrenia in childhood and early adolescence: I. Nosology, sex, and age of onset. *British Journal of Psychiatry, 169,* 361–370.

McClellan, J., & Werry, J. (1994). Practice parameters for the assessment and treatment of children and adolescents with schizophrenia. *Journal of the American Academy of Child and Adolescent Psychiatry, 33,* 616–635.

McKenna, K., Gordon, C. T., & Rapoport, J. L. (1994). Childhood-onset schizophrenia: Timely neurobiological research. *Journal of the American Academy of Child and Adolescent Psychiatry, 33,* 771–781.

Meltzer, H., & Fatemi, S. (1998). Treatment of schizophrenia. In A. Schatzberg & C. Nemeroff (Eds.), *The American Psychiatric Press textbook of psychopharmacology* (2nd ed., pp. 747–774). Washington, DC: American Psychiatric Press.

Meltzer, H., & Jayathilake, K. (1999). Low-dose loxapine in the treatment of schizophrenia: Is it more effective and more "atypical" than standard-dose loxapine? *Journal of Clinical Psychiatry, 60*(Suppl. 10), 47–51.

Mowerman, S., & Siris, S. G. (1996). Adjective loxapine in a clozapine-resistant cohort of schizophrenia patients. *Annals of Clinical Psychiatry, 8,* 193–197.

Mozes, T., Toren, P., Chernauzan, N., Mester, R., Yoran-Hegesh, R., Blumensohn, R., & Weizman, A. (1994). Clozapine treatment in very early onset schizophrenia. *Journal of the American Academy of Child and Adolescent Psychiatry, 33,* 65–70.

Nopoulos, P. C., Giedd, J. N., Andreasen, N. C., & Rapoport, J. L. (1998). Frequency and severity of enlarged cavum septi pellucidi in childhood-onset schizophrenia. *American Journal of Psychiatry, 155,* 1074–1079.

Penn, D. L., & Mueser, K. T. (1996). Research update on the psychosocial treatment of schizophrenia. *American Journal of Psychiatry, 153,* 607–617.

Physicians' Desk Reference. (53rd ed.). (1999). Montvale, NJ: Medical Economics.

Piscitelli, S. C., Frazier, J. A., McKenna, K., Albus, K. E., Grothe, D. R., Gordon, C. T., & Rapoport, J. L. (1995). Plasma clozapine and haloperidol concentrations in adolescents with childhood-onset schizophrenia: Association with response. *Journal of Clinical Psychiatry, 55*(Suppl. B), 94–97.

Pool, D., Bloom, W., Mielke, D. H., Roniger, J. J., & Gallant, D. M. (1976). A controlled evaluation of loxitane in 75 adolescent schizophrenic patients. *Current Therapeutic Research, 19,* 99–104.

Quintana, H., & Keshavan, M. (1995). Case study: Risperidone in children and adolescents with schizophrenia. *Journal of the American Academy of Child and Adolescent Psychiatry, 34,* 1292–1296.

Rapoport, J. L., Giedd, J. N., Blumenthal, J., Hamburger, S., Jeffries, N., Fernandez, T., Nicolson, R., Bedwell, J., Lenane, M., Zijdenbos, A., Paus, T., & Evans, A. (1999). Professive cortical change during adolescence in childhood-onset schizophrenia: A longitudinal magnetic resonance imaging study. *Archives of General Psychiatry, 56,* 649–654.

Realmuto, G., Erickson W., Yellin, A., Hopwood, J., & Greenberg, L. (1984). Clinical comparison of thiothixene and thioridazine in schizophrenic adolescents. *American Journal of Psychiatry, 141,* 440–442.

Rehabilitation Act of 1973, 29 U.S.C. § 791 *et seq.*

Remschmidt, H., Schulz, E., & Herpertz-Dahlmann, B. (1996). Schizophrenic psychoses in childhood and adolescence: A guide to diagnosis and drug choice. *CNS Drugs, 6,* 100–112.

Remschmidt, H., Schulz, E., & Martin, P. (1994). An open trial of clozapine in thirty-six adolescents with schizophrenia. *Journal of Child and Adolescent Psychopharmacology, 4,* 31–41.

Remschmidt, H. E., Schulz, E., Martin, M., Warnke, A., & Trott, G. E. (1994). Childhood-onset schizophrenia: History of the concept and recent studies. *Schizophrenia Bulletin, 20,* 727–745.

Ross, R. G., Olincy, A., Harris, J. G., Radant, A., Hawkins, M., Adler, L. E., & Freedman, R. (1999). Evidence of bilineal inheritance of physiological indicators of risk in childhood-onset schizophrenia. *American Journal of Medical Genetics, 88,* 188–199.

Schulz, S. C., Findling, R., Wise, A., Friedman, L., & Kenny, J. (1998). Child and adolescent schizophrenia. *Psychiatric Clinics of North America, 21,* 43–56.

Schwab, S. G., Hallmayer, J., Lerer, B., Albus, M., Borrmann, M., & Honig, S. (1998). Support for a chromosome 18p locus conferring susceptibility to functional psychoses in families with schizophrenia, by association and linkage analysis. *American Journal of Human Genetics, 63,* 1139–1152.

Shaw, S. H., Kelly, M., Smith, A. B., Shields, G., Hopkins, P. J., & Loftus, J. (1998). A genome-wide search for schizophrenia susceptibility. *American Journal of Medical Genetics, 81,* 364–376.

Simeon, J., Carey, N., Wiggins, D., Milin, R., & Hosenbocus, S. (1995). Risperidone effects in treatment-resistant adolescents: Preliminary case reports. *Journal of Child and Adolescent Psychopharmacology, 5,* 69–79.

Spencer, E., & Campbell, M. (1994). Children with schizophrenia: Diagnosis, phenomenology, and pharmacotherapy. *Schizophrenia Bulletin, 20,* 713–725.

Spencer, E., Kafantaris, V., Padron-Gayol, M., Rosenberg, C., & Campbell, M. (1992). Haloperidol in schizophrenic children: Early findings from a study in progress. *Psychopharmacology Bulletin, 28,* 183–186.

Stahl, S. M. (1999). Selecting an atypical antipsychotic by combining clinical experience with guidelines from clinical trials. *Journal of Clinical Psychiatry, 60*(Suppl. 10), 31–41.

Tolbert, H. A. (1996). Psychoses in children and adolescents: A review. *Journal of Clinical Psychiatry, 57*(Suppl. 3), 4–8.

Towbin, K., Dykens, E., & Pugliese, R. (1994). Clozapine for early developmental delays with childhood-onset schizophrenia: Protocol and 15-month outcome. *Journal of the American Academy of Child and Adolescent Psychiatry, 33,* 651–657.

Turetz, M., Mozes, T., Toren, P., Chernauzan, N., Yoran-Hegesh, R., Mester, R., Wittenberg, N., Tyano, S., & Weizman, A. (1997). An open trial of clozapine in neuroleptic-resistant childhood-onset schizophrenia. *British Journal of Psychiatry, 170,* 507–510.

van Os, J., & Marcelis, M. (1998). The ecogenetics of schizophrenia: A review. *Schizophrenia Research, 32,* 127–135.

Werry, J. S., McClellan, J. M., Andrews, L. K., & Ham, M. (1994). Clinical features and outcome of child and adolescent schizophrenia. *Schizophrenia Bulletin, 20,* 619–630.

Wildenauer, D. B., & Schwab, S. G. (1999). Chromosome 8 and 10 workshop. *American Journal of Medical Genetics, 88,* 239–243.

Zahn, T. P., Jacobsen L. K., Gordon, C. T., McKenna, K., Frazier, J. A., & Rapoport, J. L. (1997). Autonomic nervous system markers of psychopathology in childhood-onset schizophrenia. *Archives of General Psychiatry, 54,* 904–912.

Zuddas, A., Pintor, M., & Cianchetti, C. (1996). Risperidone for negative symptoms [Letter]. *Journal of the American Academy of Child and Adolescent Psychiatry, 35,* 838–839.

10

TICS AND TOURETTE'S DISORDER

Gilles de la Tourette's disorder (TD) is a primarily genetic neuropsychiatric disorder with the essential symptoms of numerous motor tics and one or more vocal tics (American Psychiatric Association, 1994). A tic is a recurrent, nonrhythmic, stereotypical, brief motor movement or vocalization that occurs without warning. Motor tics may include grimacing; nose twitching; licking; body rocking; shudders; and eye blinking, eye rolling, or wide-eyed opening. Vocal tics can include sniffing, grunting, coughing, throat clearing, and coprolalia (i.e., spontaneous, unprovoked interruption of speech flow with various obscenities). Motor and vocal tics can be classified as either simple (e.g., eye blinking, grunting) or complex (e.g., stomping feet, repeating one's own words or sounds). Onset of TD occurs before age 18 years. Criteria include tics that occur for more than 1 year causing significant impairment in occupational, social, or emotional functioning, with tic-free periods lasting no longer than 3 months. Although natural history data are limited, TD is often life-long, with periods of remission ranging from weeks to years. In many cases, however, symptoms diminish during adolescence and adulthood. Sometimes symptoms disappear by early adulthood.

There are various types of tic disorders, including TD, chronic motor

This chapter was written in part with the assistance of Cora E. Ezzell, James E. Edwards, and Walter D. Hiott, Department of Psychiatry and Behavioral Sciences, Medical University of South Carolina.

and chronic vocal tic disorders, and transient tic disorders. It should be noted that although the prevalence of TD is fairly low, the prevalence of tic disorders in general is much higher and is estimated to occur in 5%–24% of children (Singer et al., 1995). Some experts suggest that tic disorders exist on a continuum from least severe (transient tics) to most severe (TD; Kurlan, 1994). In general, the more severe the tic disorder, the more severe the functional impairment. TD occurs at higher rates in males than in females. The prevalence of TD is estimated at 1 to 8 cases per 1,000 males and between 0.1 and 4 cases per 1,000 females (Nolan & Gadow, 1997). These varying rates within gender are attributed to differences in samples (clinic vs. community), instrumentation (structured interview vs. screening tool), and age distribution (Peterson, Leckman, & Cohen, 1995). Researchers who use structured interviews with clinic samples may overestimate TD cases because of the low sensitivity of assessment instruments in distinguishing between presence of mild tics and overt TD (Kurlan, 1994; Pierre, Nolan, Gadow, Sverd, & Sprafkin, 1999). Community estimates may underrepresent the number of cases because of underreporting symptoms on assessment screening measures (Peterson et al., 1995).

COMORBIDITIES

Individuals diagnosed with TD often experience one or several comorbid conditions, including obsessive–compulsive disorder (OCD), attention deficit hyperactivity disorder (ADHD), and learning disabilities. In fact, some investigators have suggested that the severity of tic disorders is associated with higher rates of emotional and behavioral disturbances (Pierre et al., 1999). A review of these comorbidities follows.

Obsessive–Compulsive Disorder

TD and OCD are demonstrated related disorders (Como, 1995; Miguel et al., 1995; Pauls, Towbin, Leckman, Zahner, & Cohen, 1986; Peterson et al., 1995; Spencer et al., 1998; Swedo & Leonard, 1994). Researchers suggest a genetic vulnerability as the basis for the expression of either TD or OCD (Comings & Comings, 1987). Moreover, there is a high incidence of OCD in families of children with TD. Similarly, individuals with OCD and their family members appear to have a high rate of TD, tic disorders, or both (Pierre et al., 1999). One interpretation of this literature is that TD and OCD are separate but related disorders. However, Comings (1995) provided an argument that OCD and TD may represent different placements on a wide spectrum of one neuropsychiatric disorder. Some evidence in support of this position was presented by Leonard et al. (1992), who demonstrated that approximately 60% of patients initially referred for obsessive–compulsive traits without tics subsequently displayed tics at 2–7 years following the initial baseline assessment. In their sample, nearly one quarter of the patients met diagnostic criteria for TD. Children and adolescents who eventually met criteria for TD had an earlier onset of symptoms related to OCD than did those who did not develop TD. These data have been supported more recently in an investigation by Pierre et al. (1999), who found higher rates of symptoms related to OCD than did children who were later without TD. Rapoport, Swedo, and Leonard (1992) observed that males with an early onset of OCD may be at higher risk for developing tics. Other investigators (George, Trimble, Ring, Sallee, & Robertson, 1993; Pierre et al., 1999) indicated that individuals with OCD and TD, compared with individuals with OCD alone, may have different symptom profiles, with the comorbid group exhibiting more aggressive behavior. However, documenting comorbidity is difficult because of the similarities between a compulsion and a tic. Some individuals with TD, for example, also have complex behavioral rituals that occur as part of their tics (Rapoport et al., 1992; Sallee & Spratt, 1998).

In contrast to the evidence suggesting that OCD and TD may represent a continuum of one disorder, other evidence suggests that they are two distinct, albeit frequently comorbid, disorders. For example, the selective serotonin reuptake inhibitors (SSRIs) that have been demonstrated to manage OCD-related symptoms effectively (Brown & Sawyer, 1998) are not particularly effective in treating symptoms of TD (Swedo & Leonard, 1994). Similarly, neuroleptic agents appear to be effective in reducing tic severity and frequency but have not been found to be beneficial in managing symptoms of OCD (Miguel et al., 1995). Miguel et al. also noted that the onset of OCD and TD is associated with different symptoms. OCD without comorbid TD is preceded by cognitive phenomena (ideas, thoughts, and images) and anxiety but not sensory phenomena (unpleasant physical sensations). In contrast, tics in TD without comorbid OCD are preceded by sensory phenomena but not by cognitive phenomena or anxiety.

Attention Deficit Hyperactivity Disorder

Individuals with TD also frequently display symptoms of ADHD (Gadow, Nolan, Sprafkin, & Sverd, 1995; Gadow, Sverd, Sprafkin, Nolan, & Ezor, 1995; Nolan, Gadow, & Sprafkin, 1999; Peterson et al., 1995; Pierre et al., 1999; Singer et al., 1995; Walkup, Scahill, & Riddle, 1995). Studies show significant overlap between the two disorders. For example, Knell and Comings (1993) investigated 131 TD probands and found that 60% of their relatives were diagnosed with ADHD, based on earlier psychiatric diagnostic criteria, and that over 33% of family members had ADHD as defined in the current psychiatric nomenclature. Randolph,

Hyde, Gold, Goldberg, and Weinberger (1993) found that more severe tic symptoms were associated with greater impairments on measures of attention and impulse control in monozygotic twin pairs with TD. In a review of the literature, Comings (1995) pointed out that both TD and ADHD are associated with a range of behavioral problems and that children who experience these comorbidities also have relatives who exhibit a high frequency of externalizing behavioral disorders.

Not all genetic studies have supported a relationship between TD and ADHD, however (Wodrich, Benjamin, & Lachar, 1997). For example, in a more recent investigation comparing psychiatric patients with TD to those without TD, ADHD was present in over half of the TD sample (Wodrich et al., 1997), but this rate was not significantly greater than the rate in the comparison sample. As Peterson et al. (1995) observed, the nature of TD may make it difficult to define attention disturbances accurately. That is, the deleterious effects of tics on cognitive and motoric functioning often make it inherently difficult to assess attention and impulse control problems, and this could inadvertently yield a spurious overestimation of the occurrence of ADHD in individuals with TD.

In summary, whether TD and ADHD represent one disorder with different genotypes or share the same genes is not clear. Greater research efforts need to be directed toward delineating the genetic relationship between ADHD and TD, and particularly in developing more precise diagnostic methods to capture better the existing association between the two disorders.

Learning Disabilities

A high prevalence of learning difficulties in children with TD has been documented in several studies (Schuerholz, Baumgardner, Singer, Reiss, & Denckla, 1996; Singer, Schuerholz, & Denckla, 1994; Walkup et al., 1995). Other investigators have also provided evidence that a relatively high percentage of children receiving special education services meet diagnostic criteria for TD (Comings, Himes, & Comings, 1990; Kurlan, Whitmore, Irvine, McDermott, & Como, 1994). Schuerholz et al. (1996) reported that learning disabilities were present in 23% of their total TD sample, but learning disabilities were only present in those children who had comorbid ADHD. They were not found in children who had only TD. Thus, the association between TD and learning disabilities remains unclear.

Many factors may be responsible for the high occurrence of learning problems in children with TD. Such neuropsychological problems as impairments in executive functioning, learning-related sequelae more directly related to tic severity, sedative effects of neuroleptic medication, the demoralizing aspect of a stigmatizing diagnosis like TD, and the existence of other behavioral disturbances like ADHD and OCD could all contribute to compromised learning (Singer et al., 1994).

An association between tic severity and impairment in neuropsychological functioning has been demonstrated in several studies. Individuals evidencing more severe tics have shown poorer performance on such neuropsychological measures as the Trail Making Test and the Grooved Pegboard Test (Bornstein, 1990; Yeates & Bornstein, 1994), both of which are psychometric measures that assess attention and fine-motor control. Randolph et al. (1993) found that twins with a greater intensity and frequency of tic symptoms evidenced more impaired attention, visuospatial perception, and motoric functioning.

Other Disorders

TD also coexists with a range of other psychiatric disorders. Oppositional defiant disorder (ODD) and conduct disorder frequently co-occur with ADHD (Barkley, 1998) and so are frequently comorbid with TD (Gadow, Nolan, et al., 1995; Nolan & Gadow, 1997; Pierre et al., 1999). Thus, children with TD also may have problems with lying, stealing, fire setting, aggression, and relationship difficulties.

Links between depression and TD have been demonstrated in other studies (Rapoport et al., 1992; Wodrich et al., 1997). Children with TD show a high prevalence of anxiety disorders (e.g., phobias; Pierre et al., 1999). This is not surprising given that OCD is itself classified as an anxiety disorder.

DEVELOPMENTAL COURSE

The developmental course of TD is quite varied, but several general trends have been identified in longitudinal studies designed to assess its natural history. During childhood, TD develops gradually with one or more transient episodes of mild motor or vocal tics followed by the occurrence of more frequent and severe tics (Sallee & Spratt, 1998). Facial tics tend to emerge first (Kurlan, 1994; Sallee & Spratt, 1998). During the next phase, tics pervade the rest of the body, starting with the head and neck before proceeding to the upper and then lower extremities. The development of vocal tics, which typically is subsequent to the occurrence of motor tics, also is often gradual, starting with random vocalizations that eventually develop into words and phrases. For children with comorbid attention problems, attention difficulties usually emerge concurrently with the tics (Gadow, Nolan, et al., 1995). In contrast, obsessive–compulsive symptoms emerge after the appearance of tics in individuals with comorbid obsessive–compulsive features. In adolescence, symptoms often diminish. Peterson et al. (1995) hypothesized that this is due to an adolescent's increasing capacity for self-control. The disease course is unclear at any rate, as some adolescents show marked improvement but others have exacerbated levels of aggression, impulsivity, obsessions, compulsions, and severe anxiety.

Genetic and Familial Patterns

A comprehensive review of the genetic and familial patterns of tics and TD can be found in Brown and Ievers (1999). In general, they suggested that TD is a familial syndrome wherein a child receives the genetic basis for developing a tic disorder. This type of inheritance is referred to as *genetic vulnerability*. Research indicates that approximately 8% of relatives of TD probands also meet criteria for the disorder (Pauls, Raymond, Leckman, & Stevenson, 1991), a rate that is significantly higher than that found in the general population.

Despite this strong genetic evidence, the presence of the TD gene (or genes) does not appear to be sufficient to produce the disorder (Kurlan, 1994). Current genetic research is focused on localizing the genes responsible for expression of TD, which it is hoped will increase understanding of the genetic–biological risk factors associated with the expression of the disorder.

Neurobiological Findings

Strong biological basis for TD and the involvement of numerous brain structures and systems in its expression are indicated. The functions of the brain hypothesized to be involved in the disorder include the caudate nucleus, basal ganglia, frontal cortex, and reticular activating system (Kurlan, 1994; Malison et al., 1995). There also is some evidence suggesting that the neurotransmitter dopamine is involved in the expression of the disorder. Refer to the *Glossary of Terms* at the end of this book for definitions of medical terminology.

Children with TD show asymmetries in the caudate nucleus and basal ganglia compared with individuals without the disorder, which further supports a neurobiological substrate for TD (Hyde & Weinberger, 1995; Peterson et al., 1995; Singer, Waranch, Brown, Carson, & Mellitis, 1993). Additionally, positron emission tomography, or PET scans, reveal an increase in metabolic activity in the frontal cortex of individuals with TD (Braun et al., 1995). Electroencephalographic (EEG) technology is another technique used to assess neurological functioning. Earlier studies using EEG technology revealed different patterns between individuals with and without TD, but subsequent investigations have been equivocal. EEG studies of sleep patterns have found that, compared with individuals without TD, those with the disorder have abnormal arousal patterns suggestive of a dysfunctional reticular activating system (Sallee & Spratt, 1998). These differences are especially striking in individuals who have comorbid ADHD and TD (Allen, Singer, Brown, & Salem, 1992).

Studies investigating neurobiological correlates of TD have consisted of small samples and included children with comorbid conditions, making additional studies on the biological markers of the disorder necessary, in addition to comparison studies of biological markers of disorders that are frequently comorbid with TD (e.g., ADHD, learning disabilities). In addition, studies that compare TD pediatric samples with their peers with comorbid conditions will shed light on the biological markers that are unique to TD. Clearly, this is a ripe area for future inquiry.

Assessment

When evaluating TD, a thorough assessment that includes the presenting problem, the type and frequency of tics, age of onset, factors that exacerbate or attenuate the disorder, and general course of tics is most appropriate. Sallee and Spratt (1998) suggested that the clinician define and describe motor and verbal tics because parents may need assistance identifying tics, particularly more complex ones.

Tic disorders fall into one of four categories: TD, chronic motor or vocal tic disorder, transient tic disorder, and tic disorder not otherwise specified (American Psychiatric Association, 1994). When tics are present, diagnosis depends on the age of onset of the disorder, tic frequency and duration, and the type of tic exhibited. However, to qualify for any tic-associated diagnosis, there must be marked distress or significant impairment in social, educational/occupational, or other important areas of functioning. Moreover, symptoms cannot be directly attributable to the physiological effects of a drug substance or to another medical or neurological condition.

Tics must also be distinguished from other neurological disorders that involve abnormal motor movements, including Wilson's disease, multiple sclerosis, or head injuries. Similarly, tics must be distinguished from myoclonic movements (i.e., brief shocklike muscle contractions), stereotypical movements that are often seen in children diagnosed with pervasive developmental disorders, and the psychotic or disorganized behaviors that may occur in individuals with thought disorders. Lastly, tics should be differentiated from the compulsions that frequently occur in individuals diagnosed with OCD.

Objective assessment of TD is important, particularly if pharmacotherapy is a component of the treatment plan. Several clinician, parent, and self-report rating scales are available to assess various dimensions of tics, including number, frequency, intensity, complexity, and interference (i.e., the degree to which planned actions or speech are impeded by the tic symptoms). Clinician rating scales that are available include the Shapiro Tourette's Syndrome Severity Scale (A. K. Shapiro & Shapiro, 1984), the Tourette's Syndrome Global Scale (Harcherik, Leckman, Detler, & Cohen, 1984), and the Yale Global Tic Severity Scale (Leckman et al., 1989).

Our review of the literature revealed two self-report measures, one of which may also be completed by caregivers. The Motor Tic, Obsessions, and Compulsions, Vocal Tic Evaluation Survey (Gaffney, Sieg, & Hellings, 1994) is a self-report measure consisting of five subscales: motor tics, vocal tics, obsessions, compulsions, and associated symptoms (e.g., echolalia, echopraxia, coprolalia, and copropraxia). The Daily Record of Treatment (A. K. Shapiro, Shapiro, Young, & Feinberg, 1988) is a self-report measure that may also be used by caregivers. The scale is particularly appropriate for medication trials as it allows assessment of behaviors (i.e., motor and vocal tics, in addition to other symptoms of TD) on a daily basis.

MEDICAL INTERVENTIONS

Psychotropic medications are widely used to control tic symptoms, and reportedly more than 70% of children and adolescents with TD have taken medication as part of their treatment program (Gadow, 1993). As with all psychotropic agents, the health care provider should be judicious in prescribing medication for patients with tic disorders because of the adverse effects associated with many of the psychotropic agents for this disorder. No medications are known to suppress tic symptoms completely. When the issue of efficacy is considered simultaneously with adverse effects, those psychotropic medications currently available must be considered carefully. For the management of tic disorders, medications that frequently are most efficacious have the highest side-effect profile. This is in comparison with those low-potency agents that have relatively fewer adverse effects. The concept of using "as little medication as possible" is relevant in the treatment of TD, but psychotropic medications at some dosage remain an important treatment option.

The practitioner should have readily delineated target symptoms to be addressed and should educate the patient and family on these treatment goals. For example, an appropriate goal in treating tics is to reduce the symptoms to a tolerable level (Castellanos, 1998), whereas a less reasonable goal is complete suppression of tic behavior. The lowest possible medication dose should always be the standard of care. Consequently, as with all of the disorders discussed previously in this book, pharmacotherapy of TD is a clinical art as well as a science. The practitioner must evaluate exacerbations and remissions of the disorder, monitor changes in symptoms, evaluate adverse effects of medication, and adjust dosages accordingly.

Various pharmacotherapies are available to the practitioner to manage

TD. These include the neuroleptics, the stimulants, and the alpha^2 adrenergic agonists. We review these classes of medications in accordance with their prevalence of use. A summary of these psychotropic medications that have been validated in double-blind trials for use with children and adolescents with TD is presented in Table 10.1.

Neuroleptics

Neuroleptics were the first class of psychotropic medications that improved symptoms associated with TD. They are widely considered to be the drugs of choice in treating marked to severe tic symptoms or in managing mild tics, particularly when TD is comorbid with moderate to severe ADHD (Castellanos, 1998; Kurlan, 1997; Leckman, 1995). Of interest is the finding that children with TD are believed to have a lower threshold for neuroleptic-associated adverse effects, particularly extrapyramidal symptoms (Chappell, Scahill, & Leckman, 1996). Extrapyramidal symptoms refer to Parkinson-like syndromes, including muscular rigidity, tremor, slow heart beat, shuffling walk, and drooling. Neuroleptic agents must be administered judiciously with children and adolescents because pediatric patients have been found to exhibit more adverse effects than their adult counterparts (Werry & Aman, 1996). Few investigations have carefully evaluated both the efficacy and safety of neuroleptic agents for children and adolescents. Some pediatric psychopharmacologists are concerned that the use of these agents exceeds their demonstrated suitability for children (Brown, Lee, & Donegan, 1998; Brown & Sawyer, 1998). In fact, the only two psychotropic agents with approved indication for the management of TD are the high potency neuroleptics haloperidol (Haldol) and pimozide (Orap).

Haloperidol (Haldol) has been the most commonly prescribed medication for the management of TD (Brown & Ievers, 1999). It is effective in suppressing tic behaviors, with response rates approaching 70%–80% (Chappell, Leckman, & Riddle, 1995; Kurlan, 1997; Sallee, Nesbitt, Jackson, & Sethuraman, 1997). However, a major adverse effect of haloperidol is marked sedation (Ernst et al., 1999), which is particularly important for children in the classroom setting. Frequently, children with TD have comorbid learning difficulties, and the astute practitioner should recognize the cognitive toxicities associated with neuroleptics when decisions are made on medication. Other major adverse effects of haloperidol include akathisia, acute dystonia, and Parkinsonian symptoms (Brown & Sawyer, 1998), some of which are transitory and some of which may be more permanent. As with adult patients, tardive dyskinesia has been noted to be an adverse effect that is associated with the high-potency neuroleptic agents in pediatric populations (Wolfe & Wagner, 1993). Tardive dyskinesia is characterized by rhythmic, repetitive stereotypical movements, including suck-

TABLE 10.1

Medications Clinically Validated in Double-Blind Trials for Use With Children and Adolescents With Tics/Tourette's

Generic Name (Trade Name)	Children mg/kg/day	Adolescents mg/kg/day	Treatment Outcome	Adverse Effect
Clonidine (Catapres)	0.1–0.8	0.1–0.8	Reduction in impulsivity, inattention, overactivity, disruptive behaviors, and tics.	Sedation, hypotension, depression, and cardiac arrhythmias.
Fluoxetine (Prozac)	10.0–40.0	10.0–40.0	Reduction of obsessive–compulsive symptoms, but not effective for management of tics.	Nausea, diarrhea, dyspepsia, weight loss, motor restlessness, and social disinhibition.
Guafacine (Tenex)	0.5–3.0	0.5–3.0	Reduction of impulsivity, inattention, overactivity, disruptive behaviors, and motor/vocal tics.	Hypotension and sedation.
Haloperidol (Haldol)	0.25–6.0	1.0–16.0	Reduction of motor and vocal tics.	Sedation, anticholinergic symptoms, acute dystonia, akathisia, cardiac arrhythmias, parkinsonian symptoms, tardive dyskinesia.
Pimozide (Orap)	0.5–25.0	5–25.0	Reduction of motor and vocal tics.	Hepatic toxicity, tardive dyskinesia, cardiac arrhythmia, neuroleptic malignant syndrome. Reports of sudden death at high doses.
Risperidone (Risperdal)	Not yet established	2.0–10.0	Reduction of motor and vocal tics.	Neuroleptic withdrawal dyskinesia and dystonia upon abrupt cessation.

Note. Sources include Arzimanoglou (1998); Leckman et al. (1991); Peterson and Cohen (1998); Sallee, Nesbit, Jackson, and Sethuraman (1997); and Tollefson, Birkett, Koran, and Genduso (1994). ADHD = attention deficit hyperactivity disorder.

ing and smacking of the lips, shifting of the chin, thrusting of the tongue in and out of the mouth, and jerking movements of the body. Because dyskinesias and other adverse effects are typically dose related, a low dose of medication with pediatric populations is typically initiated (e.g., 0.25 to 0.5 mg/kg of body weight total dose per day), followed by careful monitoring of both beneficial and adverse effects (Peterson & Cohen, 1998).

Pimozide (Orap) is the only neuroleptic medication marketed in the United States for the treatment of TD. Pharmacological trials that have compared pimozide with haloperidol have not been entirely conclusive. One investigation reported pimozide to be equally effective to haloperidol (E. Shapiro et al., 1989), and another study found pimozide to be more efficacious than haloperidol in managing TD symptoms (Sallee et al., 1997). Other studies have been equally compelling and have found reduced motor and vocal tics in children with TD (A. K. Shapiro & Shapiro, 1984). Although pimozide may be less sedating and result in fewer acute dystonic reactions compared with haloperidol, some of the adverse effects associated with this agent are potentially deleterious. Specifically, it has potential adverse cardiac toxicities, including cardiac arrhythmias (Rosenberg, Holttum, & Gershon, 1994; E. Shapiro et al., 1989), and there have been some reports of sudden death at high doses (e.g., 60 to 70 mg/day; Fulop et al., 1987). For this reason, a thorough cardiac history should be obtained, as well as a baseline and ongoing electrocardiogram, particularly during changes in medication dose. One investigation provided data to indicate a withdrawal dyskinesia upon sudden cessation of the medication (Mennesson, Klink, & Fortin, 1998). Thus, the health care provider must always promote and assess adherence to the medication regimen.

Two major clinical trials have demonstrated efficacy (defined as reducing the severity of tics by at least 65%) of haloperidol and pimozide (Sallee et al., 1997; E. Shapiro et al., 1989). The use of these typical agents is mainly limited by their side-effect profile. If the adverse effects of a neuroleptic are unacceptable, then the clinical literature supports the possible use of alternative neuroleptic drug therapy (Cepeda, 1997). More recently, because of the adverse effects associated with neuroleptic agents, there has been increased use of atypical neuroleptics and other psychotropic medications, including tricyclic antidepressant (TCAs) agents, benzodiazepines, and clonidine (Catapres).

Recent research has focused on whether risperidone (Risperdal), an atypical neuroleptic, has demonstrated efficacy in reducing tic behaviors (Bruun & Budman, 1996; Diantoniis, Henry, Partridge, & Soucar, 1996; Stamenkovic, Aschauer, & Kasper, 1994; van der Linden, Briggeman, & van Woerkom, 1994). Lombroso et al. (1995) found risperidone to be effective in reducing tic frequency and intensity. Lombroso et al. (1995) and van der Linden et al. (1994) found that risperidone reduces tic frequency by nearly 50%. Because anecdotal evidence suggests that risperidone reduces the risk of tardive dyskinesia, this agent shows particular promise in managing TD in pediatric populations. Because of the potential of neuroleptic-related withdrawal dyskinesia or dystonia upon abrupt cessation of these agents, the astute practitioner must carefully assess risks for non-compliance. In support of this notion, Rowan and Malone (1997) reported the occurrence of a "Tourette-like syndrome" (motor and vocal tics) with abrupt cessation of risperidone. As with all neuroleptic agents, risperidone should be introduced slowly, starting at a low dose (e.g., 0.5 mg) and titrating the medication slowly until desired target symptoms (i.e., reduced tics) have responded and safety has been thoroughly established (Brown et al., 1998).

Polypharmacy (the use of more than one psychotropic agent) has also been addressed in the literature. The few investigations that have examined this issue generally indicate that the practitioner must be particularly cautious in this practice. For example, Budman, Sherling, and Bruun (1995) found that the risk of extrapyramidal symptoms is increased with the combined use of paroxetine (Paxil) and haloperidol (Haldol), causing a severe, acute dystonic reaction in one child. Other studies have demonstrated improvement in symptoms with the use of multiple pharmacological agents. For example, Hawkridge, Stein, and Bouwer (1996) demonstrated improvement in tic and OCD symptoms with the combined use of a neuroleptic agent and an SSRI in their sample of 4 children. Silver, Shytle, Philipp, and Sanberg (1996) noted a brief improvement in TD symptoms with the combined use of transdermal nicotine patches and neuroleptic drug therapy. Unfortunately, research on the pharmacotherapy of TD has lagged behind clinical practice. This mandates additional clinical trials.

Stimulants

As noted earlier, TD is frequently comorbid with ADHD (Brown & Ievers, 1999; Peterson et al., 1995), and practitioners are challenged with managing both disorders simultaneously. Although stimulants are used most frequently to manage symptoms associated with ADHD (Brown, Dingle, & Dreelin, 1997; Brown et al., 1998), there is some clinical evidence suggesting that the use of stimulants may exacerbate motor tics, stereotyped behaviors, or other symptoms associated with TD (Brown et al., 1997). Moreover, a small percentage of children with ADHD who receive stimulant medication have been found to develop tics, although clinical reports have suggested that these are typically transitory and reversible upon cessation of medication (see Bennett, Brown, Craver, & Anderson, 1999; Brown et al., 1997; Brown & Sawyer, 1998). Adverse effects of stimulant medications have been reported in the clinical literature (Bennett et al., 1999), so greater efforts toward systematic controlled methodology have been made in researching the effects of these sympathomimetic medications on children with comorbid TD and ADHD.

Sprafkin and Gadow (1996) emphasized the importance of careful and unbiased assessment of premedication (i.e., stimulant medication) symptoms, variability in TD symptomatology over time, and any possible associations between stimulant medication and tic exacerbation. In a controlled clinical trial investigating the effects of methylphenidate (Ritalin) in boys diagnosed with comorbid ADHD and TD, Gadow, Nolan, and Sverd (1992) observed children in a classroom setting for 6 weeks. Results revealed that methylphenidate reduced overactive and disruptive behavior in the classroom and physical aggression on the playground. Parent ratings of children's behavior revealed similar results (Sverd, Gadow, Nolan, Sprafkin, & Ezor, 1992). Most important, methylphenidate was found to reduce the occurrence of vocal tics at school. No differences were found, however, during routine clinical laboratory assessments. Of the 11 children studied, only 1 boy experienced motor tic exacerbation. Gadow, Sverd, Sprafkin, Nolan, and Grossman (1999) studied changes in ADHD behaviors and motor and vocal tics during long-term treatment with methylphenidate. No evidence was found that motor tics or vocal tics changed in frequency or severity during maintenance therapy. The investigators concluded that long-term management with methylphenidate therapy of children with TD appears to be safe and effective for ADHD behaviors in many children with mild to moderate tic disorders.

More recent double-blind studies of stimulant medications, including methylphenidate and dextroamphetamine (Dexadrine), conducted by Gadow and associates (Gadow, Nolan, et al., 1995; Gadow, Sverd, Sprafkin, et al., 1995; Gadow et al., 1999; Nolan et al., 1999), have revealed important data to suggest that stimulant medication appears to be a safe and effective treatment for ADHD in children with comorbid tic disorder. Despite these encouraging findings, Gadow et al. (1999) recommended careful monitoring to rule out the possibility of drug-induced tic exacerbation in individual patients.

Castellanos et al. (1997) studied the effects of methylphenidate and dextroamphetamine on tic severity in boys with ADHD comorbid with TD. Findings revealed that relatively high doses of methylphenidate and dextroamphetamine produced increases in tic severity that were sustained on higher doses of Dexedrine but attenuated on methylphenidate. The results were interpreted to suggest that a substantial minority of these patients with comorbidity had consistent exacerbation of tic symptoms while receiving stimulant drug therapy. In addition, the majority experienced improvement in ADHD symptoms. It is noteworthy that methylphenidate resulted in fewer adverse effects than did dextroamphetamine. In the clinical setting, families of children diagnosed with TD comorbid with ADHD should be informed of the potential of stimulants to worsen tic symptoms.

If a trial of stimulants is elected, careful monitoring should always be the standard of care.

Alpha^2 Adrenergic Agonists

In recent years, clonidine (Catapres) has been used to manage symptoms associated with TD. For many clinicians, clonidine therapy represents a first-line treatment for the management of this disorder (Peterson & Cohen, 1998). This medication has traditionally been used to reduce blood pressure and heart rate. Despite its widespread clinical use in child psychiatric populations, few double-blind, placebo-controlled trials evaluating the efficacy of clonidine for decreasing tic symptoms could be located in the literature (Borison, Ang, Hamilton, Diamond, & Davis, 1983; Goetz et al., 1987; Leckman et al., 1991). These studies have included both adults and children, and little is known about the safety of these agents for children. Studies using subjective ratings have included behavioral observations of the frequency of motor and vocal tics as dependent measures. Although these data are encouraging, findings were not replicated in a crossover study of 34 children with comorbid ADHD (Peterson & Cohen, 1998). Because of the potentially severe adverse cardiac effects associated with clonidine therapy, medication compliance must be carefully evaluated. Deleterious effects may occur upon abrupt cessation of the medication. Health care providers must carefully balance safety with efficacy. Needless to say, patient education regarding compliance is imperative. Guafacine (Tenex), another alfa^2 adrenergic agonist that appears to less sedating and hypotensive than clonidine, may provide a safe alternative therapy for children with ADHD in the presence of tics (Chappell et al., 1995). More systematic controlled trials of clonidine therapy are needed.

Other Medications

Other psychotropic agents, including TCAs such as imipramine (Tofranil) and desipramine (Norpramin), and SSRIs such as sertraline (Zoloft) and fluoxetine (Prozac), have been studied in children with TD (Parraga, Kelly, Parraga, Cochran, & Maxim, 1994). Scahill et al. (1997) found that fluoxetine was useful for the management of obsessive–compulsive symptoms in some patients with TD, but it was not effective for the management of tics. However, a combination of neuroleptic drug therapy and fluoxetine therapy resulted in improvement in OCD and tic symptoms.

Singer et al. (1995) examined the ability of clonidine and desipramine (Norpramin) to modify behaviors associated with ADHD. A double-blind, placebo-controlled trial revealed that improvement with desipramine was always superior to that noted with clonidine. On the basis of their data, Singer et al. (1995) suggest that desipramine may be a useful alternative for the management of symptoms of ADHD in children with TD.

Unfortunately, clinical use of many psychotropic agents and polypharmacy has far exceeded the extant research about the safety and efficacy of these medications. Clearly, controlled clinical trials are needed that have sufficient sample sizes and careful measurements that can assess target symptoms and safety across settings and situations. Studies must be mounted that can evaluate both the short-term and the long-term efficacy of these medications.

Summary

In summary, most children and adolescents diagnosed with TD receive at least one trial of psychotropic medication. Medication treatment is complex and is frequently dictated according to comorbidity. The potential adverse effects of neuroleptics cannot be underestimated. Studies on the use of stimulants in children with comorbid ADHD and TD are encouraging, but much more research will need to be conducted before concluding the safety of these agents for children and adolescents with tic disorders. There are other pharmacological agents and treatments (e.g., transcranial magnetic stimulation) that may be promising for future use, although few systematic, controlled trials have been conducted to confirm their safety or efficacy. This is a fertile area for investigation. All psychotropic agents must be used cautiously and judiciously and as an adjunct with other psychotherapies.

PSYCHOSOCIAL INTERVENTIONS

The psychosocial interventions used most frequently for the management of the symptoms associated with tic disorders are the behavioral therapies. Such approaches can either target the tic directly, as in contingency management and competing response training, or target the tic indirectly via the contingencies that maintain the tic, using techniques like relaxation training and self-monitoring. Because of the discrete, observable, and measurable nature of tics, classic behavioral approaches manage the disorder particularly well (Peterson & Azrin, 1993).

Behavioral Interventions

The use of behavioral interventions should be considered in the management of children and adolescents with TD for many reasons. First, as noted above, pharmacological interventions are often not effective or at best only partially effective for managing tics (Brown & Ievers, 1999).

Second, when pharmacotherapy is terminated, tics often return to baseline level, and hence, another level of intervention is frequently warranted. Third, behavioral interventions should be considered when health care providers or parents are concerned about real or perceived adverse effects of pharmacotherapy. Finally, behavioral interventions are often useful to manage associated comorbidities, including ADHD and ODD, as well as other co-occurring problems that are pervasive in children with TD (e.g., general peer and social problems, social withdrawal, and embarrassment regarding tics).

The behavioral approaches that have shown the most promise in managing TD are reviewed briefly below. These include awareness training or self-monitoring, relaxation training, massed negative practice, habit reversal (e.g., competing response training), and contingency management. A description of each technique is summarized and relevant research is presented.

Awareness Training/Self-Monitoring

Awareness training or self-monitoring was initially developed by Nelson (1977) to manage aggressive behavior. Since that time, its application has broadened to include the treatment of tics and TD. The treatment requests that the child recognize and record the occurrence of each tic by using a wrist counter or small notebook. For awareness training to be successful, the child must be able to identify accurately when the tic occurs, including the identification of the situation in which the tic occurs. Practice using a mirror and feedback from the clinician or the child's parent often is useful in achieving these conditions (Azrin & Nunn, 1973). Furthermore, immediate, as opposed to delayed, recording of the tic is necessary (King, Scahill, Findley, & Cohen, 1999). Rather than recording tics throughout the day, several discrete time periods of approximately 5–10 minutes may be chosen during which tics may be recorded.

Relaxation Training

As noted earlier, increased stress is a factor that often exacerbates the frequency of tic behaviors. It follows that relaxation training would be appropriate in reducing tic frequency. Relaxation training was developed by Jacobson (1938) in the form of progressive muscle relaxation and was adapted for use in psychiatric populations by Wolpe (1958) as part of a systematic desensitization treatment for anxiety disorders. Since then, its use has been applied to treating tics and TD. Relaxation training is based on the premise that one cannot be in a simultaneously aroused and relaxed state. Thus, teaching individuals relaxation skills should counteract the anxiety that presumably accompanies tics. Relaxation techniques include progressive muscle relaxation, deep or diaphragmatic breathing, visual imagery, and self-statements. Several studies suggest that relaxation is a particularly promising intervention for the management of tics.

Massed Negative Practice

Until recently, massed negative practice has been the most widely used behavioral treatment approach for managing tics (King et al., 1999; Peterson & Azrin, 1993). In this approach, the child is asked to perform the tic movement rapidly and with as much effort as possible for a specified period of time, interspersed with periods of rest (Peterson & Azrin, 1993). This method is based on the premise that the individual fatigues from performing the tic movement, resulting in reactive inhibition and an eventual reduction in tic behaviors. Peterson and Azrin (1993) reviewed studies using this approach and noted an overall 60% reduction in tic behaviors following the use of massed negative practice. Long-term benefit, however, is less clear.

Habit Reversal

Habit reversal, developed by Azrin and Nunn (1973), is a multimodal treatment in which the individual is instructed to engage in competing responses to prevent the occurrence of tics. Awareness training, relaxation training, habit control motivation, and generalization training also are used in conjunction with competing response training as part of habit reversal. With competing response training, the child is instructed to tense muscles that are opposed to the tic. In addition to this technique, Azrin and Nunn (1973) also recommended that the muscle tensing must be sustainable for several minutes to produce awareness of the muscles involved in the movement, and that the muscle tensing must be socially unobtrusive and easily compatible with ongoing behaviors. In this approach, the opposing muscles are contracted for 1 to 2 minutes contingent on either the occurrence of the tic or the urge to emit the tic.

Contingency Management

Contingency management is based on operant conditioning theory and the notion that desirable behaviors (e.g., tic-free periods) can be increased with the use of reinforcement, and undesirable behaviors (e.g., tics) can be decreased with the use of punishment. Generally, contingency management is implemented by someone other than the child, such as a parent, caretaker, or teacher. Several case studies have used contingency management, and most have shown favorable results. It should be noted, however, that many of these studies have relied on the use of contingency management in combination with other behavioral techniques. Thus, the efficacy of contingency management used alone is not entirely clear.

Although the use of contingency management requires a great deal of motivation from both the patient and the family and ongoing effort and determination from parents and teachers, the principles that presumably make it effective are often those used to control the disruptive behaviors that frequently accompany TD. Clearly, an advantage of these techniques is that they serve a dual purpose in diminishing tic behaviors and increasing prosocial behaviors. Moreover, the use of positive reinforcement is particularly recommended, as children with TD often receive little positive attention because of the stigmatizing nature of the disorder and the social consequences that frequently ensue (e.g., withdrawal from normal peer activities).

Other Treatments

Other psychosocial treatments for TD include psychoeducation, school consultation, and family psychotherapy (Scahill, Ort, & Hardin, 1993; Scahill, Walker, Lechner, & Tynan, 1993). Moreover, traditional psychotherapy, including dynamic and interpersonal approaches, are sometimes used to manage affective and interpersonal difficulties that at times accompany TD (King et al., 1999). More traditional cognitive therapies also have been used to assist children in managing the stress associated with their symptoms (Mansdorf, 1995). The children are instructed in self-talk so that they might use these strategies in psychologically threatening situations (e.g., "Their staring at me can't hurt me"), which should in turn assist these children in coping with the disorder and its associated stressors.

Summary

Behavioral strategies appear to be the treatment of choice in terms of the psychosocial management of TD. All techniques reviewed have demonstrated some success in managing the symptoms associated with TD. The specific treatment chosen for any case will depend on many factors, including the severity of tics, comorbid disorders, and the age and developmental level of the child. Future research in this area should continue to conduct dismantling studies to examine the efficacy of specific therapeutic modalities, in addition to long-term follow-up studies to assess the durability of behavioral therapy in managing TD.

SELECTION OF AN APPROPRIATE INTERVENTION

When given the array of pharmacological and behavioral interventions that are available for managing TD, the practitioner is faced with several alternatives from which to choose. The choice of a particular intervention depends on several factors, including (a) the target behaviors selected for intervention and the appropriate treatment techniques available to manage the symptoms, (b) the frequency and severity of the specific target behaviors, (c) the history of previous therapies in the management of the symptoms, (d) those resources available either within the family or the health care system to manage the target behaviors, and finally (e) treatment acceptability by parents and teachers as well as the child who is receiving the intervention.

It is well known that many caregivers and children initially may be opposed to pharmacological interventions, and for this reason the health care provider may wish to begin an appropriate behavioral intervention, providing an excellent opportunity for collaboration with a psychologist or other practitioner. For example, the parents may be requested to maintain careful recordings of the behaviors so as to determine the efficacy of the behavioral intervention. If the recordings reveal that the behavioral therapy is of little efficacy, parents may elect a pharmacological approach to manage the child's TD symptoms whereby this treatment may be more acceptable, particularly if a child has been refractory to a trial of behavioral therapy. Pharmacological intervention would necessarily require the collaboration of a physician. Finally, a combined intervention may be particularly appropriate for TD when it is comorbid with another psychiatric disorder (e.g., OCD or ADHD) where the symptoms are impairing a number of areas in the child's life (e.g., family, peers, and school) and there is a need for immediate management of symptoms. This would necessitate collaborative practice. In recent years, there have been an increasing number of clinical trials comparing the efficacy of behavioral approaches with pharmacological therapies and the combination of these treatments (e.g., MTA Cooperative Group, 1999) to guide the selection of treatment interventions. Thus, the astute practitioner will always wish to consult the existing literature as a framework for selecting a particular intervention or combinations of treatments for managing TD or associated comorbid conditions.

CONCLUSION

Several recent advances in both the behavioral and psychopharmacological management of TD are due in part to a greater understanding of the developmental course, comorbidities, and genetic and familial patterns of this disorder. TD first appears during childhood, typically with the emergence of motor tics, and it may often persist throughout adolescence and adulthood. The degree of impairment during later life is variable. Numerous studies have documented the overlap between TD and other psychiatric disorders, including ADHD and ODD, and developmental disorders including learning disabilities. However, additional research is warranted to delineate the genetic links between TD and these other disorders. TD clearly has a strong biological or genetic basis, or both, as documented by investigations of brain imaging, familial linkage studies, and biological markers of the disorder. Additional research comparing these indices in individuals with TD to individuals with TD and comorbid conditions will be a fruitful area for investigation.

Most psychotherapies targeting TD are behavioral interventions. These include relaxation, habit reversal, contingency management, competing response training, and self-monitoring. Although the short-term efficacy of these approaches has been well documented, their long-term efficacy remains an area for further investigation. A clear limitation of the research on behavioral interventions for TD is that very few dismantling studies have been conducted. Because many behavioral approaches use multiple interventions simultaneously, the relative efficacy of each intervention alone is largely unknown. Moreover, there is little known about the match of specific interventions to specific types of pathology and comorbidity patterns. Future well-controlled studies assessing the effectiveness of single interventions will provide valuable information to clinicians on which interventions are most effective for specific individuals under specific circumstances.

Psychopharmacology is also a widely used option for the management of TD. Health care providers have several psychotropic agents from which to choose, including neuroleptics, stimulants, and alpha^2 adrenergic agonists. As with all psychotropic medications, several caveats apply to the use of these agents in the management of TD, and the practitioner must be judicious in choosing medication for a particular patient. Investigating the use of other agents, including the SSRIs, is a good direction for additional studies. Further research must be conducted that carefully addresses the emergence of tics when stimulants are used.

Finally, little is known about integrating psychopharmacotherapy and behavioral interventions for the management of TD. Although each of these therapies has demonstrated efficacy, the combined effects remain largely unknown. This will require significant collaboration among providers of psychological services and physicians. Further investigation needs to be conducted on multimodal approaches in which controlled trials are conducted that compare pharmacological approaches with behavioral therapies, in addition to the combination of these treatments. It is, unfortunately, our general conclusion that empirical studies have lagged significantly behind clinical practice. We anticipate that as collaboration concomitantly increases and more is known about the disorder, an increase in treatment studies will guide clinical efforts with these children and enhance their quality of life.

REFERENCES

Allen, A. J., Singer, H. S., Brown, J. E., & Salem, M. M. (1992). Sleep disorders in Tourette's syndrome: A primary or related problem? *Pediatric Neurology, 8,* 275–280.

American Psychiatric Association. (1994). *Diagnostic and statistical manual of mental disorders* (4th ed.). Washington, DC: Author.

Arzimanoglou, A. A. (1998). Gilles de la Tourette syndrome. *Journal of Neurology, 245,* 761–765.

Azrin, N. H., & Nunn, R. G. (1973). Habit reversal: A method of eliminating nervous habits and tics. *Behavior Research and Therapy, 11,* 619–628.

Barkley, R. A. (1998). *Attention-deficit hyperactivity disorder: A handbook for diagnosis and treatment* (2nd ed.). New York: Guilford Press.

Bennett, F., Brown, R. T., Craver, J., & Anderson, D. (1999). Stimulant medication. In A. Morgan (Ed.), *Pediatric clinics of North America* (pp. 924–944). Philadelphia: Saunders.

Borison, R. L., Ang, L., Hamilton, W. J., Diamond, B. I., & Davis, J. M. (1983). Treatment approaches in Gilles de la Tourette syndrome. *Brain Research Bulletin, 11,* 205–208.

Bornstein, R. A. (1990). Neuropsychological performance in children with Tourette's syndrome. *Psychiatry Research, 33,* 73–81.

Braun, A. R., Randolph, C., Stoetter, B., Mohr, E., Cox, C., Vladar, K., Sexton, R., Carson, R. E., Herscovitch, P., & Chase, T. N. (1995). The functional neuroanatomy of Tourette's syndrome: An FDG-PET study. II: Relationship between regional cerebral metabolism and associated behavioral and cognitive features of the illness. *Neuropsychopharmacology, 13,* 151–168.

Brown, R. T., Dingle, A., & Dreelin, B. (1997). Neuropsychological effects of stimulant medication on children's learning and behavior. In C. R. Reynolds & E. Fletcher-Janzen (Eds.), *Handbook of clinical child neuropsychology* (2nd ed., pp. 539–572). New York: Plenum Press.

Brown, R. T., & Ievers, C. E. (1999). Gilles de la Tourette's syndrome. In S. Goldstein & C. R. Reynolds (Eds.), *Handbook of neurodevelopmental and genetic disorders in children* (pp. 185–215). New York: Guilford Press.

Brown, R. T., Lee, D., & Donegan, J. E. (1998). Psychopharmacotherapy in children and adolescents. In C. R. Reynolds & T. Gutkin (Eds.), *Handbook of school psychology* (pp. 822–862). New York: Wiley.

Brown, R. T., & Sawyer, M. G. (1998). *Medications for school-age children.* New York: Guilford Press.

Bruun, R. D., & Budman, C. L. (1996). Risperidone as a treatment for Tourette's syndrome. *Journal of Clinical Psychiatry, 57,* 29–31.

Budman, C. L., Sherling, M., & Bruun, R. D. (1995). Combined pharmacotherapy risk. *Journal of the American Academy of Child and Adolescent Psychiatry, 34,* 263–264.

Castellanos, F. X. (1998). Tic disorders and obsessive–compulsive disorder. In B. T.

Walsh (Ed.), *Child psychopharmacology* (pp. 1–28). Washington DC: American Psychiatric Press.

Castellanos, F. X., Giedd, J. N., Elia, J., March, W. L., Ritchie, G. F., Hamberger, S. D., & Rapoport, J. L. (1997). Controlled stimulant treatment of ADHD and comorbid Tourette's syndrome: Effects of stimulant and dose. *Journal of the American Academy of Child and Adolescent Psychiatry, 36,* 589–596.

Cepeda, M. (1997). Nonstimulant psychotropic medication: Desired effects and cognitive–behavioral adverse effects. In C. R. Reynolds & E. Fletcher-Janzen (Eds.), *Handbook of clinical child neuropsychology* (2nd ed., pp. 539–572). New York: Plenum Press.

Chappell, P. B., Leckman, J. F., & Riddle, M. A. (1995). The pharmacologic treatment of tic disorders. *Child Adolescent Psychiatry Clinics of North America, 4,* 197–216.

Chappell, P. B., Riddle, M. A., Schill, L., Lynch, K. A., Schultz, R., Arnsten, A., Leckman, J. F., & Cohen, D. J. (1995). Guafacine treatment of comorbid ADHD and Tourette's syndrome: Preliminary clinical experience. *Journal of the American Academy of Child and Adolescent Psychiatry, 34,* 1140–1146.

Chappell, P. B., Scahill, L. D., & Leckman, J. F. (1996). Future therapies of Tourette's syndrome. *Neurologic Clinics, 15,* 429–450.

Comings, D. E. (1995). Tourette's syndrome: A behavioral spectrum disorder. *Behavioral Neurology of Movement Disorders, 65,* 293–303.

Comings, D. E., & Comings, B. J. (1987). Hereditary agoraphobia and obsessive–compulsive behaviour in relatives of patients with Gilles de la Tourette's syndrome. *Behavioral Neurology of Movement Disorders, 65,* 281–291.

Comings, D. E., Himes, J. A., & Comings, B. G. (1990). An epidemiological study of Tourette's syndrome in a single school district. *Journal of Clinical Psychiatry, 51,* 462–469.

Como, P. G. (1995). Obsessive–compulsive disorder in Tourette's syndrome. *Behavioral Neurology of Movement Disorders, 65,* 281–291.

Diantoniis, M. R., Henry, K. M., Partridge, P. A., & Soucar, E. (1996). Tics and risperidone. *Journal of the American Academy of Child and Adolescent Psychiatry, 35,* 839–840.

Ernst, M., Zametkin, A. J., Jons, P. H., Matochik, J. A., Pascuavaca, D., & Cohen, R. M. (1999). High presynaptic dopaminergic activity in children with Tourette's disorder. *Journal of the American Academy of Child and Adolescent Psychiatry, 38,* 86–94.

Fulop, G., Phillips, R. A., Shapiro, A. K., Gomes, J. A., Shapiro, E., & Nandie, M. (1987). EKG changes during haloperidol and pimozide treatment of Tourette's disorder. *American Journal of Psychiatry, 144,* 673–675.

Gadow, K. D. (1993). A school-based medication evaluation program. In J. L. Matson (Ed.), *Handbook of hyperactivity in children* (pp. 186–219). Needham Heights, MA: Allyn & Bacon.

Gadow, K. D., Nolan, E., Sprafkin, J., & Sverd, J. (1995). School observations of children with attention-deficit hyperactivity disorder and comorbid tic disorder: Effects of methylphenidate treatment. *Developmental and Behavioral Pediatrics, 16,* 167–176.

Gadow, K. D., Nolan, E. E., & Sverd, J. (1992). Methylphenidate in hyperactive boys with comorbid tic disorders: II. Short-term behavioral effects in school settings. *Journal of the American Academy of Child and Adolescent Psychiatry, 31,* 462–471.

Gadow, K. D., Sverd, J., Sprafkin, J., Nolan, E. E., & Ezor, S. N. (1995). Efficacy of methylphenidate for attention-deficit hyperactivity disorder in children with tic disorder. *Archives of General Psychiatry, 52,* 444–455.

Gadow, K. D., Sverd, J., Sprafkin, J., Nolan, E. E., & Grossman, S. (1999). Long-term methylphenidate therapy in children with comorbid attention deficit hyperactivity disorder and chronic multiple tic disorder. *Archives of General Psychiatry, 56,* 330–336.

Gaffney G. R., Sieg, K., & Hellings, J. (1994). The MOVES: A self-rating scale for Tourette's syndrome. *Journal of Child and Adolescent Psychopharmacology, 4,* 269–280.

George, M. S., Trimble, M. R., Ring, H. A., Sallee, F. R., & Robertson, M. M. (1993). Obsessions in obsessive–compulsive disorder with and without Gilles de la Tourette's syndrome. *American Journal of Psychiatry, 150,* 93–97.

Goetz, C. G., Tanner, C. M., Wilson, R. S., Carroll, V. S., Como, P. G., & Shannon, K. M. K. (1987). Clonidine and Gilles de la Tourette's syndrome: Double-blind study using objective rating methods. *Annals of Neurology, 21,* 307–310.

Harcherik, D. F., Leckman, J. F., Detler, J., & Cohen, D. J. (1984). A new instrument for clinical studies of Tourette's syndrome. *Journal of American Academy of Child Psychiatry, 5,* 71–76.

Hawkridge, S., Stein, D. J., & Bouwer, C. (1996). Combined pharmacotherapy for TS and OCD [Letter]. *Journal of the American Academy of Child and Adolescent Psychiatry, 35,* 703–704.

Hyde, T. M., & Weinberger, D. R. (1995). Tourette's syndrome: A model neuropsychiatric disorder. *Journal of the American Medical Association, 239,* 498–511.

Jacobson, E. (1938). *Progressive relaxation.* Chicago: University of Chicago Press.

King, R. A., Scahill, L., Findley, D., & Cohen, D. J. (1999). Psychosocial and behavioral treatments. In J. F. Leckman & D. J. Cohen (Eds.), *Tourette's syndrome—Tics, obsessions, compulsions: Developmental psychopathology and clinical care* (pp. 338–359). New York: Wiley.

Knell, E. R., & Comings, D. E. (1993). Tourette's syndrome and attention-deficit hyperactivity disorder: Evidence for a genetic relationship. *Journal of Child Psychology and Psychiatry, 54,* 331–337.

Kurlan, R. (1994). Hypothesis II: Tourette's syndrome is part of a clinical spectrum that includes normal brain development. *Archives of Neurology, 51,* 1145–1150.

Kurlan, R. (1997). Tourette's syndrome: Treatment of tics. *Neurologic Clinics, 15,* 403–409.

Kurlan, R., Whitmore, D., Irvine, C., McDermott, M. P., & Como, P. G. (1994). Tourette's syndrome in a special education population: Preliminary findings. *Neurology, 51,* 1145–1150.

Leckman, J. F. (1995). Risperidone treatment of children and adolescents with chronic tic disorders: A preliminary report. *Journal of the American Academy of Child and Adolescent Psychiatry, 34,* 1147–1152.

Leckman, J. F., Hardin, M. T., Riddle, M. A., Stevenson, J., Ort, S. I., & Cohen, D. J. (1991). Clonidine treatment of Gilles de la Tourette's syndrome. *Archives of General Psychiatry, 48,* 324–328.

Leckman, J. F., Riddle, M. A., Hardin, M. T., Ort, S. I., Swartz, K. L., Stevenson, J., & Cohen, D. J. (1989). The Yale Global Tic Severity Scale (YGTSS): Initial testing of a clinical-rated scale of tic severity. *Journal of the American Academy of Child and Adolescent Psychiatry, 28,* 566–573.

Leonard, H. L., Lenane, M. C., Swedo, S. E., Rettew, D. C., Gershon, E. S., & Rapoport, J. L. (1992). Tics and Tourette's syndrome: A 2- to 7-year follow-up of 54 obsessive compulsive children. *American Journal of Psychiatry, 149,* 1244–1251.

Lombroso, P. J., Scahill, L., King, R. A., Lynch, K. A., Chappell, P. B., Peterson, B. S., McDougle, C. J., & Leckman, J. F. (1995). Risperidone treatment of children and adolescents with chronic tic disorders: A preliminary report. *Journal of the American Academy of Child and Adolescent Psychiatry, 34,* 1147–1152.

Malison, R. T., McDougle, C. J., van Dyck, C. H., Seahill, L., Baldwin, R. M., Seibyl, J. P., Price, L. H., Leckman, J. F., & Innis, R. B. (1995). B SPECT Imaging of striatal dopamine transporter binding in Tourette's disorder. *American Journal of Psychiatry, 152,* 1359–1361.

Mansdorf, I. J. (1995). Tic disorders. In R. T. Ammerman & M. Hersen (Eds.), *Handbook of child behavior therapy in the psychiatric setting* (pp. 323–340). New York: Wiley.

Mennesson, M., Klink, B. A., & Fortin, A. H. (1998). Case study: Worsening Tourette's disorder or withdrawn dystonia? *Journal of the American Academy of Child and Adolescent Psychiatry, 37,* 785–788.

Miguel, E. C., Coffey, B. J., Baer, L., Savage, C. R., Rauch, S. L., & Jenike, M. A. (1995). Phenomenology of intentional repetitive behaviors in obsessive–compulsive disorder and Tourette's disorder. *Journal of Clinical Psychiatry, 56,* 246–255.

MTA Cooperative Group. (1999). A 14-month randomized clinical trial of treatment strategies for attention deficit/hyperactivity disorder. *Archives of General Psychiatry, 56,* 1073–1086.

Nelson, R. O. (1977). Assessment and therapeutic functions of self-monitoring. In M. Hersen, R. M. Eisler, & P. M. Miller (Eds.), *Progress in behavior modification.* (Vol. 5, pp. 57–69). New York: Academic Press.

Nolan, E. E., & Gadow, K. D. (1997). Children with ADHD and tic disorder and their classmates: Behavioral normalization with methylphenidate. *Journal of the American Academy of Child and Adolescent Psychiatry, 36,* 597–604.

Nolan, E. E., Gadow, K. D., & Sprafkin, J. (1999). Stimulant withdrawal during long-term therapy in children with comorbid attention-deficit hyperactivity disorder and chronic multiple tic disorder. *Pediatrics, 103,* 730–737.

Parraga, H. C., Kelly, D. P., Parraga, M. I., Cochran, M. K., & Maxim, L. T. (1994). Combined psychostimulant and tricyclic antidepressant treatment of Tourette's syndrome and comorbid conditions in children. *Journal of Child and Adolescent Psychopharmacology, 4,* 113–122.

Pauls, D. L., Raymond, C. L., Leckman, J. F., & Stevenson, J. M. (1991). A family study of Tourette's syndrome. *American Journal of Human Genetics, 48,* 154–163.

Pauls, D. L., Towbin, K. E., Leckman, J. F., Zahner, G. E. P., & Cohen, D. J. (1986). Gilles de la Tourette's syndrome and obsessive–compulsive disorder: Evidence supporting a genetic relationship. *Archives of General Psychiatry, 43,* 1180–1182.

Peterson, A. L., & Azrin, N. H. (1993). Behavioral and pharmacological treatments for Tourette syndrome: A review. *Applied and Preventive Psychology, 2,* 231–242.

Peterson, B. S., & Cohen, D. J. (1998). The treatment of Tourette's syndrome: Multimodal, developmental intervention. *Journal of Clinical Psychiatry, 59* (Suppl. 1), 62–72.

Peterson, B. S., Leckman, J. F., & Cohen, D. J. (1995). Tourette's syndrome: A genetically predisposed and an environmentally specified developmental psychopathology. In D. Cicchetti & D. J. Cohen (Eds.), *Developmental psychopathology: Risk, disorder and adaptation* (Vol. 2, pp. 213–242). New York: Wiley.

Pierre, C. B., Nolan, E. E., Gadow, K. D., Sverd, J., & Sprafkin, J. (1999). Comparison of internalizing and externalizing symptoms in children with attention-deficit hyperactivity disorder with and without comorbid tic disorder. *Developmental and Behavioral Pediatrics, 20,* 170–176.

Randolph, C., Hyde, T. M., Gold, J. M., Goldberg, T. E., & Weinberger, D. R. (1993). Tourette's syndrome in monozygotic twins: Relationship of tic severity to neuropsychological function. *Archives of Neurology, 50,* 725–728.

Rapoport, J. L., Swedo, S. E., & Leonard, H. L. (1992). Childhood obsessive compulsive disorder. *Journal of Clinical Psychiatry, 53,* 11–16.

Rosenberg, D. R., Holttum, J., & Gershon, S. (1994). *Textbook of pharmacotherapy for child and adolescent psychiatric disorders.* New York: Brunner-Mazel.

Rowan, A. B., & Malone, R. P. (1997). Tics with risperidone withdrawal [Letter]. *Journal of the American Academy of Child and Adolescent Psychiatry, 36,* 162–163.

Sallee, F. R., Nesbit, L., Jackson C., & Sethuraman, G. (1997). Relative efficacy of haloperidol and pimozide in children and adolescents with Tourette's disorder. *American Journal of Psychiatry, 154,* 1057–1062.

Sallee, F. R., & Spratt, E. G. (1998). Tics and Tourette's disorder. In T. Ollendick & M. Hersen (Eds.), *Handbook of child psychopathology* (3rd ed., pp. 337–353). New York: Plenum.

Scahill, L., Ort, S. I., & Hardin, M. T. (1993). Tourette's syndrome: Part 1. Definition and diagnosis. *Archives of Psychiatric Nursing, 7,* 203–208.

Scahill, L., Riddle, M., King, R. A., Hardin, M. T., Rasmussen, A., Makuch, R., & Leckman, J. F. (1997). Fluoxetine has no marked effect on tic symptoms in patients with Tourette's syndrome: A double-blind, placebo-controlled study. *Journal of Child and Adolescent Psychopharmacology, 7,* 75–85.

Scahill, L., Walker, R. D., Lechner, S. N., & Tynan, K. E. (1993). Inpatient treatment of obsessive compulsive disorder in childhood: A case study. *Journal of Clinical Psychiatric Nursing, 6,* 5–14.

Schuerholz, L. J., Baumgardner, T. L., Singer, H. S., Reiss, A. L., & Denckla, M. B. (1996). Neuropsychological status of children with Tourette's syndrome with and without attention deficit hyperactivity disorder. *Neurology, 46,* 958–965.

Shapiro, A. K., & Shapiro, E. (1984). Controlled study of pimozide vs. placebo in Tourette's syndrome. *Journal of the American Academy of Child and Adolescent Psychiatry, 23,* 161–173.

Shapiro, A. K., Shapiro, E. S., Young, J. G., & Feinberg, T. (1988). *Gilles de la Tourette syndrome.* New York: Raven Press.

Shapiro, E., Shapiro, A. K., Fulop, G., Hubbard, M., Mandeli, J., Nordlei, J., & Phillips, R. (1989). Controlled study of haloperidol, pimozide, and placebo for the treatment of Gilles de la Tourette's syndrome. *Archives of General Psychiatry, 46,* 722–730.

Silver, A. A., Shytle, R. D., Philipp, M. K., & Sanberg, P. R. (1996). Case study: Long-term potentiation of neuroleptics with transdermal nicotine in Tourette's syndrome. *Journal of the American Academy of Child and Adolescent Psychiatry, 35,* 1631–1636.

Singer, H. S., Brown, J., Quaskey, S., Rosenberg, L. A., Mellitis, E. D., & Denckla, M. B. (1995). The treatment of attention deficit hyperactivity disorder in Tourette's syndrome: A double-blind placebo-controlled study with clonidine and desipramine. *Pediatrics, 95,* 74–81.

Singer, H. S., Schuerholz, L. J., & Denckla, M. B. (1994). Learning difficulties in children with Tourette's syndrome. *Journal of Child Neurology, 10,* 58–61.

Singer, H. S., Waranch, H. R., Brown, J., Carson, K., & Mellitis, D. (1993, October). *Relaxation therapy: An alternative treatment for Tourette's syndrome?* Paper presented at the meeting of the Child Neurology Society, New York.

Spencer, T., Biederman, J., Harding, M., O'Donnell, D., Wilens, T., Faraone, S., Coffey, B., & Geller, D. (1998). Disentangling the overlap between Tourette's disorder and ADHD. *Journal of Child Psychology and Psychiatry and Allied Disciplines, 39,* 1037–1044.

Sprafkin, J., & Gadow, K. D. (1996). Double-blind versus open evaluations of stimulant drug response in children with attention-deficit hyperactivity disorder. *Journal of Child and Adolescent Psychopharmacology, 6,* 215–228.

Stamenkovic, M., Aschauer, H., & Kasper, S. (1994). Risperidone for Tourette's syndrome. *Lancet, 344,* 1577–1578.

Sverd, J., Gadow, K. D., Nolan, E. E., Sprafkin, J., & Ezor, S. N. (1992). Methylphenidate in hyperactive boys with comorbid tic disorder. *Advances in Neurology, 58,* 271–281.

Swedo, S. E., & Leonard, H. L. (1994). Childhood movement disorders and obsessive compulsive disorder. *Journal of Clinical Psychiatry, 55,* 32–37.

Tollefson, G. D., Birkett, M., Koran, L., & Genduso, L. (1994). Continuation treatment of OCD: Double-blind and open-label experience with fluoxetine. *Journal of Clinical Psychiatry, 55,* 69–76.

van der Linden, C., Briggeman, R., & van Woerkom, T. C. A. M. (1994). Serotonin-dopamine antagonist and Gilles de la Tourette's syndrome: An open pilot dose-titration study with risperidone. *Movement Disorders, 9,* 687–688.

Walkup, J. T., Scahill, L., & Riddle, M. A. (1995). Disruptive behavior, hyperactivity, and learning disabilities in children with Tourette's syndrome. *Advances in Neurology, 65,* 259–272.

Werry, J. S., & Aman, M. G. (Eds.). (1996). *Practitioner's guide to psychoactive drugs for children and adolescents.* New York: Plenum.

Wodrich, D. L., Benjamin, E., & Lachar, D. (1997). Tourette's syndrome and psychopathology in a child psychiatry setting. *Journal of the American Academy of Child and Adolescent Psychiatry, 36,* 1618–1624.

Wolfe, D. V., & Wagner, K. D. (1993). Tardive dyskinesia, tardive dystonia, and tardive Tourette's syndrome in children and adolescents. *Journal of Child and Adolescent Psychopharmacology, 3,* 175–198.

Wolpe, J. (1958). *Psychotherapy by reciprocal inhibition.* Stanford, CA: Stanford University Press.

Yeates, K. O., & Bornstein, R. A. (1994). Attention deficit disorder and neuropsychological functioning in children with Tourette's syndrome. *Neuropsychology, 8,* 65–74.

GLOSSARY OF TERMS

This glossary provides definitions of medical and psychological terms associated with pediatric psychopharmacology.

Acetylcholine: A neurotransmitter that exerts excitation on skeletal muscle fibers and inhibition on heart muscle fiber. Involved in learning, memory, and sleep.

Acute dystonia: Medication side effect usually seen shortly after treatment begins that includes severe motor spasms in the jaw, neck, tongue, and back. Can cause breathing difficulties by creating esophageal restriction.

Adrenergic: Nerve fibers that, when stimulated, release epinephrine.

Agranulocytosis: Toxicity of bone marrow resulting in white blood count depletion. Complications could include death from opportunistic infection. Necessitates weekly blood monitoring.

Akathisia: A constellation of medication side effects that includes feelings of restlessness, muscle tension, foot tapping, and rocking from foot to foot. Apathy and negative affect may also be present.

Akinesia: Behavioral component of Parkinsonian symptoms. Identified by apathy and affective blunting. Difficult to distinguish from negative symptoms of schizophrenia.

Allele: One of two or more different genes containing specific inheritable characteristics that occupy corresponding positions on paired chromosomes.

Anticholinergic side effects: Interference with cholinergic receptors that leads to cognitive impairment, blurred vision, dry mouth, and constipation.

Ataxia: Defective muscular coordination

Benzodiazepine: A classification of antianxiety medications that are hypothesized to enhance GABA (gamma-aminobutryic acid), the main inhibitory neurotransmitter in the central nervous system (e.g., Ativan, Klonopin, and Xanax).

Cholinergic: Nerve endings that liberate acetylcholine, which is thought to play an important role in the transmission of nerve impulses at synapses and myoneural junctions.

Coprolalia: Morbid desire to use sacrilegious or obscene words in ordinary conversation.

Dopamine: Catecholamine neurotransmitter involved with movement, attention, learning, and addictions. Dopaminergic receptor activity in brain thought to be influential in course of schizophrenia.

Echolalia: The often pathological repetition of what is said by other people as if echoing them.

Epinephrine: Hormone secreted by the adrenal medulla that is a vasoconstrictor.

Extrapyramidal symptoms: A constellation of medication side effects causing odd muscular reactions due to the antipsychotics' action on dopamine receptors (D2). Includes acute dystonia, akathisia, akinesia, and Parkinsonian side effects.

Galactorrhea: Continuation of lactation of flow of milk at intervals after cessation of nursing.

Hyperphagia: Abnormally increased appetite of food frequently associated with injury of the hypothalamus.

Neuroleptic: Drug that modifies psychotic behaviors.

Neuroleptic malignant syndrome: Condition marked by exceptionally high fever, rigidity, unstable pulse and blood pressure, and altered consciousness. May be fatal if not treated promptly.

Norepinephrine: A hormone produced by the adrenal medulla that is a vasoconstrictor.

Parkinsonian side effects: Occurs after 2 to 3 weeks of therapeutic treatment with antipsychotics. Symptoms may include tremor, drooling, balance problems, and movement difficulties. Anticholinergic medications such as benztropine used to ameliorate condition.

Reticular activating system: Alerting system of the brain essential in initiating and maintaining wakefulness, attention, and introspection.

Selective serotonin reuptake inhibitor (SSRI): A classification of antidepressant medications that affect the neurotransmitter serotonin (e.g., Anafranil, Paxil, Prozac, and Zoloft).

Serotonin: Neurotransmitter involved in regulation of mood, appetite, sleep, arousal, and aggressive behaviors. Serotenergic receptor activity in brain also thought to contribute to schizophrenia.

Tardive dyskinesia: Appears after long-term (3 months or more) treatment with antipsychotics. Generally appears as abnormal involuntary movement of the mouth, face, tongue, and neck. May be irreversible.

Titration: Gradually increasing medication by known quantities to determine drug efficacy.

Tricyclic antidepressant (TCA): A classification of antidepressant medications that are hypothesized to potentiate the adrenergic synapses by blocking the reuptake of norepinephrine at the nerve endings (e.g., Elavil, Norpramin, Pamelor, and Tofranil).

Withdrawal dyskinesia: Similar to tardive dyskinesia; however, onset occurs because of rapid withdrawal of neuroleptic medication. Condition usually resolves itself.

INDEX

for psychotic symptoms, 188–191
Cognitive–behavioral interventions
  for anxiety disorders, 78
  conceptual basis, 77, 174
  efficacy, 78, 174–175
  for mood disorders, 175
  relapse risk, 175
  technique, 77–78
Collaborative practice
  acceptability of treatment and, 51–52
  family role in, 48
  managed care and, 58–59
  in monitoring medication effectiveness,
    39–40
  training for, 14
Community-based services, 58
  interventions with externalizing behav-
    iors, 120
Comorbidity
  anxiety disorders, 66–67
  attention-deficit/hyperactivity disorder,
    106–107, 122, 205–206
  autistic spectrum disorders, 151–152
  bipolar disorder, 151–152
  conduct disorder, 106–107, 122
  enuresis, 88–89
  externalizing disorders, 122
  implications for psychopharmacother-
    apy, 5, 6
  mental retardation, 134
  obsessive–compulsive disorder, 204–
    205
  oppositional defiant disorder, 106–107,
    122
  posttraumatic stress disorder, 69
  research needs, 14–16
  Tourette's syndrome, 204–207, 221–
    222
Conduct disorder
  clinical features, 104
  comorbidity, 106–107, 122
  developmental course, 106
  etiological influences, 105–106, 122
  medical interventions, 107–116, 122
  psychosocial interventions, 116–120,
    123
  stimulant use and, 108
Contingency management
  for anxiety disorders, 77
  for tic disorder management, 219–220
Cost considerations
  access to care and, 53

in managed care, 58
rationale for psychologist prescription
  privileges, 11
Curriculum-based measurement, 27–28

Depressive disorders
  in autism, 151–152
  classification, 163
  comorbid mental retardation, 137–140
  epidemiology, 164
  etiology, 164–165
  gender differences, 164, 165
  medical interventions, 166–174, 176
  psychosocial intervention, 174–176
  symptoms, 164
Desensitization therapy, 76–77
Desipramine, 73, 113
  for mood disorders, 170
  for Tourette's syndrome, 216–217
Desmopressin, 91
Dextroamphetamine, 110
  tic management and, 215–216

Education and training of practitioners, 4
  argument against psychologist prescrip-
    tion privileges, 12
  in biological bases for psychopathology,
    10
  for collaborative practice, 14
  levels of, for psychopharmacology, 13–
    14, 18
  rationale for psychologist prescription
    privileges, 11
Elimination disorders. See Encopresis; En-
    uresis
Emotional functioning, assessment and
    monitoring, 33–34
Encopresis
  assessment, 94–95
  clinical features, 93
  definition, 93
  etiology, 94
  incidence, 93–94
  treatment, 95–96, 97
Enuresis
  assessment, 88–89
  associated medical disorders, 88–89
  definition, 87
  diagnostic criteria, 88

Loxapine
adverse effects, 191–192
for psychotic symptoms, 191–192

Managed care, 11, 53, 58–59
Massed negative practice, 219
Memory function, assessing, 27
Mental retardation
assessment, 134–135
behavioral problems in, 134
comorbid disorders, 134, 137–142
co-occurring symptoms, 137
definition, 133–134
diagnostic criteria, 134
functional adaptive components, 134
management of injurious behaviors,
142–143
medical interventions, 135–144
perseverative behavior in, 143–144
pharmacotherapy concerns, 135–137
psychosocial interventions, 144–145
stereotyped behavior in, 143–144
stimulant effects, 140–142
Methylphenidate, 110–112, 140, 141,
149–150
tic management and, 215–216
Modeling interventions, for anxiety disorders, 77
Monitoring
for adverse effects, 23, 34–35
clomipramine therapy, 70
collaborative practice in, 39–40, 41
commitment to change, 8
designing medication-monitoring protocols, 8–9, 36–39, 40–41
early identification of psychotic symptoms, 193–195
emotional functioning, 33–34
externalizing behavior, 30–33
family's acceptance of intervention,
35–36
interpreting medication-monitoring
findings, 9
measures of academic functioning, 25–
30
measures of social functioning, 34
mental retardation patients, 135–136
oversight, 40
psychologist role in, 8–9, 40, 41
role of intervention team, 9
selecting outcome measures, 25

stimulant use in Tourette's syndrome
timing considerations, 37
tricyclic antidepressant therapy, 113
Monoamine oxidase inhibitors
cautions, 113
for managing externalizing behaviors,
113
Mood disorders
in autism, 151–152
classification, 163
in mental retardation, 137–140
See also Bipolar disorder; Depressive
disorders

Naltrexone, 149
adverse effects monitoring, 35
Nefazodone, 172
Neurobiological dysfunction
in autistic spectrum disorders, 146
in schizophrenia, 187
in Tourette's syndrome, 208–209
See also Neurotransmitter dysfunction
Neuroleptic medications
adverse effects, 115, 143, 188, 211–
213
for managing externalizing behaviors,
114–115
for patient with mental retardation,
142–143
for psychotic symptoms, 188
for Tourette's syndrome, 211–214
See also specific agent
Neurotransmitter dysfunction
in attention-deficit/hyperactivity disorder, 102
in patient with mental retardation,
142
in Tourette's syndrome, 208
Nortriptyline, 113, 172–173

Obsessive–compulsive disorder, 65–66
clinical features, 67
diagnosis, 67
epidemiology, 67
medical interventions, 70, 74, 75
psychosocial interventions, 78–79
risk, 67
symptoms in autistic spectrum disorders, 150–151

role of psychologists, 3–4, 6–9, 17
for Tourette's syndrome management,
  221, 222
treatment planning, 5–6
trends in pediatric practice, 4
Psychosocial intervention, 7–8
  acceptability, 50, 51
  adherence, 50–51
  anxiety disorders, 76–79, 79–80
  autistic spectrum disorders, 152–153,
    154
  effectiveness, 39
  encopresis management, 95–96
  enuresis management, 91, 92–93
  externalizing behaviors, 116–120, 123
  implications of psychologist prescrip-
    tion privileges, 12–13
  mental retardation, 144–145
  mood disorders, 166, 174–176
  psychotic disorders, 193–196
  Tourette's syndrome, 217–220, 222
Psychotic disorders, 166
  assessment, 186
  classification, 185
  clinical conceptualization, 185
  diagnostic criteria, 186
  differential diagnosis, 186
  early identification, 193–195
  educational placement, 195
  etiology, 187
  family support, 193, 194
  long-term prognosis, 187–188
  medical interventions, 188–193, 196
  multimodal treatment, 193, 196
  psychosocial interventions, 193–196
  treatment team approach, 193

Quetiapine, 148

Race/ethnicity
  help-seeking behaviors and, 53–54
  treatment acceptability and, 52
  treatment settings, 58
Relaxation training, 218–219
Response prevention, 78–79
Risperidone, 115, 174
  adverse effects, 148, 192–193
  for autistic syndromes, 147–148
  for mental retardation patient, 142,
    143
  for psychotic symptoms, 192–193
  for Tourette's syndrome, 213–214

Schizophrenia. See Psychotic disorders
Schools
  interventions with externalizing behav-
    iors, 120
  management of psychotic disorders in,
    195
  as treatment setting, 58
  See also Academic performance; Teach-
    ers
Selective serotonin reuptake inhibitors,
  113–114
  for anxiety disorders, 75
  for managing externalizing behaviors,
    113–114
  for obsessive–compulsive behaviors in
    autism, 150–151
  pediatric pharmacotherapy, 166–169,
    176
  side effects, 114
  See also specific agent
Self-injurious behaviors
  in autism, 145, 147–148, 149
  in patient with mental retardation,
    142–143
Self-monitoring, 218
Separation anxiety, 65, 66–67
  medical interventions, 73, 74
Sertraline, 75, 150, 173, 216
Settings for treatment, 58
  encopresis management, 96
Severity of disorder, acceptability of treatment and, 51
Social functioning
  assessment and monitoring, 34
  behavioral intervention with external-
    izing behaviors, 119
  stimulant use and, 108, 109–110
Social phobia, 65–66
  medical interventions, 74, 75
Social validity perceptions, 50–53
Sociocultural factors
  cultural sensitivity of practitioners, 59
  obstacles to care, 53
  treatment acceptability and, 52
Stimulants
  for ADHD treatment, 107–112, 214–
    216
  adverse effects, 109–110
  aggressive behavior and, 108
  cautions, 110
  individual differences, 34–35
  long-term use, 108–109, 110

Stimulants (*continued*)
   for managing externalizing behaviors, 107–112, 122–123
   monitoring, 34–35
   for patient with mental retardation, 140–142
   social functioning and, 108, 109–110
   Tourette's syndrome and, 214–216
Substance abuse, 66
Symptom targeting, 24–25
   monitoring externalizing behavior, 31–32
   Tourette's syndrome treatment, 210
Systematic desensitization. *See* Desensitization therapies

Tardive dyskinesia, 211–213
Teachers
   in academic performance assessment, 26–27
   assessment of treatment acceptability, 56
Termination of treatment, premature, 48
Therapeutic relationship, cultural sensitivity in, 59
Thioridazine, 142–143, 149, 193
Thiothixene, 193
Tics
   assessment, 209
   defined, 203
   in Tourette's syndrome, 203, 207
Tourette's syndrome
   assessment and monitoring, 31–32, 209–210
   attention-deficit/hyperactivity disorder and, 205–206, 214–216
   classification, 203–204
   comorbid disorders, 204–207, 221–222
   developmental course, 203, 207–210
   diagnostic criteria, 203
   genetic factors, 204, 206, 208, 221–222
   learning difficulties in, 206–207
   medical interventions, 210–217, 222
   neurobiological findings, 208–209

   obsessive–compulsive disorder and, 204–205
   prevalence, 204
   psychopharmacotherapy, 221, 222
   psychosocial interventions, 217–220, 222
   stimulant use and, 109
   symptoms, 203
   treatment planning, 24–25, 210, 220–221
Trazodone, 113
Treatment planning, 5–6
   assessing family's acceptance of intervention, 35–36
   autistic spectrum disorders, 146–147
   collaborative practice in, 39–40
   designing medication-monitoring protocols, 8–9
   empirically supported intervention, 7–8
   family participation, 48
   goal-setting, 7
   outcome measurement and, 24–25
   psychologist's role, 7, 8–9, 17–18
   readiness for change and, 8, 56–58, 59–60
   research needs, 14–16
   stages of change model in, 49, 59
   symptom targeting, 24–25
   Tourette's syndrome, 210, 220–221
   treatment adherence and, 48
Tricyclic antidepressants, 112–113
   pediatric pharmacotherapy, 166–169, 176
   See also specific agent

Utilization, barriers to, 47

Valproic acid, 137–140, 173–174
Venlafaxine, 114, 137, 173
Violent behavior, exposure to
   in conduct disorder etiology, 106
   in posttraumatic stress disorder etiology, 69
   See also Aggressive behavior

ABOUT THE AUTHORS

LeAdelle Phelps, PhD, is professor and director of the School Psychology Program in the Department of Counseling, School, and Educational Psychology at the State University of New York at Buffalo. She is a Fellow of the American Psychological Association (APA) Division 16 (School Psychology) and a member of Divisions 40 (Clinical Neuropsychology) and 54 (Society of Pediatric Psychology). She has published more than 75 journal articles and book chapters on such diverse health-related topics as eating disorders, prenatal alcohol and cocaine exposure, and lead poisoning. She edited *Health-Related Disorders in Children and Adolescents: A Guidebook for Understanding and Education* (APA, 1998) and is editor of *Psychology in the Schools.*

Ronald T. Brown, PhD, ABPP, is professor and chairman in the Department of Health Professions and is professor of pediatrics and associate dean in the College of Health Professions at the Medical University of South Carolina. He is past president of the Society for Pediatric Psychology, Division 54 of the American Psychological Association (APA), and is editor-elect of the *Journal of Pediatric Psychology.* Dr. Brown is a Fellow of the APA and the American Psychological Society and is a Diplomate of the American Board of Professional Psychology. He has authored more than 125 published reports, chapters, and books and is on the editorial boards of more than 10 scholarly journals in the fields of clinical child and school psychology.

Thomas J. Power, PhD, is associate professor of School Psychology in Pediatrics at the University of Pennsylvania School of Medicine. He is also director of the Center for Management of Attention Deficit Hyperactivity Disorder (ADHD) and the Community Schools Program at the Children's

Hospital of Philadelphia. He serves as associate editor of *School Psychology Review* and has authored numerous journal articles and book chapters on assessment and intervention for children with ADHD and integrating the health and educational systems of care for children and families. He is the coauthor of several books, including *Homework Success for Children With ADHD: A Family–School Intervention Program; The Clinician's Practical Guide to ADHD;* and *AHDH Rating Scale–IV: Checklist, Norms, and Clinical Interpretation.*